ONE WEEK

in Ordinary Time

Psalms, Canticles, Sayings of Jesus,
& Readings on the Christian Life

compiled by
Stephen Joseph Wolf

idjc.org

One Week in Ordinary Time
Copyright © 2016
Stephen Joseph Wolf
All rights reserved. No part of this book may be
copied or reproduced in any form or by any means,
except for the songs understood by the publisher to be in the
public domain or the inclusion of brief quotations in a review,
without the written permission of the publisher.

For the holy name YHVH or Yahweh,
the Hebrew word for "my Lord" (*Adonai*) is used,
pronounced *ah-duh-'nigh*. See page 442 for the
other choices made in this meditation rendering.

Most of the Songs have been altered,
and some are marked for an alternate melody.
Original texts for most of these and the music tunes
are available on www.nethymnal.org.

Most of the Antiphons are **Sayings of Jesus** drawn from Sunday
Gospel readings: In the Sunday Lectionary, the Old Testament
readings have connections with the Gospel reading, and the
Responsorial Psalm is a response to the Old Testament reading.
This means that on any given Sunday there is a
relationship between the Gospel reading and the Psalm.
The Antiphons were chosen based on this relationship.

Most of the Psalms and Canticles appear here
on the same day of the week as in the four-week cycle
of the *Liturgy of the Hours*. See page 450 for a comparison.

The Antiphon for the Gospel Canticle of Night Prayer
is as sung at the Abbey of Gethsemani.

Cover art is by Stephen Joseph Wolf

ISBN 978-1-937081-50-8

published by idjc press
printed and disbributed by Ingram

idjc.org

One Week in Ordinary Time

	SUN	MON	TUE	WED	THU	FRI	SAT
READINGS	18	77	145	213	275	337	400

traditionally in the middle of the night, or at any hour of the day

	SUN	MON	TUE	WED	THU	FRI	SAT
PROPHETS	30	90	161	227	286	349	411

following Readings, or at any hour of the day

	SUN	MON	TUE	WED	THU	FRI	SAT
MORNING	38	96	170	234	293	357	420

in the first hour of daylight

	SUN	MON	TUE	WED	THU	FRI	SAT
DAYTIME	54	112	184	248	306	369	432

midmorning or midday or midafternoon

	SUN	MON	TUE	WED	THU	FRI	SAT
EVENING	62	126	196	259	319	381	4

at dusk, the hour of the gloaming

	SUN	MON	TUE	WED	THU	FRI	SAT
NIGHT	73	140	208	271	333	394	14

at bedtime

Traditional Doxology recited after each psalm or canticle

Glory to the Father and to the Son
and to the Holy Spirit,
As it was in the beginning, is now,
and will be forever. Amen.

The **Antiphon** is then traditionally repeated after the doxology.

SOLEMNITY GOSPELS in ORDINARY TIME	441
ACKNOWLEDGEMENTS	442
INDEX of SONGS	445
INDEX of PSALMS	447
INDEX of CANTICLES	
& READINGS on THE CHRISTIAN LIFE	448
INDEX of ANTIPHONS & RESPONSORY VERSES	449
PSALTER COMPARISON	450

VIGIL of SUNDAY
(Saturday Evening)

+ *God, come to my assistance;*   Psalm 70:2
Lord, make haste to help me!

Glory to the Father and to the Son and to the Holy Spirit: as it was in the beginning, is now, and will be forever.
Amen.

Now thank we all our God
With heart and hands and voi-ces,
Who won-drous things has done,
In whom this world re-joi-ces;
Who from our mo-thers' arms
Has blessed/ us on our way
With count-less gifts of love,
And still is ours to-day.

All praise and thanks to God
Our Ab-ba now be giv-en,
With Son and Spir-it as
They reign in high-est heav-en:
The one e-ter-nal God,
Whom heav-en and earth a-dore!
For thus it was, is now,
And shall be ev-er-more.

Text: Martin Rinckart, 1636 (see Ecclesiastes 50:22-24)
translation by Catherine Winkworth, 1858, altered
Music: 67 67 66 66, NUN DANKET; Johann Cruger, 1648

PSALM 113

Antiphon *No servant can serve two lords,*
and so you cannot serve
God and mammon.   Lk 16:13

Hallelujah! Praise Adonai!
Praise, you who serve Adonai!
Praise the name Adonai!
Blessed be the name of Adonai
from now and to forevermore.

From the rising of the sun to its setting
praised be the name Adonai.
Exalted over all the nations is Adonai,
the glory above the heavens.

Who is like our God Adonai,
sitting enthroned on high,
leaning to look down
on the heavens and the earth?

The One who raises the poor from dust
and lifts up the needy from ash heaps
to sit with princes, the princes of the people,
who settles the childless woman in a home,
a happy mother of children.
Hallelujah! Praise Adonai!

Glory to the Father and to the Son and to the Holy Spirit:
as it was in the beginning, is now, and will be forever. Amen.

Repeat antiphon.

PSALM 116:10-19

Antiphon   *As I, the Lord and Teacher, washed your feet,*
so also are you to wash the feet of each other.

Jn 13:14

I believed it and so said,
"I am greatly afflicted."
I said when it dismayed me,
"Everyone is a liar."

How can I repay to Adonai
all the goodness to me?
I will lift the cup of salvation
and I will call on the name of Adonai.

My vows to Adonai I will now fulfill
in the presence of all the people.
Precious in the eyes of Adonai
are the saints to the death.

O, Adonai, I am truly your servant,
your servant and child of your maidservant;
you freed me from the chains.
I will offer to you the sacrifice of thanksgiving
and I will call on the name of Adonai.

My vows to Adonai I will now fulfill
in the presence of all the people,
in courts of the house of Adonai,
in your midst, Jerusalem.
Hallelujah! Praise Adonai!

Glory...   Antiphon

PSALM 122

Antiphon	*Amen I tell you,*	
	you will be with me in paradise.	Lk 23:43

I rejoiced with those saying to me,
"Let us go to Adonai's house."
Our feet stand in your gates, Jerusalem.

Jerusalem is built like a city
formed together, a compact.
There the tribes go up,
the tribes of Adonai.

Make it in Israel a statute
to praise the name of Adonai,
for there stand the thrones of justice,
thrones of the house of David.

Pray for the peace of Jerusalem!
May those who love you be secure.
May peace be within your walls,
security within your citadels.

For the sake of my sisters and brothers and friends
now I will say, "Peace be with you."
For the sake of the house of our God Adonai
I will seek your prosperity.

Glory…

Antiphon

PSALM 141

Antiphon *Blessed are the merciful,*
for they will receive mercy. Mt 5:7

Adonai, I call to you; be quick to come to me.
Hear my voice when I call to you.
May my prayer be as incense before you,
lifting my hands in evening sacrifice.

Set guard, Adonai, over my mouth.
Keep watch over the door of my lips.
Let my heart not be drawn to evil matter,
to join in wicked deeds with their doers
or to eat of their delicacies.

Let the just person strike me with kindness
and rebuke me with oil on my head;
my head will not refuse this,
my prayer is ever against evil deeds.

Their rulers will drop over cliff edge;
they will learn that my words were well spoken:
"As a plower breaks up the earth
  our bones were scattered at the mouth of Sheol."

But on you, Lord Adonai, are my eyes,
and in you I take refuge;
my soul you do not give over to death.

Keep me from the hands of the snares
and from the traps of those doing evil.
When they fall together into their nets,
keep me in safety.

Glory... Antiphon

VIGIL OF SUNDAY (Saturday Evening)

PSALM 142

Antiphon *Let the light of you shine before humanity,*
that they may see your good works
and give glory to your Father in heaven.   Mt 5:16

My voice cries to Adonai;
my voice asks for mercy from Adonai,
before whom I pour out my complaint,
before whom I tell my trouble.
When my spirit grows faint within me
then you know my way.

In the path where I walk
they hid a snare for me.
Look right and see:
the one with concern for me
has fled away from me for refuge;
there is no one who cares for my life.

I cry to you, Adonai,
and say you are my refuge,
my portion in the land of the living.
Listen, El, to my cry,
for I am in desperate need.

Rescue me from the strong pursuers;
set my soul free from prison to praise your name.
The righteous ones will gather about me
because you will be good to me.

Glory…

Antiphon

PHILIPPIANS 2:6-11

Antiphon

*Do nothing out of selfishness
or for vainglory,
but humbly deem others
as greater than yourselves.* Phil 2:3

Christ Jesus, though in the form of God,
did not deem equality with God something to grasp,
but emptied himself,
taking the form of a slave,
coming in human likeness.

And being found in human fashion,
he humbled himself,
becoming obedient until death,
and death on a cross.

And so God highly exalted him,
and gave to him the name above every name,
that in the name of Jesus every knee should bend,
of heavenly beings and earthly beings,
and beings under the earth;

And every tongue confess
to the glory of God the Father
that Jesus Christ is Lord.

Glory...

Antiphon

VIGIL OF SUNDAY (Saturday Evening)

READING   **ROMANS 11:30-36**

As you then disobeyed God,
but now have received mercy
by way of these disobediences,
so also others have disobeyed in the same mercy
so that they also may now receive mercy.
For God locked up all in disobedience
so that God may show mercy to all.
O the depth
of riches and wisdom and knowledge of God;
how inscrutable the judgments
and unsearchable the ways,
for who has known the mind of the Lord?
Or who has been the Lord's counselor?
Or who has given anything to the Lord to be repaid?
Because of God, through God, and to God
all things are.
To God is the doxa-glory for the eons. Amen.

RESPONSORY   Ps 111:2,4,10

Great are the works of the Lord…
                 …pondered by all who delight in them.

Praise enduring for deeds of wonder…
                 …pondered by all who delight in them.

Glory to the Father and to the Son and to the Holy Spirit:
                 …Great are the works of the Lord,
                   pondered by all who delight in them.

GOSPEL CANTICLE OF MARY   **LUKE 1:46-55**

Antiphon   *My soul magnifies the Lord,*
           with Abraham and his descendants forever.

+ My soul is stretched full with praise of the Lord,
  and my spirit, beyond joy in God, my Savior,
  who chose to lay eyes on this humble servant.

  Behold, now and forward,
  each and every age will call me blessed,
  for the Mighty One did great things to me.
  Holy is the name and the mercy
  to generations and generations,
  the ones fearing the One,

  Who scattered the haughty of mind and heart,
  pulled the powerful off their high place,
  and lifted with dignity the humble in need.

  The hungering are filled with good things,
  the rich are sent away empty,
  and servant Israel is given relief

  with a memory of mercy to remember,
  the promise spoken to our ancestors,
  to Abraham and his descendants forever.

Glory…

                                                Antiphon

VIGIL OF SUNDAY (Saturday Evening)

INTERCESSIONS
- Lord, make your Church ever new…
- Watch over our pope and bishops…
- Keep us united in our diversity…
- Inspire leaders with your justice…
- Keep married couples in love…
- For respect for the dignity of the human person…
- For a culture of vocations all over the world…
- For all who have died…

- In gratitude for blessings…; Abba thank you.
- For the sins of this day…; Lord Jesus have mercy.
- With concerns over tomorrow…; Holy Spirit help.

Our Fath-er, who art in heav-en,
hal-lowed be thy name;
thy king dom come, thy will be done
on earth as it is in heav-en.

Give us this day our dai-ly bread,
and for-give us our tres-pass-es,
as we for-give those who tres-pass a-gainst/ us;
and lead us not in-to temp-ta/-tion,
but de-liv-er us from e\-vil.

+ *May the Lord bless us, protect us from all evil,*
  and bring us to everlasting life. ***Amen.***

SUNDAY NIGHT I
(Saturday Night)

+ *God, come to my assistance;* Psalm 70:2
  Lord, make haste to help me!

Glory...

Ye sons and daugh\-ters of\ the King,
With heav'n-ly hosts\ in glo\-ry sing,
To-day the grave\ has lost\ its sting: Al-le-lu-ia!

On that first morn\-ing of\ the week,
Be-fore the day\ be-gan\ to break,
The Ma-rys went\ their Lord\ to seek: Al-le-lu-ia!

An an-gel bade\ their sor\-row flee,
By speak-ing thus\ un-to\ the three:
"Your Lord is gone\ to Gal\-i-lee":   Al-le-lu-ia!

That night th'A-pos\-tles met\ in fear,
A-midst them came\ their Lord\ most dear
And said, "Peace be\ un-to\ you here":   Al-le-lu-ia!

Bless-ed are they\ that have\ not seen
And yet whose faith\ has con\-stant been,
In life e-ter\-nal they\ shall reign: Al-le-lu-ia!

And we with ho\-ly Church\ u-nite,
As ev-er-more\ is just\ and right,
In glo-ry to\ the King\ of light: Al-le-lu-ia!

Al-le-lu-ia\! Al-le\-lu-ia! Al-le-lu-ia!

PSALM 4

Antiphon *You are witnesses of these things,* Lk 24:46
the Christ to suffer, and rise on the third day.

When I call, answer me, righteous God.
From distress you give me relief.
Be merciful to me and hear my prayer.

Until when, human, will you shame the glory?
Until when will you love delusion and seek the lie?
Know that Adonai set apart the faithful for Adonai
and will hear when I call.

When you tremble, do not sin.
Search within your heart and on your bed.
Offer sacrifices of goodness, and trust Adonai.

Many are asking,
"Who can show us good?
 Adonai, let the light of your faces shine upon us."

You put joy in my heart, more joy
than when their grain and new wine abound.
In the peace of God's face I will lie down and sleep,
for you alone, Adonai, make me dwell in safety.

Glory...

                                                             Antiphon

Song text: see John 20; attrib. to Jean Tisserand, d. 1494;
translated by John M. Neal, 1851, altered
Music: 888, O FILII ET FILIAE; Chant Mode II,
Airs sur les hymnes sacrez, odes et noels, 1623

PSALM 134

Antiphon *Be not afraid.*

Mt 10:26, 14:27, 17:17, 28:10,...;
Mk 6:50,...; Lk 5:10, 12:4,...;
Jn 6:20,...

Come and bless Adonai,
all you servants of Adonai,
and you ministers at night
in the house of Adonai.

Lift up your hands in the sanctuary
and bless Adonai!
May you be blessed from Zion by Adonai,
the One Making heavens and earth.

Glory…

Antiphon

READING **DEUTERONOMY 6:4-7**

Hear, Israel! The Lord our God is the one Lord!
Love the Lord, your God, with all your heart,
and with all your soul, and with all your strength.
These commands I am giving you this day
to be the commands on your heart.
Impress them on your children,
and talk about them when you sit in your house
and when you walk on the road,
when you lie down,
and when you get up.

SUNDAY NIGHT I (Saturday Night)

RESPONSORY Ps 31:6

Into your hands, Lord,…   …*I commend my spirit.*

You have redeemed us, Lord God of truth.
 …*I commend my spirit.*

Glory to the Father and to the Son and to the Holy Spirit:
 …*Into your hands, Lord,*
 I commend my spirit.

Antiphon

> *Lord, save/ us!*
> *Save/ us while\ we are a-wake\,*
> *pro-tect us while we are a-sleep,*
> *that we may keep our watch/ with Christ/*
> *and when we sleep\, rest/ in his\ peace.*

GOSPEL CANTICLE of SIMEON **LUKE 2:29-32**

+ Now, Master, you set free your servant
 according to your word in peace;

 my eyes have seen your salvation,
 which you have prepared
 before the face of all the peoples,

 a light for revelation to the nations
 and glory for your people, Israel.

Glory Antiphon

+ *May the all-powerful Lord*
 grant us a restful night and a peaceful death. **Amen**.

HAIL MARY…

SUNDAY READEADINGS

+ *Lord, open my lips* Psalm 51:17
and my mouth will declare your praise.

Glory…

On this day, the first of days,
God the Fa-ther's Name we praise;
Who, cre-a-tion's Lord and Spring
Did the world from dark-ness bring.

On this day th'e-ter-nal Son
Ov-er death has tri-umph won;
On this day the Spir-it came
Bring-ing gifts of liv-ing flame.

Fa-ther, who did fash-ion me
Im-age of your-self to be,
Fill me with your love div-ine,
Let my ev'ry thought be thine.

God, the bless-ed Three-in-One,
Dwell with-in my heart a-lone;
As you give your-self to me
May I give my-self to thee.

Text: *Le Mans Breviary*, 1748,
Hymns Ancient and Modern, Henry W. Baker, 1861, altered
Music: 77 77 LUBECK, 77 77, *Gesanbuch*
by Johann A. Freylinghausen, 1704

PSALM 95

Antiphon *Where two or three are gathered in my name,*
there am I in the midst of them.

Mt 18:20

Come, let us sing to Adonai;
let us shout to our saving Rock.
Come, let us extol Adonai
with thanksgiving and with song.

Adonai is the great El,
the great King above all those little "g" gods,
holding in hand the depths of earth
and peaks of mountains,
the sea and dry land formed by that hand.

Come, let us worship and bow
and kneel before Adonai who made us.
For God is our God, and we are the people
of the pasture and flock and care of our God.

"If today you hear the voice
 do not harden your heart,
 as at Meribah and the desert day at Massah
 where your ancestors tested me;
 they tried me though they saw my deeds.

 For forty years was my anger on that generation,
 the people straying in their heart;
 and so they did not know my ways
 and were unable to enter my rest."

Glory...   Antiphon

PSALM 1

Antiphon   *Blessed are the poor in spirit,*
              for theirs is the kingdom of heaven.   Mt 5:3

Blessings are on the human being
who stands not in wicked counsel,
who walks not on the path of sinners,
nor sits in the seat of mockers,
but rather delights in the law of Adonai
and meditates on it by day and by night.

This blessed one is like a tree
planted by streams of water
which yields fruit in the season
and its leaf withers not
and prosperity finds what this one does.

Not so those who do wicked,
but rather like the chaff blown in the wind
those who do wicked
will be unable to stand in the judgment
nor sinners in the assembly of the just.

Adonai watches over the way of the just
and wicked ways will perish.

Glory...   Antiphon

PSALM 2

Antiphon   *Wind blows where it will and you hear its sound*
              not knowing from where it comes and goes away;
              so with everyone who is born of the Spirit.   Jn 3:8

PSALM 2

Why do nations rage and peoples plot vanity?
Kings of the earth make their stand
and ruling ones gather together
against Adonai and Adonai's anointed one:
"Let us break their chains,
 let us throw off their fetters."

The One enthroned in the heavens laughs,
the Lord scoffs and rebukes them.
In anger and in wrath the Lord terrifies them.
"I indeed installed my king
 on my holy hill of Zion.

 I will proclaim a decree of Adonai who said,
 'You are my son, this day I have begotten you.
 Ask of me and nations are your inheritance,
 and your possession to the ends of earth.
 You will rule them with a scepter of iron
 and dash them to pieces of what potters make.'

 Kings, now be wise! Rulers of earth, be warned!
 Serve Adonai with fear; rejoice with trembling!
 Kiss my son, lest he be angry
 and you be destroyed
 for in a moment he can flare up in wrath.

 Blessings on all
 who take refuge in him."

Glory...

Antiphon

PSALM 3

Antiphon
*Whoever does and teaches
these commandments
will be called great
in the Kingdom of heaven.* Mt 5:19

How many, Adonai, are the foes,
many rising against me,
many saying of me,
"No deliverance by God for this self!"

But you, Adonai, shield around me,
my glorious One, you lift my head.
My voice cries to Adonai
who answers me from the holy hill.

I lie down and I sleep;
and I wake because Adonai sustains me.
I will have no fear of tens of thousands of people
who are drawn up on every side against me.

Arise, Adonai! Deliver me, my God!
You struck the jaw of enmity
and broke the teeth of badness.
From Adonai is the deliverance.
May your blessing be on your people.

Glory…

Antiphon

PSALM 66

Antiphon
*The harvest is plenty
but workers are few;
ask the Lord of the harvest
to cast workers into the harvest.*   Lk 10:2

Shout to God all the earth!
Sing the glory of the name!
Offer glory and praise to God!
Say to God, "How awesome are you;
  how great are your deeds."

Before you and your power
those in enmity cringe.
All of the earth bow down to you,
they sing praise to you,
they sing praise to your name.

Come and see the deeds of God who is awesome,
the works on behalf of all sons and daughters.
God turned the sea into dry land;
through the river they passed on foot.

Let us rejoice in God.
God rules forever with power,
with eyes watching the nations.
Let no rebels rise up.

Peoples, bless our God!
Make heard the praise!
God preserves our life among the living,
and lets not our foot to slip.

PSALM 66, continued

God, you tested us, refined us as silver is refined.
You let us be brought into prison,
you let burdens be put on our backs,
you let human beings ride over our head.

We went through the fire and through the waters
and you brought us to the place of freedom.

I will come to your temple with burnt offerings,
I will fulfill to you my vows, promised on my lips,
spoken in a time of trouble.

Sacrifices of fat animals I will sacrifice to you;
with offerings of rams I will offer bull and goats.

Come! Listen! Let me tell all who fear God
what God has done for my very self.
To God my mouth cried out
with praise on my tongue.

Had I cherished sin in my heart
the Lord would not have listened.
Surely God listened and heard my voice of prayer.

Blessed be God, who rejected not my prayer
nor took from within me
the Lord's own hesed-mercy.

Glory…

Antiphon *The harvest is plenty*
but workers are few;
ask the Lord of the harvest
to cast workers into the harvest.   Lk 10:2

PSALM 104

Antiphon
*Peace to you;
as the Father has sent me,
so I send you;
receive the Holy Spirit.* Jn 20:21

Blessed be Adonai, my soul!
My God, Adonai, you are beyond measure.
Splendor and majesty clothe you,
wrapped in light as a garment,

stretching out over the heavens like the tent,
laying beams on the waters of the upper chambers.
You make a chariot of the clouds,
riding on wings of wind,
making messengers of the winds
and servants of flaming fire.

You have set foundations on earth,
unmoveable for ever and ever.
Deep is your garment, covering the earth;
above the mountains the waters stood.

At your rebuke, they then fled;
at the sound of your thunder they took flight.
They flowed over mountains
and went down into valleys
to the places you assigned for them.
You set a boundary they are not to cross;
never again are they to cover the earth.

PSALM 104, continued

You make springs of water pour into ravines;
between the mountains they flow.
They give water to all beasts of the field;
they quench the thirst of donkeys.
Birds of the air nest in branches beside them;
they give you their song.

You water mountains from your upper chambers;
by the fruit of your works the earth is satisfied.
You make grass grow for the cattle
and plants for human beings to cultivate

to bring forth food from the earth,
wine to make glad the human heart,
oil to make faces shine,
and bread to sustain the human heart.

They are all Adonai's well watered trees,
cedars of Lebanon planted
where birds make their nests,
and the pine tree where the stork makes a home,
mountains, the high ones, for wild goats,
and crags, a refuge for rock-badgers.

You mark off seasons by the moon,
and know the going down of the sun.
You bring darkness
and all beasts of the forest prowl in the night.
The young lions roar for prey
seeking their food from God.

The sun rises, they steal away,
and into their dens they lie down.
Human beings go out to do their work
and labor until the evening.

How varied are your works, Adonai!
All of them in wisdom you made.
The earth is full of your creatures.

There is the sea, vast and spacious;
living creatures countless there,
small ones and large ones.
There ships go about
and leviathan which you formed for frolic.

All of them look to you
to give them food at their time.
You give to them and they gather,
you open your hands
and they are goodly satisfied.

You hide your face and they are terrified,
you take away their breath and they die
and to their dust they return.
You breathe your Spirit, and they are created,
and you renew the faces of earth.

May the glory of Adonai endure to forever.
May Adonai rejoice in the works:
looking at the earth, she trembles,
touching the mountains, they smoke.

PSALM 104, continued

I will sing to Adonai during my life
and sing praise to my God while I still am.
May my meditation be found pleasing.
I rejoice in Adonai.
May sin vanish from the earth
and the wicked be so no more.

Bless Adonai, my soul! Hallelujah!

Glory...

Antiphon *Peace to you;*
as the Father has sent me,
so I send you;
receive the Holy Spirit. Jn 20:21

READING	Year I	Year II
Baptism	Isaiah 42:1-9	Isaiah 49:1-9
week 2	Romans 4	Genesis 9
3	Romans 8:1-17	Genesis 18
4	Romans 11:25-36	Genesis 27:1-29
5	1 Corinthians 1:1-17	Genesis 39
6	1 Corinthians 6:12-20	1 Thessalonians 1:1-2:12
7	1 Corinthians 10:14-11:1	2 Corinthians 1:1-14
8	1 Corinthians 14:20-40	2 Corinthians 7
9	James 2:1-13	Galatians 1:1-12
10	Sirach 46	Philipians 1:1-11
11	Joshua 24	Isaiah 44:21-45:3
12	Judges 13	Zechariah 3 & 4
13	1 Samuel 5 & 6	Nehemiah 3 & 4
14	1 Samuel 17	Proverbs 1 & 2
15	2 Samuel 1	Job 1
16	2 Samuel 15 & 16	Job 11

SUNDAY READINGS

17	1 Kings 9	Job 28
18	1 Kings 19	Obediah
19	2 Kings 4:8-44	Jonah 1 & 2
20	Ephesians 1:1-14	Ecclesiastes 1
21	Ephesians 4:17-24	Titus 1
22	2 Kings 14	1 Timothy 5:3-25
23	Amos 7	2 Peter 1:1-11
24	Hosea 8	Esther 1 & 2
25	Isaiah 6	Tobit 1
26	Micah 3	Judith 1 & 2 & 3
27	Isaiah 22:1-14	Sirach 1
28	Zephaniah 3	Sirach 10
29	2 Kings 22 & 23	Sirach 26
30	Jeremiah 23	Wisdom 1
31	2 Kings 24 & 25	Wisdom 8
32	Ezekiel 2 & 3	1 Macabees 1:1-25
33	Ezekiel 16	1 Macabees 4
34	Daniel 7	Daniel 7

or SHORT READING **REVELATION 7:9-12**

I saw, behold, a crowd too great to number, out of every nation and tribe and people and tongue, standing before the throne and before the Lamb clothed in white robes and with palms in their hands. They cried out with a loud voice saying, *Salvation to our God sitting on the throne, and to the Lamb.* And all the angels stood around the throne with the elders and the four living creatures, and fell on their faces before the throne and worshipped God, saying: *Amen, blessing and glory and wisdom and thanks and honor and power and strength to our God to the eons of the eons. Amen.*

Let us bless the Lord. *Thanks be to God.*

SUNDAY PROPHETS

Praise to the Lord,
the Al-migh-ty, the King of cre-a-tion!
O my soul, praise the Lord,
who is our health and sal-va-tion!
Join the full throng; Wake, harp and psal-ter and song;
Sound forth in glad ad-o-ra-tion!

Praise to the Lord,
the on-ly One, the Ma-ker of heav-en,
It is the Lord who made the earth,
the seas and all in them.
Can we yet see   How our de-sire\ and need
Meet in our Lord's will and un-ion.

Praise to the Lord,
who brings our work to pros-per be-fore us;
Who from the heav-ens sent
    the mer-cy riv-er in-to us.
Pon-der a-new   What the Al-migh-ty can do,
Who in div-ine love be-friends us.

Praise to the Lord,
oh let all that is in us sing prais-ing!
All that has life and breath,
come forth and with us sing prais-ing!
Let the A-men   Sound from all peo-ple a-gain;
Glad-ly sing wor-ship and prais-ing!

> Text: from Nehemiah 9:6, Joachim Neander, 1679;
> translated by Catherine Winkworth, 1863, altered;
> verse 2 by Stephen J. Wolf, 2009
> Music: 14 14 4 7 8 LOBE DEN HERREN; *Straslund Gesangbuch*, 1665

DANIEL 3:52-57

Antiphon *God sent the Son into the cosmos*
not to condemn
but that the cosmos might be saved
through him.   Jn 3:17

Blessed are you, O Lord, God of our ancestors,
praiseworthy and exalted above all forever.

Blessed is your glorious and holy name,
praiseworthy and exalted above all forever.

Blessed are you in the temple of your sacred glory,
praiseworthy and exalted above all forever.

Blessed are you on your royal throne,
praiseworthy and exalted above all forever.

Blessed are you who sit high on the cherubim
   and look into the depths,
praiseworthy and exalted above all forever.

Blessed are you in the dome of heaven,
to be hymned and glorified forever.

Bless the Lord, all you works of the Lord,
sing praise and high exaltation forever.

Glory…

Antiphon

ISAIAH 33:2-10

Antiphon *Our hope of resurrection has dawned.*

Be gracious to us, Adonai; for you we long;
be our strength in the mornings
and our salvation in times of distress.

At the voice of thunder peoples flee,
at your rising the nations scatter
and your plunder is harvested
as a harvesting by the young locust,
like a swarm of locusts pouncing.

Dwelling on the height, exalted is Adonai,
who will fill Zion with justice and righteousness,
who will be the sure foundation for your seasons,
the rich store of salvation, wisdom and knowledge;
fear of Adonai is the treasure.

Look! Their brave ones cry in the street,
envoys of peace in bitter weeping.
Highways are deserted, road travel ceases,
treaties are broken, cities are despised,
and no one is respected.

The land mourns and wastes away,
Lebanon withers in shame.
The Sharon is like the Arabah;
dropping are Bashan and Carmel.
"Now will I arise," says our Lord,
"Now will I be exalted, now will I lift up."

Glory...   Antiphon

HOSEA 6:1-6

Antiphon *At table in the house of Matthew*
many sinners came and sat
with Jesus and his disciples.   Mt 9:10

Come and let us return to Adonai,
who let us be torn up but will heal us,
who let us be injured but will bind our wounds,

who will revive us after two days
and restore us on the third day
that we may live in the presence.

So let us know,
let us press on to know Adonai,
who will appear coming as the sun rises,
who will come to us like the winter rain,
watering the earth like spring rain.

What can I do with you Ephraim?
What can I do with you Judah?
Your loyal love is like morning mist,
and like the early dew that disappears.

For this I cut to pieces with the prophets
and have slain with words of my mouth
and judgments of lightning shining:
For it is mercy that I desire and not sacrifice,
knowledge of God rather than burnt offerings.

Glory…

                                                              Antiphon

JEREMIAH 7:3b-7

Antiphon
Deal with your neighbor with justice;
oppress no alien, orphan, or widow;
shed no innocent blood;
and follow no other "god."   Jer 7:5b.6

This says Adonai Sabaoth, God of Israel:
"Reform your ways and your actions
 and I may live with you in this place!

Trust you not in words of deception to say,
'Temple of Adonai,
 Temple of Adonai,
 Temple of Adonai.'

If indeed to reform
you change your ways and your actions,
if to deal you deal with each other with justice,

you oppress no alien, orphan or widow,
you shed no more innocent blood in this place,
you follow no other "gods" to your own harm,

then will I let you live in this place
in the land I gave to your ancestors
from ever and to ever."

Glory...

Antiphon

READING   **EZEKIEL 37:1-14**

The hand of Adonai was on me, and brought me out by the Spirit of Adonai and set me in the middle of the valley full of bones, and led me among them back and forth, to see many great ones on the floors of the valley and to see the very dry ones, and asking me, "Son of man, can these bones live?"

And I said, "You, Sovereign Adonai, you know." And then to me, "Prophesy to these bones and say to them, the dry bones,

'Hear the word of Adonai! This Sovereign Adonai says to these bones: See! I am making breath enter into you and you will come to life, and I will attach to you tendons, and I will make flesh come upon you, and I will cover skin on you, and I will put breath in you, and you will come to life; and then you will know that I am your Adonai.'"

So I prophesied as I was commanded, and as I prophesied a noise came with a sight: rattling bones coming together bone to bone. And I saw a sight, tendons on them and flesh appeared, and skin covered them over, but there was no breath in them.

Then saying to me, "Prophesy to the breath! Prophesy, son of man, and say to the breath, 'This says Sovereign Adonai: Come from the four winds, breath, and breathe into these slain that they may live!'"

So I prophesied as I was commanded and the breath entered into them, and they came to life, and they stood up on their feet, a very very vast army.

EZEKIEL 37:1-14, continued

And then to me, "Son of man, these bones are the whole house of Israel. See how they say, 'Our bones are dried up and our hope is gone and we are cut off from ourselves.' Prophesy, therefore, and say to them,

'This says Sovereign Adonai: See! Opening your graves, I will bring you, my people, up from your graves and I will bring you back to the land of Israel. Then you will know that I am Adonai, when I open your graves and bring you to me, my people, and I will put my Spirit in you and you will live, and I will settle you in your land.

Then you will know that I Adonai have spoken and I have done it, declares Adonai.'"

RESPONSORY   Luke 18:13; 22:69

Lord Jesus Christ, Son of the living God…
> …*have mercy on us.*

You are seated at the right hand of the Father…
> …*have mercy on us.*

Glory to the Father and to Son and to the Holy Spirit:
> …*Lord Jesus Christ, Son of the living God,*
> *have mercy on us.*

HYMN, TE DEUM

O God, we praise you and know you as Lord.
Father everlasting, all the earth does worship you.
To you all angels cry aloud,
    the heavens, all powers,
    and cherubim and seraphim continually:

Holy, Holy, Holy, Lord God Sabaoth;
heaven and earth are filled to the full
with the majesty of your glory.
The glorious company of Apostles praise you;
in good gathering the Prophets praise you;
the noble testimony of Martyrs praise you;
the holy Church all over the world know you:
  Our Father, in majesty infinite,
  your true and only Son,
  and Holy Spirit Comforter.
You, Christ, are the King of glory
  and everlasting Son of the Father.
Taking it onto yourself to deliver humanity,
  you did not avoid the virgin womb.
Overcoming the harsh death
  you opened the kingdom of heaven to all believers.
You sit at the right hand of God
  in the glory of the Father.
And we believe you will come to be our judge.
Day by day in every place
  we give you thanks and ever praise your name.
Help your servants redeemed by your blood
  and number them with the saints in eternal glory.
Save your people and bless your heritage;
  govern us, Lord, and lift us to forever.
Keep us this day, Lord, without sin.
  Have mercy on us, Lord, have mercy;
  Let your mercy rest upon us.

Let us bless the Lord. *Thanks be to God.*

SUNDAY MORNING

+ *God, come to my assistance;*   Psalm 70:2
  Lord, make haste to help me!

  Glory...

Ho-ly, **ho-ly**, **ho-ly**, Lord God Al-migh-ty!
Ear-ly in the morn-ing our song shall rise to thee;
Ho-ly, ho-ly, ho-ly, mer-ci-ful and migh-ty!
God in Three Per-sons, bless-ed Trin-i-ty!

Ho-ly, ho-ly, ho-ly! All the saints a-dore thee,
Cast-ing down their gold-en crowns
                       a-round the glass-y sea;
Cher-u-bim and ser-a-phim fall-ing down be-fore thee,
Who was, and is, and ev-er-more shall be.

Ho-ly, ho-ly, ho-ly! Though con-fu-sion hide you,
Glo-ry shin-ing through the blurr
                       of cloud-ed hu-man view;
You a-lone are ho-ly; there is none be-side you:
Per-fect and pure, your love in all you do.

Ho-ly, ho-ly, ho-ly! Lord God Al-migh-ty!
All cre-a-tion praise your name in earth & sky & sea.
Ho-ly, ho-ly, ho-ly, mer-ci-ful and migh-ty!
God in Three Persons, bless-ed Trin-i-ty!

Text: From Revelation 4:8; by Reginald Heber, 1827, altered
Music: 11 12 12 10, NICAEA; John B. Dykes, 1861

PSALM 63:1-8

Antiphon *Watch ready, for you know*
neither the day nor the hour.   Mt 25:13

God, you are my God;
you I earnestly seek.
My soul, she thirsts for you,
my body, he longs for you,
as in a land with no water, dry and weary.

So in the sanctuary I saw you,
beheld you in your power and glory.
Your love is better than life itself;
my lips will glorify you.

So I will bless you
in all the ways I am alive;
in your name I will lift up my hands.
As with fatness and richness,
my soul will be satisfied;
with singing lips my mouth will sing praise.

When I remember you on my bed,
through night watches I think of you,
you who are my savior;
then in the shadow of your wings I sing.
My soul stays close to you;
your right hand upholds me.

Glory...

Antiphon

DANIEL 3:57-90

Antiphon *Taking the five loaves and the two fishes,*
looking up to heaven,
he blessed,
and broke,
and gave them to the disciples
to set before the crowd. Lk 9:16

Bless the Lord, all you works of the Lord,
exalt and sing praise to forever.
Angels of the Lord, bless the Lord,
You heavens, bless the Lord,
All you waters above the heavens, bless the Lord,
All you powers, bless the Lord,
Sun and moon, bless the Lord,
Stars of heaven, bless the Lord.

All you rain and dew, bless the Lord,
All you winds, bless the Lord,
You fire and heat, bless the Lord,
You ice and cold, bless the Lord,
You dews and showers, bless the Lord,
You snows and frosts, bless the Lord,
You nights and days, bless the Lord,
You light and darkness, bless the Lord,
You lightning and clouds, bless the Lord.

Let the earth bless the Lord,
exalt and sing praise to forever.
You mountains and hills, bless the Lord,
All things growing on the earth, bless the Lord,
You seas and rivers, bless the Lord,
You springs and ponds, bless the Lord,
You sea monsters and all swimmers, bless the Lord,
All you birds of the air, bless the Lord,
All you wild beasts and cattle, bless the Lord,
You sons and daughters, bless the Lord.

O Israel, bless the Lord,
exalt and sing praise to forever.
You priests of the Lord, bless the Lord,
You servants of the Lord, bless the Lord,
You spirits and souls of the just, bless the Lord,
You holy and humble in heart, bless the Lord,
Hananiah, Azariah, and Mishael, bless the Lord,
exalt and sing praise to forever…

Give thanks to the Lord, who is good,
whose mercy endures to forever.
Bless the God of "gods,"
all you who worship the Lord;
sing praise and give thanks to the One God
whose mercy endures to forever.

(*No doxology*)

Antiphon

PSALM 93

Antiphon *Do you ask if I am a king from yourself
or have others told you about me?* Jn 18:34

Adonai reigns, robed in majesty;
robed is Adonai
and belted with strength.

The world is firmly established;
she cannot be moved.
Your throne was set up from long ago;
from eternity you are.

The flooding sea lifted up, Adonai,
the seas lifted their voice;
the floods lifted up their pounding.

More than roaring thunders of great waters
or mighty breakers of the sea,
mighty in the height is Adonai.

Your statutes stand very firm;
your house, Adonai,
is adorned in holiness
for all the length of days.

Glory…

Antiphon

PSALM 118

Antiphon *I am the good shepherd,
and I know mine
and mine know me.* Jn 10:14

Give thanks to Adonai who is good,
whose mercy is to forever.

Let Israel now declare:
mercy to forever.
Let the house of Aaron declare:
mercy to forever.
Let those who fear Adonai declare:
mercy to forever.

In anguish I cried to Adonai
who answered me with freedom.
Adonai is with me,
I will not be afraid.
What can a mortal human do to me?
Before enmity I keep this in mind:
Adonai is with me, ready to help me.

Better to take refuge in Adonai
than to trust in the human;
Better to take refuge in Adonai
than to trust in a prince;

PSALM 118, continued

All the nations surrounded me,
indeed did they surround me;
in the name of Adonai indeed I cut them.
They swarmed around me like bees,
they crackled like thorns in a fire;
in the name of Adonai indeed I cut them.

To push back they pushed me back to fall
but Adonai came to my help.
Adonai became my strength and my song
and became to me salvation.
Shout joy and victory
in your tents, you righteous.

Adonai's right hand does a mighty thing,
Adonai's right hand lifted high.
Adonai's right hand does a mighty thing.
I will not die; I will live
and proclaim these deeds indeed.
To chasten, Adonai let me be chastened,
but did not give me to death.

Open for me the gates of righteousness;
I will enter through them
and give thanks to Adonai.
This is Adonai's gate,
where righteous ones may enter.
I will give thanks to you for you answered me
and you became to me salvation.

The stone they rejected as builders
became the cornerstone.
With Adonai this happened
and it is marvelous in our eyes.
This is the day Adonai has made;
let us rejoice in it and be glad.

Adonai, save now!
Adonai, grant success now!
Blessed is the one coming in the name of Adonai;
We bless you from Adonai's house.
Our El Adonai has enlightened us.

Join with boughs the festal procession
up to the horns of the altar.
To you, my God, I will give thanks.
You, my God, I will exalt.
Give thanks to Adonai who is good,
whose mercy is to forever.

Glory…

Antiphon	*I am the good shepherd,*	
	and I know mine	
	and mine know me.	Jn 10:14

PSALM 148

Antiphon	*This I command,*	
	that you love one another.	Jn 15:17

Hallelujah! Praise Adonai!
Give praise from the heavens!
Give praise in the heights.
Give praise all you angels.
Give praise all you hosts.

Give praise sun and moon.
Give praise all stars shining.
Give praise, you heavens of the heavens
and waters above the skies.

Let them praise the name Adonai,
who commanded and they were created,
who set them in place forever,
to forever the decree Adonai gave,
not to pass away.

Praise Adonai, you earth,
give praise you creatures of the sea
and all in the deep,
you lightning and hail,
you snow and cloud,
you wind of the storm,
all who do Adonai's bidding,

mountains and hills,
fruit trees and cedars,
wild animals and all cattle,
small creatures and birds of flight,

kings of the earth and the nations,
princes and all people ruling on earth,
young men and also maidens,
old men and children:

Let them praise the name Adonai
whose name alone is exalted,
whose splendor is above earth and the heavens,
who raised a horn for the people,

praise of all the saints,
of the sons and daughters of Israel,
of people close to the Lord.
Hallelujah! Praise Adonai!

Glory...

                                                            Antiphon

PSALM 149

Antiphon   *John the Baptist told his disciples,*
This joy of mine is full;
it is fitting for the Christ to increase
and for me to decrease.   Jn 3:30

Hallelujah! Praise Adonai!
Sing to Adonai a new song,
praise in the assembly of saints.
Let Israel rejoice in their Maker,
let the people of Zion be glad in their King.

Let them praise the name
with dance, tambourine and harp.
Let them make music for Adonai
who delights in Adonai's people.

Adonai crowns humble ones with salvation
and lets saints rejoice in honor
and sing for joy on their beds.
Praises of God be in their mouths
and a two-edged sword in their hands.

Retribution on the nations
and punishment on the peoples
binding royalty in restraint
and nobility in rings of iron:
the judgment decreed for them,
such is the glory of the saints.
Hallelujah! Praise Adonai!

Glory...   Antiphon

SUNDAY MORNING

PSALM 150

Antiphon *Be merciful
as your Father is merciful.* Lk 6:36

Hallelujah! Praise Adonai!
To El in the sanctuary, give praise.
In the mighty heavens, give praise.
For the works of power, give praise.
For surpassing greatness, give praise.

With sounding of trumpet, give praise.
With harp and lyre, give praise.
With tambourine and dance, give praise.
With flute and string, give praise.

With cymbals clashing, give praise.
With cymbals resounding, give praise.
Let all that has breath praise Adonai!
Hallelujah! Praise Adonai!

Glory…

Antiphon

READING **2 TIMOTHY 2:1-13**

And so you, my child, be empowered by the grace in Christ Jesus. And the things you heard from me through many witnesses, commit these to faithful people who will be competent to also teach others.

2 TIMOTHY 2:1-13, continued

Suffer ill as a good soldier of Jesus Christ. No soldiers are involved with the affairs of life, so that they may please those who enlisted them. And also in athletics one is not crowned without competing by the rules. It is best if the laboring farmer is the first to partake of crops. Ponder what I say, for the Lord will give you understanding in all things.

Remember Jesus Christ, raised from the dead, of the seed of David: this is my gospel, in which I suffer and am in chains as if an evildoer. But the word of God has not been chained. And so I endure all things for the chosen ones, that they also may obtain salvation in Christ Jesus with eternal glory.

Faithful is the word: If we died with him, we shall also live with him; if we endure, we shall also reign with him; if we deny, that one will also deny us; if we disbelieve, that one remains faithful, for he cannot deny himself.

RESPONSORY   Is 12:4,5

We give thanks to you, O Lord,…

...*calling on your name.*

We proclaim and make known your deeds…

...*calling on your name.*

Glory to the Father and to the Son and to the Holy Spirit:
...*We give thanks to you, O Lord,
calling on your name.*

GOSPEL CANTICLE OF ZECHARIAH — **LUKE 1:68-79**

Antiphon *Lord, you have raised salvation,*
saving strength from your own servant.

+ Blessed be the Lord the God of Israel
who chose a people,
visited them to bring redemption,
and raised salvation in the house of David,
saving strength from God's own servant,

 speaking from the age of the prophets
through the mouth of the holy prophet:
Salvation out of enmity,
even out of those who hate us,

 to show our ancestors how mercy works,
and to remember the holy promise of the Lord,
the covenant made for our father Abraham,
calming our fear and making us free
to serve God as holy and righteous and just
in the Lord's presence all our days.

 And you also child
will be called a prophet of the Most High
for you will go before the Lord to prepare his way
and give to his people a knowledge of salvation
known in accepting forgiveness of their sins.

 From the deepness of God's mercy on us,
a sun rising from the height will visit to appear
to those who sit in the dark or shadow of death,
and to guide our feet into the way of peace.

Glory... Antiphon

Gospel Reading for Sunday,

	Year A	Year B	Year C
Baptism of the Lord	Matthew 3:13-17	Mark 1:7-11	Luke 3:15-16,21-22
Trinity Sunday	John 3:16-18	Matthew 28:16-20	John 16:12-15
Corpus Christi	John 6:51-58	Mark 14:12-16,22-26	Luke 9:11b-17
Sun Week 2	John 1:29-34	John 1:35-42	John 2:1-11
3	Matt 4:12-23	Mark 1:14-20	Lk 1:1-4; 4:14-21
4	Matt 5:1-12a	Mark 1:21-28	Luke 4:21-30
5	Matt 5:13-16	Mark 1:29-39	Luke 5:1-11
6	Matt 5:17-37	Mark 1:40-45	Lk 6:17,20-26
7	Matt 5:38-48	Mark 2:1-12	Luke 6:27-38
8	Matt 6:24-34	Mark 2:18-22	Luke 6:39-45
9	Matt 7:21-27	Mark 2:23-3:6	Luke 7:1-10
10	Matt 9:9-13	Mark 3:20-35	Luke 7:11-17
11	Matt 9:36-10:8	Mark 4:26-34	Lk 7:36 - 8:3
12	Matt 10:26-33	Mark 4:35-41	Luke 9:18-24
13	Matt 10:37-42	Mark 5:21-43	Luke 9:51-62
14	Matt 11:25-30	Mark 6:1-6	Lk 10:1-12,17-20
15	Matt 13:1-23	Mark 6:7-13	Lk 10:25-37
16	Matt 13:24-43	Mark 6:30-34	Lk 10:38-42
17	Matt 13:44-52	John 6:1-15	Luke 11:1-13
18	Matt 14:13-21	John 6:24-35	Lk 12:13-21
19	Matt 14:22-33	John 6:41-51	Lk 12:32-48
20	Matt 15:21-28	John 6:51-58	Lk 12:49-53
21	Matt 16:13-20	John 6:60-69	Lk 13:22-30
22	Matt 16:21-27	Mk 7:1-8,14-15,21-23	Lk 14:1,7-14
23	Matt 18:15-20	Mark 7:31-37	Lk 14:25-33
24	Matt 18:21-35	Mark 8:27-35	Luke 15:1-32
25	Matt 20:1-16a	Mark 9:30-37	Luke 16:1-13
26	Matt 21:28-32	Mk 9:38-43,45,47-48	Lk 16:19-31

27 Matt 21:33-43	**27** Mark 10:2-16	**27** Luke 17:5-10
28 Matt 22:1-14	**28** Mark 10:17-30	**28** Lk 17:11-19
29 Matt 22:15-21	**29** Mark 10:35-45	**29** Luke 18:1-8
30 Matt 22:34-40	**30** Mark 10:46-52	**30** Luke 18:9-14
31 Matt 23:1-12	**31** Mark 12:28b-34	**31** Luke 19:1-9
32 Matt 25:1-13	**32** Mark 12:38-44	**32** Lk 20:27-38
33 Matt 25:14-30	**33** Mark 13:24-43	**33** Luke 21:5-19

Christ the King

34 Matt 25:31-46	**34** John 18:33b-37	**34** Lk 23:35-43

PETITIONS FOR THE CONSECRATION TO GOD
OF THE DAY AND ITS WORK

- For the Church and her ministry and apostolates…
- For secular authorities and all serving as stewards…
- For people who are poor or sick or in sorrow…
- For peace and the basic needs of each human being…
- For justice for migrant workers and refugees…
- For starving children awakening our conscience…
- For people living in subhuman conditions…
- For human beings unjustly imprisoned or enslaved…
- For workers in degrading or unsafe conditions…
- For laborers where treated as mere tools for profit…
- In gratitude for blessings and grace…
- For those who have asked for my prayer…
- For those for whom I have promised to pray…
- For those who weigh on my heart…

OUR FATHER…

+ *May the Lord bless us, protect us from all evil,
and bring us to everlasting life.* **Amen**.

SUNDAY DAYTIME

+ *God, come to my assistance;* Psalm 70:2
  Lord, make haste to help me!

  Glory...

Come, Ho-ly Spir_it, who ev-er One
Are with the Fa\-ther and/ the Son;
Come, Ho-ly Spir_it, our souls pos-sess
With your full flood of\ ho-li-ness;
With your full flood of\ ho-li-ness.

In will and deed, by heart and tongue,
With all our pow-ers, your praise/ be sung;
Light up in love our hu-man frame,
Till others catch the\ liv-ing flame;
Till others catch the\ liv-ing flame.

Fa-ther Al-migh-ty, hear now our cry
Through Je-sus Christ\ our Lord/ most high,
Who with the Ho-ly Spir-it and Thee
Do live and reign e\-ter-nal-ly;
Do live and reign e\-ter-nal-ly.

Text: attributed to Ambrose of Milan,
Nunc Sancte nobis Spiritus, d.397; translated by John Henry Newman,
Tracts for the Times, 1836, altered
Music: LAMBILLOTTE, LM; with repeat;
Louis Lambillotte, SJ, 1796-1855
Popular melody for: *Come, Holy Ghost, Creator Blest...*

PSALM 119:1-8
Aleph

Antiphon *You have heard it said,*
an eye for an eye and a tooth for a tooth;
but I tell you,
do not resist an evil doer.   Mt 5:38,39

Blessed are ones of your blameless way,
who walk by your law, Adonai.
Blessed are ones keeping your statutes,
seeking you with all their heart.

They do no wrong;
they walk in your ways.
You laid down your precepts
for full obedience.

Oh, that my ways were steadfast,
obedient to your decrees.
Then I would have no shame
when pondering all your commands.

I will praise you with a sincere heart
so to learn your righteous laws.
I will obey your decrees;
utterly forsake me not.

Glory…

Antiphon

PSALM 119:9-16
Beth

Antiphon   *It has been written,*
You shall worship the Lord your God
and only your God shall you serve.   Lk 4:8

How can a young one keep the purity way?
By living as is your word.
With all my heart I seek you;
let me not stray from your commands.

I hid your word in my heart
to sin not against you.
Be praised, Adonai.
Teach me your decrees.

I recount with my lips
all the laws of your mouth.
I rejoice in the way of your statutes
as in great riches.

I meditate on your precepts
and ponder your ways.
I delight in your decrees
and will not neglect your word.

Glory…

Antiphon

PSALM 23

Antiphon   *For I was hungry and you gave me to eat,*
thirsty and you gave me drink,
a stranger and you welcomed me,
naked and you clothed me,
ill and you cared for me,
in prison and you came to me.   Mt 25:35,36

Adonai is my shepherd; nothing do I lack.
My Lord lays me down in green pastures
and leads me beside still quiet waters,
restoring my soul
and guiding me in paths of justice
for the Lord's own namesake.

So when I walk in the deep dark valley
I will not fear for you are with me,
your rod and staff a comfort to me.

A table you prepare before me
in the presence even of enmity.
My head you anoint with oil
and my cup is overflowing.

Surely goodness and mercy will chase me
all the days of my life
and I will dwell in the Lord's own house
for the length of days.

Glory…

                                              Antiphon

PSALM 76

Antiphon   *The Son of humanity is Lord also of the sabbath.*
Mk 2:28

God is known in Judah; great in Israel is the Name.
In Salem is God's tent, in Zion the dwelling place.
There flashes broke the arrow,
shield and sword and weapons of war.

Giver of Light, you are,
more majestic than mountains of game.
Human beings of valiant heart lie plundered;
they sleep their sleep
and warriors can no more lift up their hands.
At your roar, O God of Jacob,
both chariot and horse lie still.

You are feared, you.
Who can stand before you when you are angry?
From the heavens you pronounced judgment;
when God rose for the judgment
to save all the afflicted of the land,
the land feared and she was quiet.

Even the wrath of humanity comes to praise you,
and you hold close the survivor of wrath.
Make vows! Fulfill vows to your God Adonai!
Let all the neighbors of God bring their gift
to the One rightly feared,
who checks the spirit of princes of the earth,
the One rightly feared by the kings and the queens.

Glory...   Antiphon

PSALM 119:161-168
Shin

Antiphon *Give them food yourselves.* Lk 9:13

Rulers persecute me for no reason
but at your word my heart trembles.
I rejoice in your promise
like one finding great spoil.

I hate and abhor falsehood;
it is your law I love.
Seven times daily I praise you
for your righteous laws.

Great peace comes to ones loving your law;
they do not stumble.
I wait for your salvation, Adonai;
I follow your commands.

My self she obeys your statutes,
for greatly do I love them.
I obey your precepts and statutes
for all my ways are before you.

Glory…

Antiphon

PSALM 119:169-176
Taw

Antiphon
*Do you believe
because you have seen me?
Blessed are those not seeing
but believing.*

Jn 20:29

May my cry come before you, Adonai,
as your word gives me understanding!
May my prayer come before you;
as you promise deliver me!

May praise of my lips overflow
for you teach me your decrees.
May my tongue sing your word
for all your righteous commands.

May your hand be a help to me
for your precepts I have chosen.
I long for your salvation, Adonai,
and your law is my delight.

Let my soul live that she may praise you;
may your laws sustain me.
I wandered like one lost sheep.
Seek your servant
for I forget not your commands.

Glory…

Antiphon

READING **HEBREWS 12:18-24**

You have not approached a mountain that can be felt, having been set on fire, and to darkness and to deep gloom and to whirlwind and to a trumpet sound and to a voice of words, such that hearers beg that not a word be added to them; for they could not bear the thing being charged: If even a beast touches the mountain, it will be stoned. So fearful was what appeared that Moses said, *I am terrified and trembling.*

But you have approached Zion, to the mountain and a city of the living God, to a heavenly Jerusalem, and to myriads of angels, to an assembly and a church of firstborn ones enrolled in heaven, and to God the judge of all people, and to spirits of the just who are made perfect, and to Jesus the mediator of a new covenant, and to a sprinkling of blood that speaks better than that of Abel.

RESPONSORY Ps 147:5

Great is our Lord… *…and mighty in power.*

Unlimited in understanding… *…and mighty in power.*

Glory to the Father and to the Son and to the Holy Spirit:
…Great is our Lord, and mighty in power.

Lord\, have mer-cy.
>*Christ\, have mer-cy.*
>>Lord\, have mer-cy.

SUNDAY EVENING

+ *God, come to my assistance;* Psalm 70:2
  Lord, make haste to help me!

  Glory...

A

Praise God, from whom all bless-ings flow;
Praise God, all crea-tures here be-low;
Praise God a-bove, ye heav'n-ly host,
Praise Fa-ther, Son, and Ho-ly Ghost.

For maj-es-ty and migh-ty deeds,
With blast of horn and tam-bou-rine,
With harp and dance and flute and string,
Let ev'-ry hu-man breath now sing.

Give praise to reach the migh-ty dome,
Give praise with cym-bals, crash-ing sound,
Give praise with lyre and bless-ed skill,
Praise God to wake the ho-ly hill.

Praise God, from whom all bless-ings flow;
Raise hands, all crea-tures here be-low;
Praise God, our Fa-ther and the Son
And Ho-ly Spir-it, Three in One.

Text: from Psalm 150; verse 1 by Thomas Ken, 1695, altered;
verses 2,3 by Stephen J. Wolf, 2009
Music: OLD HUNDREDTH, LM, Louis Bourgeois,
first published in *Genevan Psalter*, 1551

SUNDAY EVENING

B

Lord, your al-migh\-ty Word
Cha-os and dark/\-ness heard, And took their flight;
Hear us we hum-bly pray,
And where the gos-pel day
Sheds not its glo-rious ray, Let there be light!

Sa-vior, you came\ to give
Those who in shad/\-ows live Heal-ing and sight,
Health to the sick in mind, Sight to the in-ly blind,
Now to all hu-man-kind Let there be light!

Spir-it of truth\ and love,
Life-giv-ing, ho/\-ly dove, Speed forth your flight!
Move on the wa-ter's face
Bear-ing the lamp of grace,
And in earth's sad-dest place, Let there be light!

Holy and bless\-ed Three,
Glo/-rious Trin/\-i-ty, Wis-dom, love, might;
Bound-less as o-cean tide, Roll-ing in full-est pride,
Through the world far and wide, Let there be light!

Text: Based on Genesis 1:3, *Thou Whose Almighty Word*,
John Marriott, 1813, altered
Music: 664 6664, ITALIAN HYMN (MOSCOW),
Felice de Giardini, 1769

PSALM 110:1-6a,7

Antiphon   *Get the people to recline
in groups of about fifty.*   Lk 9:14

Adonai said to my Lord:
"Sit at my right hand
  until I make enmity as a footstool for your feet."
A scepter of your might
Adonai will extend from Zion,
and rule in the midst of enmity!

Your people are willing on the day of conflict.
In majestic holiness from the womb of the dawn
to you is the dew of your youth.
Adonai swore and this mind will not change,
"You are a priest to forever
 in the order of Melchizedek."

The Lord at your right hand
will crush kings on the day of wrath
and will judge the nations…
and drink from a brook on the way
with head lifted up because of all this.

Glory…   Antiphon

PSALM 111

Antiphon   *Immediately stretching out his hand
Jesus took hold of Simon, and said,
Little-faith, why did you doubt?*   Mt 14:31

PSALM 111

Hallelujah! Praise Adonai!
I will extol Adonai with all my heart
in the council of the upright ones
and in the assembly.
Great are the works of Adonai,
pondered by all who delight in them.

Glorious and majestic are the deeds,
righteousness enduring to forever:
remembrance evoked of deeds of wonder
by gracious and compassionate Adonai,

providing food for ones fearing the One,
remembering the covenant to forever,
and having shown power at work,
giving the people the land of the nations.

True and just is the handiwork of Adonai,
whose precepts are worthy of trust.
Steadfast are they forever to forever,
to be done in truth and equity.

Redemption is sent for Adonai's people;
ordained to forever is the covenant.
Holy and awesome is the Name.

The beginning of wisdom is fear of Adonai,
good understanding for all who follow this.
Praise endures to eternity.

Glory…

                                          Antiphon

PSALM 112

Antiphon *Blessed are those hungering
and thirsting for what is right;
they will be satisfied.* Mt 5:6

Hallelujah! Praise Adonai!
Blessed are the ones who fear Adonai,
and delight greatly in the commandments.
Mighty in the land will that one be,
and blessed with a generation of upright children,

wealth and richness in their houses,
and righteousness enduring to forever.
Light dawns in the darkness
for the upright and gracious
and compassionate and righteous.

The good human, generous and lending,
conducts affairs with justice.
Surely to forever the good one will not be shaken;
remembered forever will the righteous one be.

The good will have no fear of bad news,
being steadfast of heart and trusting Adonai
with tranquil heart, no fear to the end,
when face to face with enmity.

The good one scatters, giving to the poor,
with righteousness enduring to forever;
the dignity of the good one will be lifted in honor.

The doers of bad things will see this and be vexed
with gnashing of teeth and a wasting away,
wicked longings coming to nothing.

Glory...

Antiphon

PSALM 114

Antiphon *I tell you, forgive; not seven times,
but to seventy times seven.*   Lk 18:22

When Israel came out from Egypt,
the house of Jacob free from people of alien tongue,
Judah became as God's sanctuary,
and Israel God's dominion.

The sea looked and fled,
the Jordan turned back.
The mountains skipped like rams
and hills like a flock of lambs.

What to you, sea, that you fled?
Jordan, that you turned back?
Mountains, that you skipped like rams?
You hills, like a flock of lambs?

Tremble, earth, at the presences of the Lord!
Tremble at the presences of the God of Jacob,
the one turning the rock into pools of waters,
hard rock into springs of waters.

Glory...

Antiphon

PSALM 115

Antiphon *Anyone who loves me will keep my word;*
my Father will love that one,
within whom we will come
and make our dwelling.   Jn 14:23

Not to us, Adonai, not to us,
but to your name give glory
because of your mercy,
because of your fidelity.
Why say the nations,
"Where now is their God?"

Our God now is in the heavens
and does all that God pleases.
Their idols are silver and gold,
made of human hands.

Made with a mouth, they cannot speak;
made with eyes, they cannot see;
made with ears, they cannot hear;
made with a nose, they cannot smell;

made with hands, they cannot feel;
made with feet, they cannot walk,
and they utter no sound from their throat.
Like them will become those who make them,
and all who trust in them.

SUNDAY EVENING

Israel, trust Adonai,
your help and your shield.
Aaron, trust Adonai,
your help and your shield.
Ones fearing Adonai, trust Adonai,
your help and your shield.

Adonai remembers us and will bless us,
will bless the house of Israel,
will bless the house of Aaron,
will bless ones fearing Adonai,
the small ones with the great ones.

May Adonai make an increase to you,
to you and to your children.
You are blessed by Adonai,
Maker of heavens and earth.

Heavens, the heavens are to Adonai,
but earth is given to children of humanity.
The dead ones do not praise Adonai,
and not all those who go down into silence.

But we, we extol Adonai,
from now and to forevermore.
Hallelujah! Praise Adonai!

Glory…

Antiphon

REVELATION 19:1b,2a,5b,6b,7

Antiphon *We are an Easter people and **alleluia** is our song.*   St. Augustine

Alleluia! Praise the Lord!
Salvation and glory and power
are to our God,
whose judgments are true and just.

Alleluia! Praise the Lord!
Praise our God, all you servants of the Lord,
you small and you great,
who hold God in awe.

Alleluia! Praise the Lord!
The Lord is reigning, our God, the Almighty.
Let us rejoice and be glad,
and we will give the glory to the Lord.

Alleluia! Praise the Lord!
The day has come for the marriage of the Lamb,
and the bride has prepared herself.

Glory...

Antiphon

READING   **2 CORINTHIANS 1:3-7**

Blessed be the God and Father of our Lord Jesus Christ, Father of compassion and God of all comfort, comforting-encouraging us in all our affliction that we may be able to comfort those in every affliction, through the comfort by which we ourselves are comforted by God. As the sufferings of Christ abound in us, so through Christ also abounds our comfort. Now when we are afflicted, it is on behalf of your comfort and salvation; when we are comforted, it is on behalf of your comfort enduring in the same sufferings which we also suffer. Our hope for you is firm, knowing that as you partake in the sufferings, so also you partake of the comfort.

RESPONSORY　　　　　　　　　　　　　　　　Ps 138:5,4

May all creation sing of your ways...
...for great is your glory.

And praise the words of your mouth...
...for great is your glory.

Glory to the Father and to the Son and to the Holy Spirit:
...May all creation sing of your ways,
for great is your glory.

GOSPEL CANTICLE OF MARY　　　　　**LUKE 1:46-55**

Antiphon　　*Join the ones who fear the One,*
　　　　　　to generations and generations forever.

+ My soul is stretched full with praise of the Lord,
  and my spirit, beyond joy in God, my Savior,
  who chose to lay eyes on this humble servant.

LUKE 1:46-55, continued

Behold, now and forward,
each and every age will call me blessed,
for the Mighty One did great things to me.
Holy is the name and the mercy
to generations and generations,
the ones fearing the One,

Who scattered the haughty of mind and heart,
pulled the powerful off their high place,
and lifted with dignity the humble in need.

The hungering are filled with good things,
the rich are sent away empty,
and servant Israel is given relief

with a memory of mercy to remember,
the promise spoken to our ancestors,
to Abraham and his descendants forever.

Glory…

Antiphon   *Join the ones who fear the One,*
           to generations and generations forever.

INTERCESSIONS
- In gratitude for blessings…; Abba thank you.
- For the sins of this day…; Lord Jesus have mercy.
- With concerns over tomorrow…; Holy Spirit help.

OUR FATHER…

+ *May the Lord bless us, protect us from all evil,*
  and bring us to everlasting life. ***Amen.***

SUNDAY NIGHT II
(Sunday Night)

+ *God, come to my assistance;* Psalm 70:2
  Lord, make haste to help me!

  Glory…

Joy-ful, joy-ful, we a-dore you,
God of glo-ry, Lord of love;
Hearts un-fold like flow'rs be-fore you,
Op'n-ing to the sun a-bove.
Melt the clouds of sin and/ sad-ness;
Drive the/ dark of doubt a-way;
Giv-er of e-ter-nal glad-ness,
Fill us with the light of day.

You are giv-ing and for-giv-ing,
Ev-er bless-ing, ev-er blest,
Well-spring of the joy of liv-ing,
O-cean depth of hap-py rest!
You our Fa-ther, Christ our/ bro-ther,
All who/ live in love are thine;
Teach us how to love each oth-er,
Ho-ly Spir-it, joy div-ine.

Text: Henry Van Dyke, 1907, altered   Music:8787D, HYMN TO JOY,
Ludwig van Beethoven,d.1827; ad.by Edward Hodges,1824

PSALM 91

Antiphon *It has been written,*
"Not on bread alone shall the human live." Lk 4:4

One who dwells in the shelter of Elyon,
in the shadow of Shaddai, will find rest.
I will say of Adonai, my refuge, my fortress:
in my God do I trust.

Surely the Lord will save you
from fowler snare, from deadly pestilence.
With the feather of the Lord you will be covered,
and under those wings you will find refuge,
shield and rampart, the faithfulness of the Lord.

You will have no fear of terror at night
nor of arrows flying by day,
of pestilence roaming in the darkness,
nor of plague that destroys at midday.

A thousand may fall at your side,
and ten thousand at your right hand;
near to you they will not come.

Observe with your eyes, simply watch;
punishment of wickedness you will see.
Make Adonai, who is my refuge,
make Elyon your dwelling.

Harm will not befall you,
nor will disaster come near your tent.
God's own Angels, the Lord will command
to guard you wherever you go.

SUNDAY NIGHT

In their hands they will lift you up;
lest your foot strike against the stone.
Upon lion and cobra you will tread,
you will trample the great lion and dragon.

"Because you cling to me, I will rescue you,
I will protect all who know my Name.
You will call upon me and I will answer.
I am with you in trouble;
I will deliver you and honor you.

In length of days I will satisfy you,
and show you my salvation."

Glory...

Antiphon

READING   **1 TIMOTHY 3:16**

We confess
that great is the mystery of our fidelity:
Who was manifested in flesh,
justified in Spirit,
seen by angels,
proclaimed among nations,
believed in the world,
and taken up in glory.

RESPONSORY   Ps 31:6

Into your hands, Lord,...   ...*I commend my spirit.*

You have redeemed us, Lord God of truth.
                                    ...*I commend my spirit.*

Glory to the Father and to the Son and to the Holy Spirit:
                                    ...*Into your hands, Lord,*
                                       I commend my spirit.

Antiphon

> *Lord, save/ us!*
> *Save/ us while\ we are a-wake\,*
> *pro-tect us while we are a-sleep,*
> *that we may keep our watch/ with Christ/*
> *and when we sleep\, rest/ in his\ peace.*

GOSPEL CANTICLE of SIMEON   **LUKE 2:29-32**

+ Now, Master, you set free your servant
  according to your word in peace;

  my eyes have seen your salvation,
  which you have prepared
  before the face of all the peoples,

  a light for revelation to the nations
  and glory for your people, Israel.

Glory   Antiphon

+ *May the all-powerful Lord*
  grant us a restful night and a peaceful death. **Amen.**

HAIL MARY...

MONDAY READINGS

+ *Lord, open my lips* Psalm 51:17
  and my mouth will declare your praise.

  Glory…

From all that dwell be/-low the\ skies,
Let the Cre-a-tor's praise a-rise;
Let the Re-deem/-er's/ Name\ be\ sung,
Through ev-'ry land, by ev-'ry tongue.

E-ter-nal are your/ mer-cies\, Lord;
E-ter-nal truth at-tends your Word.
Your praise shall sound/ from/ shore\ to\ shore,
Till suns shall rise and set no more.

In ev-'ry land be/-gin the\ song;
To ev-'ry land the strains be-long;
In cheer-ful sounds/ all/ voi\-ces\ raise,
And fill the world with loud-est praise.

see Psalm 117
Text: Isaac Watts, *The Psalms of David*, 1719;
Robert Spence, *Pocket Hymn Book*, 1780, altered
Music: DUKE STREET, LM; John Hatton, 1793

PSALM 6

Antiphon *Young man, I say to you:*
Arise! Lk 7:14

Adonai, do not rebuke me in your anger
nor discipline me in your wrath.
Show pity to me, Adonai, for I am faint!
Heal me, Adonai, for my bones are in agony
and my soul is in great anguish.

But you, Adonai, how long?
Turn, Adonai, and deliver my soul!
Save me because of your unfailing mercy!
Not from death are you remembered.
Who can praise you from Sheol?

I am worn out from my groaning;
through all the night I flood my bed with tears,
I drench my couch.
My eye grows weak with sorrow;
she fails because of all foes.

Away from me, all doers of badness,
for Adonai has heard the sound of my weeping.
Adonai has heard my cry.
Adonai accepts my prayer.
May all enmity be ashamed
and greatly dismayed,
and turn back in humble confusion.

Glory…

Antiphon

PSALM 9

Antiphon *Foxes have holes and birds of the sky nests,*
but the Son of humanity has no place
where his head may lay. Lk 9:58

I will praise Adonai with all my heart;
I will tell of all the wonderful things.
I will be glad and rejoice in you,
I will sing praise to your name, Most High.

When enmity turns back
it stumbles before you
for you upheld my right and my cause;
you sat on the throne judging justly.

You rebuked nations,
you destroyed wicked ways;
their name you blotted out to forever and ever.
Enmity is overtaken by endless ruin;
cities are uprooted and their memories perish.

Adonai reigns to forever,
set up on the throne for judgment
to judge the world fairly
and to govern peoples with justice.

Adonai is the refuge for the oppressed,
the stronghold in times of trouble.
Those who know your name will trust in you,
for you have never forsaken seekers of Adonai.

PSALM 9, continued

Sing praise to Adonai, enthroned in Zion.
Proclaim the deeds among the nations
for the One who can avenge bloodshed remembers
and does not ignore the cry of the afflicted.

Pour your grace on me, Adonai,
and see the persecution by enmity.
Lift me up from the gates of death
that I may declare all of your praises
in the gates of your daughter Zion.
I will rejoice in your salvation.

Nations fell into the pit they dug;
in the net that they hid are their own feet caught.
Adonai is known in justice;
wicked ways are ensnared in their handiwork.

The nations forgetting God return to Sheol,
but the needy will not be forgotten
nor will the hope of the afflicted ever perish.

Arise Adonai; let not the human triumph.
Let the nations be judged in your presences.
Strike the nations, Adonai,
and let them know their humanity.

Glory…

Antiphon *Foxes have holes and birds of the sky nests,*
but the Son of humanity has no place
where his head may lay. Lk 9:58

PSALM 31:1-17,20-25

Antiphon *Everyone who hears my words and does them*
will be like a wise human
who built his house on the rock. Mt 7:24

In you, Adonai, I take refuge;
let me not be shamed to forever.
Deliver me in your righteousness.
Quickly turn to me your ear! Rescue me!

Be for me a rock of refuge,
a fortress house to save me.
Since you are my rock and my fortress,
for the sake of your name
you lead me and guide me.

You free me from the trap they set for me,
for you are my refuge.
Into your hands I commend my spirit;
you redeem me, Adonai God of truth.

I hate when folks cling to worthless idols,
and I trust in Adonai.
I will be glad and rejoice in your mercy
for you saw my affliction;
you knew the anguishes of my soul.

You do not abandon me
into the hand of enmity;
you set my feet
into the spacious place.

PSALM 31, continued

Be gracious to me, Adonai,
in my distress;
my eyes and my soul and my body
grow weak with sorrow.

My life is consumed by anguish
and my years with groaning.
My strength fails because of my guilt
and my bones grow weak.

Because of enmity I am
the utter contempt of even my neighbors
and a dread to my friends
who see me on the street and flee.

I am forgotten as though dead;
my heart became like broken pottery,
for I hear the slander of many
and terror on every side
when they conspire together against me
and plot to take my life.

But I trust in you, Adonai;
I say you are my God;
my times are in your hand.
Deliver me from the hands
of enmity and pursuers.

Shine your faces on your servant!
Save me in your unfailing mercy!...

How great is the goodness
you store up for ones who fear you
and bestow on those taking refuge in you
in the sight of the children of humanity.

You hide them in the shelter of your presence;
from human intrigues you keep them
in a dwelling safe from the strife of tongues.

Blessed be Adonai for showing wonderful mercy
to me in the city besieged, and I said in my alarm,
"I am cut off from before your eyes."
Yet you heard the sound of my cries for mercy
when I called to you for help.

Love Adonai, all you saints,
Adonai faithful and preserving,
but paying back in full the arrogant.

Be strong and strengthen your heart,
all you hoping in Adonai!

Glory…

Antiphon	*Everyone who hears my words and does them will be like a wise human who built his house on the rock.* Mt 7:24

PSALM 50

Antiphon *I desire mercy and not sacrifice,*
knowledge of God rather than burnt offerings.

Hosea 6:6; Mt 9:13a, 12:7

El Elohim Adonai
speaks and summons earth
from the rising of the sun to its setting.
From Zion, perfect of beauty, God shines forth.

Our God comes and will not be silent,
before whom a fire devours,
around whom a storm is great.
The heavens at above are summoned,
and the earth to judge the people:

"Gather the ones consecrated to me,
  the ones making my covenant by sacrifice."
The heavens proclaim the righteousness of God,
the One who is the judge.

"Hear, my people, and I will speak, Israel,
  and I will testify against you;
  God, your God, am I.

Not for your sacrifices do I rebuke you,
or your burnt offerings ever before me.
I do not need a bull from your stall
or goats from your pen,

for every animal of the forest is mine,
cattle on the hills, the thousands.
I know every bird of the mountains,
and every creature of fields is mine.

Were I hungry, I would not tell it to you,
for the world is mine and all in her.
Do I eat the flesh of bulls?
Do I drink the blood of goats?

Sacrifice to God offerings of praise!
And fulfill your vows to the Most High!
Call upon me in the day of trouble;
I will deliver you and you will honor me."

But God says to those who do wicked,
"What to you to recite my commandments
or to take my covenant on your lip?
For you hate instruction
and you cast my words behind you.

When you see a thief, you join in,
and cast your lot with doers of adultery.
You use your mouth for evil
and harness your tongue to deceit.

You sit and speak against your brother and sister
and slander against your mother's children.
You did these, and I kept silent;
you thought me to be like you?

Consider now this:
there is no one to rescue
those who insist on forgetting God.
One sacrificing an offering of praise
honors me and prepares the way,
and I will show that one to the salvation of God."

Glory... Antiphon

PSALM 73

Antiphon *Any of you who do not detach*
from all your possessions
cannot be my disciple.   Lk 14:33

Surely good to Israel is El, to those pure of heart.
But my feet almost slipped,
as nearly lost were my footholds,
for I envied the arrogant
and the prosperity I have seen of the wicked.

None of them struggle with pain
and healthy are their bodies.
Human burdens are not theirs,
nor the human plagues.

So pride wraps them as a necklace
clothing on them violence.
Their eyes bulge with fat;
their conceits pass the limits of the mind.

They scoff and they speak with malice
and threaten arrogant oppression.
Their mouths lay claim to the heavens,
and their tongues to possession of the earth.

And so their people turn for themselves
and they drink up waters of abundance.
They say, "How does El know?"
and, "Is there knowledge of this to the Most High?"
See these bad doers:
even carefree of Always they increase their wealth.

Surely in vain have I kept my heart pure
and washed my hands in innocence.
But I am plagued all the day
and punished in the mornings.

If I said that I would speak as they do,
see the generation of your children
I would betray!

My efforts to understand this
are oppressive to my eyes.
Until! I entered into sanctuaries of God
and understood about their final destiny.

Surely you place them on slippery ground
and cast them down to ruins.
How sudden is their destruction,
swept away complete by terrors.
As with a dream when waking up, Lord,
their fantasy you will despise when you arise.

When my heart was wounded
and my spirits bitter
and senseless and unknowing,
I was but a brute beast before you.

Yet I am always with you;
you hold me by my right hand.
With your counsel you guide me
and will take me after the glory.

PSALM 73, continued

Who in the heavens is to me?
And with you, nothing on earth do I desire.
My flesh and my heart may fail,
but the strength of my heart is Elohim
and my portion to forever.

For see! Those far from you will perish...
But the nearness of Elohim is my good.
I have made you my refuge, Lord Adonai,
to tell of all your deeds.

Glory...

Antiphon *Any of you who do not detach
from all your possessions
cannot be my disciple.* Lk 14:33

READING	Year I	Year II
week 1	Romans 1:1-17	Genesis 1:1-2:3
2	Romans 5:1-11	Genesis 11
3	Romans 8:18-39	Genesis 19
4	Romans 12	Genesis 27:30-46
5	1 Corinthians 1:18-31	Genesis 41
6	1 Corinthians 7:1-24	1 Thessalonians 2:13-3:13
7	1 Corinthians 11:2-16	2 Corinthians 1:15-2:11
8	1 Corinthians 15:1-19	2 Corinthians 8
9	James 2:14-26	Galatians 1:13-2:10
10	Joshua 1	Philipians 1:12-26
11	Judges 2 & 3	Ezra 1 & 2 & 3
12	Judges 16	Zechariah 8
13	1 Samuel 7 & 8	Nehemiah 5 & 6
14	1 Samuel 18	Proverbs 3

15	2 Samuel 2 & 3	Job 2
16	2 Samuel 18 & 19	Job 12
17	1 Kings 10	Job 29 & 30
18	1 Kings 21	Joel 1
19	2 Kings 5	Jonah 3 & 4
20	Ephesians 1:15-23	Ecclesiastes 2
21	Ephesians 4:25-5:7	Titus 2
22	Amos 1	1 Timothy 6:1-10
23	Amos 8	2 Peter 1:12-21
24	Hosea 9	Esther 3
25	Isaiah 3	Tobit 2
26	Micah 6	Judith 4 & 5
27	Isaiah 30:1-18	Sirach 2
28	Jeremiah 1	Sirach 11
29	Nahum 1 & 2 & 3	Sirach 27 & 28
30	Jeremiah 25	Wisdom 2
31	Jeremiah 38	Wisdom 9
32	Ezekiel 4 & 5	1 Macabees 1:26-63
33	Ezekiel 17	2 Macabees 12
34	Ezekiel 36	Daniel 5

or SHORT READING **COLOSSIANS 1:3-6**

We give thanks always to God the Father of our Lord Jesus Christ praying concerning you, having heard of your faith in Christ Jesus and the love you have toward all the holy ones because of the hope being laid up for you in the heavens, which you heard previously in the word of the truth of the evangelion-gospel coming to you, as it is also bearing fruit and growing in all the world as also in you, from the day you heard and fully knew in truth the grace of God.

Let us bless the Lord. *Thanks be to God.*

MONDAY PROPHETS

A-ma-zing\ Grace! How sweet the sound
That saved a\ wretch like me.
I once\ was\ lost, but now/ am\ found,
Was blind, but\ now I see.

'**T**was grace that\ taught my heart to fear,
And grace my\ fears re-lieved.
How prec\-ious\ did that grace/ ap\-pear
The hour I\ first be-lieved.

Through ma-ny\ dan-gers, toils, and snares,
I have al\-rea-dy come.
'Tis grace\ hath\ brought me safe/ thus\ far,
And grace will\ lead me home.

When we've been\ there ten thou-sand years,
Bright shi-ning\ as the sun,
We've no\ less\ days to sing/ God's\ praise
Than when we'd\ first be-gun.

Text: John Newton, 1779
Music: NEW BRITAIN, CM, composer unknown;
Virginia Harmony, 1831

ISAIAH 2:2-5

Antiphon *Blessed are the peacemakers,*
for they will be called
sons and daughters of God.   Mt 5:9

In the last of the days
the mountain of the temple of Adonai
will be established as chief of the mountains,
raised above the hills.

All the nations will stream to it.
Many peoples will come and say,
"Come, let us go up to the mountain of Adonai,
 to the house of the God of Jacob,
 who will teach us the ways
 so we may walk in the path."

Indeed, from Zion the law will go out
and from Jerusalem the word of Adonai,
who will judge between the nations
and settle disputes for many peoples.

They will beat their swords into plowshares
and their spears into pruning hooks.
Nations will not take up the sword against nations,
and they will train for war no more.

House of Jacob, come!
Let us walk in the light of Adonai.

Glory...

Antiphon

1 CHRONICLES 29:10b-13

Antiphon   *Every thing we have to give*
               is from you, our God.   1 Chr 29:14b

Blessed are you, Lord, God of Israel,
our Father from everlasting to everlasting.

To you, our Lord, are the greatness and power
and glory and majesty and splendor
for all in the heavens and on the earth.

To you, our Lord, are the kingdom
and exaltation as head over all,
and wealth and honor from before you.

And you rule over all in your hand,
strength and power in your hand,
to exalt and give strength to all.

Now, our God, we give thanks to you
and praise your name and your glory.

Glory...   Antiphon

SIRACH 36:1-6,13-22

Antiphon   *The Lord hears the cry of the poor;*
               blessed be the Lord.   Ps 34

Come to our aid, God of all;
let all the nations be in fear of you.
Raise your hand to the foreign nations,
that they may see your might.

As you have used us to show them your holiness,
so now use them to show us your glory.
They will know as we know
that there is no God but you.

Give new signs and work new wonders;
show the splendor
of your right hand and arm…

Gather all the tribes of Jacob,
that they may inherit the land as at the beginning.
Show mercy to the people called by your name:
Israel, whom you named your firstborn.

Have pity on your holy city, Jerusalem,
the foundation for your throne.
Fill Zion with your majesty,
and your temple with your glory.

Give witness of your deeds of old;
fulfill the prophecies spoken in your name.
Reward those who have hoped in you,
and let your prophets be proven true.

Hear the prayers of your servants,
as you are good to your people.
Thus all will know to the ends of the earth
that you are God eternal.

Glory…

                                                    Antiphon

ISAIAH 42:10-16

Antiphon   *I, your Lord,*
                 have called you for justice.   Is 42:6a

Sing to Adonai a new song,
praise from the ends of the earth!

Ones going down to the sea and all in it,
and the islands, the ones living in them,
and the desert and its towns
and settlements where Kedar lives,
let them arise, let them sing for joy,

and the people of Sela
let them shout from the top of mountains.
Let them give Adonai the glory
and proclaim praise in the islands.

Adonai will march out like the mighty human
and stir up zeal like a warrior,
and shouting and raising a cry
will triumph over enmity.

I was silent for a long time
and held back in quiet;
like a woman bearing a child,
I cry out and gasp and pant.

I will lay waste mountains and hills
letting all their vegetation dry up;
I will turn rivers into islands
and dry up pools.

I will lead blind ones by ways they did not know;
along paths they did not know I will guide them.
I will turn what is dark before them into light
and rough places into smooth.

These things I will do
and I will not forsake them.

Glory…

Antiphon

READING **JEREMIAH 15:16**

Your words came and I ate them, and your word was my joy and the delight of my heart, for your name, Adonai God Sabaoth, called to me.

RESPONSORY Psalm 147:2

How good to sing praise to our God,…
…and give God the praise that is fitting.
How pleasant to sing a new song,…
…and give God the praise that is fitting.
Glory to the Father, and to Son, and to the Holy Spirit:
…How good to sing praise to our God,
and give God the praise that is fitting.

Let us bless the Lord. *Thanks be to God.*

MONDAY MORNING

+ *God, come to my assistance;*   Psalm 70:2
Lord, make haste to help me!

Glory…

A migh-ty for/-tress is\ our God,
   The bul-wark nev-er fail\\-ing;
Our help-er, God/, a-mid\ the flood
   Of mor-tal ills pre-vail\\-ing:
For still/ our an-cient\ foe
   Does seek to work us woe;
His craft and pow'r are great,
   And armed with cru-el hate,
On earth is not his e\\-qual.

Do we in our/ own strength\ con-fide?
   Our stri-ving would be los\\-ing,
Were not the Sa/-vior on\ our side,
   The Son of God's own choos\\-ing:
You ask/ who that may\ be?
   Christ Je-sus, it is he;
Lord Sab-a-oth, his name,
   From age to age the same,
And he must win the bat\\-tle.

Text: based on Ps. 46; Martin Luther, 1529;
translated by Frederick H. Hedge, d.1890, altered
Music: 87 87 66 66 7 EIN' FESTE BURG; Martin Luther, 1529

PSALM 5

Antiphon *If someone wishes to sue you*
to get your tunic,
let that one take also
the cloak. Mt 5:40

Give ear to my words, Adonai;
consider my sighing.
Listen to the sound of my cry for help,
for to you I pray, my King and my God.

Hear, Adonai, my morning voice;
with my morning request before you,
I wait.

You are not pleased with evil,
nor can the doer of evil dwell with you.
The arrogant cannot stand before your eyes.
You hate when wrong is done,
you destroy lies,
you abhor bloodshed and deceit.

By the abundance of your mercy, Adonai,
I will come into your house,
I will bow in reverence
toward your holy temple.

Lead me in your justice, Adonai;
because of enmity
make straight before me your way.

PSALM 5, continued

Their mouth has no sincerity,
their heart is destruction,
their throat an open grave,
and their tongue speaks deceit.

If you, God, declare them guilty
let their fall be by their intrigue;
let them be banished if they have sinned,
if they have rebelled against you.

But let all who take refuge in you be glad;
let them sing for joy forever.
You spread protection over them
that they may rejoice in you
and love your name.

You bless the just ones, Adonai,
surrounding them with favor as a shield.

Glory…

Antiphon *If someone wishes to sue you
to get your tunic,
let that one take also
the cloak.* Mt 5:40

PSALM 19

Antiphon
*The Samaritan did mercy
to the beaten man;
You go and do likewise.*   Lk 10:37

The heavens declare the glory of God,
and the sky proclaims the work of God's hands.
Day after day, speech pouring forth,
and knowledge on display night after night.

There is no speech
and there is no language
and no sound is heard.
Into all the earth their telling goes out
and their words to the ends of the world.

There God has pitched a tent for the sun,
and like a bridegroom coming forth,
and like a champion running the course,
rejoices.

From one end of the heavens is the rising,
to their furthest ends is the circuit,
and nothing is hidden from its heat.

The law of Adonai is perfect,
reviving the soul;
statutes of Adonai are trustworthy,
making wise of the simple;
precepts of Adonai are right ones,
giving joy of heart;

PSALM 19, continued

the command of Adonai is radiant,
giving light to eyes;
the fear of Adonai is pure,
enduring to forever;
ordinances of Adonai are sure
and altogether just;

more precious than gold,
much more than pure gold,
more sweet than honey,
the honey of honeycombs.

Your servant is being warned by them;
to keep them is a great reward.
Who can discern errors?
From those hidden from me, forgive me!

And keep your servant from willful sins!
May they not control me;
then will I be free of blame
and innocent of grave transgression.

May the words of my mouth be as pleasing
and the meditation of my heart be as pleasing
before you, Adonai,
my Rock and my Redeemer.

Glory…

Antiphon *The Samaritan did mercy*
to the beaten man;
You go and do likewise. Lk 10:37

PSALM 29

Antiphon   *A voice out of heaven: This is my Beloved Son in whom I am well pleased.*   Mt 3:17

Ascribe to Adonai, sons and daughters.
Ascribe to Adonai glory and strength.
Ascribe to Adonai the glory of the name.
Worship Adonai in holy splendor.

The voice of Adonai over the waters,
the God of glory thunders.
Adonai over mighty waters,
the voice of Adonai in power,
the voice of Adonai in majesty,
the voice of Adonai breaking cedars,

Adonai breaks the cedars of Lebanon
and makes Lebanon skip like a calf
and Sirion like a young wild ox.

The voice of Adonai strikes flashes of lightning,
the voice of Adonai shakes the desert,
Adonai shakes the desert of Kadesh.

The voice of Adonai makes the deer give birth
and strips the forests bare,
and all in the temple cry, "Glory!"

Adonai sits over the flood
and King Adonai is enthroned to forever.
Adonai gives strength to the people;
Adonai blesses the people with peace.

Glory...   Antiphon

PSALM 42

Antiphon
*When he sends forth all his own,
he goes before them,
and the sheep follow
because they know his voice.*   Jn 10:4

As a deer breathes heavy for streams of water,
so my soul throbs for you, O God.
My soul she thirsts for God, the living God.
When can I go and meet the faces of God?

My tears were my food by day and by night,
while all day they said to me,
"Where is your God?"

These things I remember
as my soul pours out before me:
How I would go with the multitude
to lead them to the house of God
sounding shouts of joy and thanksgiving,
a festive throng!

Why are you downcast, my soul,
and do you groan within me?
Wait for God, whom I will yet praise,
the saving help and presence.

My God, within me my soul she is downcast.
For this I will remember you
from the land of Jordan and the heights of Hermon,
from the Mount of Mizar:

MONDAY MORNING

Deep calls to deep
in the roar of your waterfalls.
All your waves and breakers
are swept over me.

By day Adonai directs mercy
and at night the song within me
is a prayer to the God of my life.

I say to El my Rock,
"Why do you forget me?
Why must I go about mourning,
oppressed by the enmity?"

With mortal agony in my bones,
taunted by adversity;
all day they say to me,
"Where is your God?"

Why are you downcast, my soul?
Why do you grown within me?
Wait for God, whom I will yet praise,
my saving help and God.

Glory...

Antiphon

PSALM 84

Antiphon *Why do you look for me?*
Do you not know
that I have to be in my Father's house?   Lk 2:49

How lovely are your dwellings,
Adonai Sabaoth!
My soul she yearns and even faints
for the courts of Adonai;
my heart and my flesh cry out for God alive.

Even the sparrow found a home
and the swallow a nest
where she may keep her young
near your altar, Adonai Sabaoth,
my King and my God.

Blessed are the dwellers in your house,
ever they praise you.
Blessed are the ones whose strength is in you,
who make a pilgrimage in their hearts.

Passing through the Baca Valley
springs are made and found,
pools covered over with autumn rains.
They go from strength to strength
and appear before God in Zion.

Adonai, God Sabaoth, hear my prayer!
Listen, God of Jacob; God, our shield, look!
Look on the face of your anointed!

Better is a day in your courts
than a thousand elsewhere.
Better a doorkeeper in my God's house
than to dwell in tents of the badness,

for God Adonai is sun and shield.
Adonai bestows favor and honor,
withholding no good thing
from walkers free of blame.

Adonai Sabaoth,
blessed is the one trusting in you.

Glory…

Antiphon

PSALM 90

Antiphon	*Be wary and on guard against all greed for life is not about possessions.*	Lk 12:15

You, Lord, you are our dwelling place
from generation to generation.
Before the mountains were born,
before you brought forth earth,
from eternity to eternity,
you are God.

PSALM 90, continued

You turn humans back to dust and say,
"Return, sons and daughters of humanity."
A thousand years in your eyes
are like the day yesterday that went by,
like one watch of the night.

You sweep humans into the sleep
like new grass in the morning that sprouts.
In the morning the human springs up and sprouts,
and then by the evening is withered and dry.

Indeed we can be consumed in your anger
and terrified by your indignation.
You set our faults before you,
our secrets in the light of your presences.

Indeed all our days pass away under your wrath;
we finish our years like a sigh.
Our days last for seventy years
or eighty if given the strength.

The best part of them are toil and sorrow,
passing quickly, and we fly away.
Who knows the power of your anger,
who fears your wrath?

Number our days aright;
teach, that we may gain hearts of wisdom.
How long, Adonai, until you relent?
Have compassion on your servants.

Satisfy our morning hunger
with your unfailing love
that we may sing for joy and be glad all our days.
Make us glad, equal to our affliction,
the years of trouble we have seen.

May your deeds be shown to your servants
and your splendor to their children.
May the favor of the Lord our God rest upon us
and the work of our hands be made good;
yes, make good the work of our hands.

Glory…

Antiphon	*Be wary and on guard against all greed for life is not about possessions.*	Lk 12:15

PSALM 96

Antiphon	*Render to Caesar the things of Caesar, and to God the things of God.*	Mt 22:21

Sing to Adonai a new song!
Sing to Adonai, all the earth!
Sing to Adonai and bless the name!
Proclaim salvation from day to day!

Declare among the nations the glory of the Lord!
Among all the peoples the marvelous deeds,
for great is Adonai, greatly being praised,
the one being feared above all so-called "gods."

PSALM 96, continued

For all "gods" of the nations are idols,
but Adonai made the heavens,
splendor and majesty and strength and glory
in the holy sanctuary.

Ascribe to Adonai, families of nations!
Ascribe to Adonai glory and strength!
Ascribe to Adonai the glory of the name!

Bring offerings and come into the courts!
Worship Adonai in holy splendor!
Tremble in the presence all the earth!

Say among the nations,
"Adonai reigns!"
Firmly established, the world cannot be moved
and peoples will be judged with equity.

Let the heavens rejoice and the earth be glad.
Let the sea resound and all its fullness.
Let the fields and all that is in them be jubilant,
then all the trees of the forests will sing for joy

before Adonai who comes,
who comes to govern the earth,
who will judge the world and its peoples
in justice and fidelity.

Glory...

Antiphon   *Render to Caesar the things of Caesar,*
           and to God the things of God.   Mt 22:21

READING **2 THESSALONIANS 3:7-13**

You yourselves know how good it is to imitate us.
We were not idle among you,
nor did we eat bread as a gift from anyone,
but by labor and struggle by night and by day
working, to not be a burden on any of you,
not that we have no authority,
but so that we ourselves might give to you
an example to imitate.
Even when we were with you,
we gave you as a charge
that if anyone does not wish to work,
neither let that one eat.
For we hear of some walking among you idly,
not working but walking around the working,
and to such we charge
and exhort in the Lord Jesus Christ
that from your quiet working you may eat bread.
And you, brothers and sisters,
do not lose heart in doing good.

RESPONSORY Ps 72:18,19

Blessed be the Lord, the God of Israel…
…blessed from now and to forever.
The One alone doing marvelous deeds…
…blessed from now and to forever.
Glory to the Father and to the Son and to the Holy Spirit:
…Blessed be the Lord, the God of Israel;
blessed from now and to forever.

GOSPEL READING OF THE DAY or GOSPEL CANTICLE

Antiphon   *Blessed be the Lord our God.*

CANTICLE OF ZECHARIAH   **LUKE 1:68-79**

+ Blessed be the Lord the God of Israel
  who chose a people,
  visited them to bring redemption,
  and raised salvation in the house of David,
  saving strength from God's own servant,

  speaking from the age of the prophets
  through the mouth of the holy prophet:
  Salvation out of enmity,
  even out of those who hate us,

  to show our ancestors how mercy works,
  and to remember the holy promise of the Lord,
  the covenant made for our father Abraham,
  calming our fear and making us free
  to serve God as holy and righteous and just
  in the Lord's presence all our days.

  And you also child
  will be called a prophet of the Most High
  for you will go before the Lord to prepare his way
  and give to his people a knowledge of salvation
  known in accepting forgiveness of their sins.

  From the deepness of God's mercy on us,
  a sun rising from the height will visit to appear
  to those who sit in the dark or shadow of death,
  and to guide our feet into the way of peace.

MONDAY MORNING

Gospel Reading for Monday of

Week			
	1 Mark 1:14-20	13 Matt 8:18-22	25 Luke 8:16-18
	2 Mark 2:18-22	14 Matt 9:18-26	26 Luke 9:46-50
	3 Mark 3:22-30	15 Mt 10:34 - 11:1	27 Lk 10:25-37
	4 Mark 5:1-20	16 Matt 12:38-42	28 Lk 11:29-32
	5 Mark 6:53-56	17 Matt 13:31-35	29 Lk 12:13-21
	6 Mark 8:11-13	18 Matt 14:22-36	30 Lk 13:10-17
	7 Mark 9:14-29	19 Matt 17:22-27	31 Lk 14:12-14
	8 Mark 10:17-27	20 Matt 19:16-22	32 Luke 17:1-6
	9 Mark 12:1-12	21 Matt 23:13-22	33 Lk 18:35-43
	10 Matt 5:1-12	22 Luke 4:16-30	34 Luke 21:1-4
	11 Matt 5:38-42	23 Luke 6:6-11	
	12 Matt 7:1-5	24 Luke 7:1-10	

Glory…

Antiphon

PETITIONS FOR THE CONSECRATION TO GOD
OF THE DAY AND ITS WORK

- For the Church and her ministry and apostolates…
- For secular authorities and all serving as stewards…
- For awareness of being created in the image of God…
- For acceptance of being completely loved by God…
- For discovery and discernment of our charisms…
- For people who are poor or sick or in sorrow…
- For good work for all to do in dignity…
- For peace and the basic needs of each human being…

OUR FATHER…

+ *May the Lord bless us, protect us from all evil,
and bring us to everlasting life.* ***Amen***.

MONDAY DAYTIME

+ *God, come to my assistance;*   Psalm 70:2
Lord, make haste to help me!

Glory…

Faith of our an-ces-tors, liv\-ing still,
In spite of dun-geon, fire\ and sword;
O how our hearts\ beat high\ with joy
When-'er we hear that glo/-rious Word!
Faith of our an-ces-tors, ho-ly faith!
We will be true to you till death.

Faith of our **fa\-thers**, we\ will strive
A-mong all peo-ples, as is our call;
That through the truth\ that comes\ from God,
True free-dom may be found/ by all.
Faith of our an-ces-tors, ho-ly faith!
We will be true to you till death.

Faith of our **mo\-thers**, we\ will love
Both friend and foe in all\ our strife;
Liv-ing and preach-ing as love\ knows how
By kind-ly words and vir/-tuous life.
Faith of our an-ces-tors, ho-ly faith!
We will be true to you till death.

Text: Frederick W. Faber, Jesus and Mary, 1849;
refrain by James G. Walton, 1874; altered
Music: ST. CATHERINE, LM with refrain; Henry F. Hemy, 1864;
adapted by James G. Walton, 1874

PSALM 119:17-24
Gimel

Antiphon *Come yourselves privately*
to a desert place
and rest a little. Mk 6:31

Do good to your servant;
I will live and obey your word.
Open my eyes that I may see
things of wonder in your law.

From this stranger on the earth
you hide not your commands.
My soul she is consumed all the time
with longing for your laws.

You rebuke the arrogant with a curse,
those straying from your commands.
Remove from me scorn and contempt
for your statutes I keep.

Though princes sit and slander against me
your servant will meditate on your decrees.
Indeed your statutes are my delights,
my people of counsel.

Glory…

Antiphon

PSALM 119:25-32
Daleth

Antiphon *When you pray, enter your room*
and close your door
and pray to your Father in secret.   Mt 6:6

My soul falls flat in the dust;
make me alive as is your word.
I recount my ways and you answer me;
teach me your decrees.

Let me understand your precepts
and I will ponder your wonders done.
My soul she is weary with sorrow;
strengthen me as is your word.

Keep from me the way of deceit!
Your law be gracious to me!
I choose the way of truth;
on your law I set my heart.

I hold fast to your statutes, Adonai;
let me not be shamed.
I run the path of your commands
for you set my heart free.

Glory…

Antiphon

PSALM 119:33-40
He

Antiphon   *Ones who are well*
have no need of a physician,
but the sick do…
I came not to call the righteous,
but sinners.   Mt 9:12,13b

Teach me, Adonai, the way of your decrees;
to the end will I keep her.
Give me understanding to keep your law
and obey her with all my heart.

Direct me in the path of your commands
for I delight in them.
Turn my heart to your statutes
and away from selfish gain.

Turn my eyes from sight of worthless things;
make me alive in your way.
Fulfill your promise to your servant
for to fear you in awe.

Take away my disgrace of dread
for good are your laws.
See how I long for your precepts;
in your righteousness make me alive!

Glory…

Antiphon

PSALM 7

Antiphon *Let whoever thirsts*
come to me and drink. Jn 7:37

My God, Adonai, in you I take refuge;
save me and deliver me from all who pursue me.
Like lions they want to tear me up,
rip my self to pieces with no one to rescue me.

My God, Adonai, if I deserve this,
if there is guilt on my hands,
if I did wrong to one at peace with me
or if I robbed without cause from an enemy,

then let that one pursue my self
and overtake my life
and trample my honor to the ground;
let that one put me to sleep in the dust.

Arise, Adonai, rise up in your anger
against the rages of enmity.
Awake, my God, and decree your justice
and let the assembly of peoples gather;
rule over us from the height.
Let Adonai be the judge of the peoples.

MONDAY DAYTIME 117

Judge me, Adonai,
as you judge me in justice,
as you judge my integrity, Most High.
May violence end now
and the just be secure;
search our minds and hearts, righteous God.

My shield, God Most High,
saves the upright of heart,
and judges each day with justice,
holding the threat of wrath.

If none repent, they will sharpen their sword
and bend their bow with string and make ready
with weapons of death and flaming arrows.
See, trouble is conceived and evil is pregnant,
then comes to birth disillusionment.

They dig holes and scoop them out
but fall into the pits they made.
Their trouble recoils on their heads;
on their heads their violence makes landing.

I give thanks for Adonai's justice
and sing praise to the name
of Most High Adonai.

Glory...

                                                               Antiphon

PSALM 40:2-14,17-18

Antiphon   *I have come to throw fire on the earth
and how I wish it was ablaze.*   Lk 12:49

Waiting, I waited for Adonai,
who turned to me and heard my cry,

who lifted me from the slime pit
and from the muddy mire,
and set my feet on rock,
making firm my standing place,

and put in my mouth a new song,
a hymn of praise to our God.
Many will see and fear and trust Adonai.

Blessed is the one who trusts in Adonai
and looks not to the proud
or those turning to false "gods."

Adonai, my God,
many are your deeds of wonder
and your plans cannot be equaled.
Should I speak and tell of them
they would be too many to declare.

Sacrifice and offerings you did not desire,
but my ears you pierced open for me.
Burnt offering and sin offering
you did not require.

Then I said, "Here, I have come;
 in the scroll, in the book, it is written of me:
 To do your will, my God, is my desire,
 and your law is within my heart."

I proclaim righteousness in the great assembly.
See my lips unsealed.
You, Adonai, you know!

Your righteousness I do not hide in my heart;
your faithfulness and salvation I speak.
I do not conceal your faithful mercy
from the great assembly.

Adonai, withhold not your compassion;
may your faithful mercy protect me always
for countless troubles surround around me.

My sins overtook me and I cannot see.
They are more than the hairs of my head
and my heart fails me.

Be pleased, Adonai, to save me;
Adonai, come quickly to help me!...

May all who seek you rejoice in you and be glad
and may lovers of your salvation say always,
"Let Adonai be exalted."

Yet I am poor and needy.
May the Lord think of me and not delay,
my help and my deliverer, my God.

Glory...   Antiphon

PSALM 71

Antiphon

*Amen I tell you
that no prophet is acceptable
in his or her native place.*   Lk 4:24

In you, Adonai, I take refuge;
let me not be shamed to forever.
In your justice you rescue and deliver me.
Turn your ear to me and save me!

Be to me as a rock,
and a refuge to go to always.
Command that I be saved,
for you are my rock and my fortress.
My God, deliver me from wicked hands
and the grasp of doers of violent cruelty,

for you are my hope, Lord Adonai,
my confidence since my youth.
I have relied on you from birth,
from my mother's womb you brought me forth;
my praise is ever to you.

To many I became like a portent
but you are my strong refuge.
My mouth is filled all the day
with praise of your splendor.
Cast me not away at my time of old age;
forsake me not when my strength is gone.

Enmity speaks against me;
waiting on my life, conspirers together say,
"God has abandoned that one!
  Pursue to seize,
  for no one is coming to the rescue!"
God, be not far from me.
God, come quickly to help me!

May accusations against me
perish in shame.
May scorn and disgrace
cover the desire to do harm.

But I will hope always
and add to all your praise.
My mouth will tell of your justice,
all the day of your salvation,
though I know not its measure;

I will come in mighty acts of Lord Adonai;
I will proclaim your singular justice.
You taught me, God, since my youth;
to this day I declare your marvelous deeds.

Even in my old age and gray hair
you do not forsake me, O God.
May I delcare your power to this generation,
your might to all who will come,
and your justice to the sky,
you, God, who have done great things.
Who, God, is your equal?

PSALM 71, continued

Though you let me see troubles,
many and bitter,
you will again let me live.
And from the depths of the earth
you will again bring me up.
You will restore my honor
and again you will comfort me.

With the harp instrument I will praise you
and your faithfulness, my God;
I will sing praise to you with lyre,
Holy One of Israel.
My lips will shout for joy
when I sing praise to you,
even my soul whom you redeemed.

Also my tongue will tell
all the day of your justice
for desires of some to do harm
are in shame and confusion.

Glory...

Antiphon
*Amen I tell you
that no prophet is acceptable
in his or her native place.* Lk 4:24

PSALM 82

Antiphon *One is the lawgiver and judge,*
the one able to save and destroy;
who are you
to be judging your neighbor? James 4:12

God Elohim is presiding
in the assembly of El,
giving judgment among little "g" gods:

"Until when will you defend the unjust
 and show partiality to the faces of bad doers?
 Defend the marginal and the orphans!
 Maintain the rights of the poor and oppressed!
 Rescue the weak and the needy!
 Deliver them from the hands of bad doings!"

They know nothing
and they understand nothing.
They walk in darkness
and all the foundations of earth are shaken.

 "I said, 'All of you are gods,
 sons and daughters of Elyon Most High,'
 but like all humans you too will die
 and like any prince you too will fall."

Rise up, Elohim, and judge the earth!
For yours are all of the nations!

Glory…

                                            Antiphon

PSALM 120

Antiphon *Even the Son of humanity*
did not come to be served
but to serve,
to give his life
in ransom for the many.   Mk 10:45

In my distress I call on Adonai
who answers me.
Adonai, save my soul from lips of the lie
and from the deceitful tongue.

What will be done to you
and what more will be done
to you, deceitful tongue?
The warrior arrows of war,
with coals of a broom tree made sharp.

Woe to me that I dwell in Meshech
and live among tents of Kedar.

Too long has my self lived
among haters of peace.
I am of peace,
but when I speak
they are for war.

Glory...

Antiphon

READING   **1 THESSALONIANS 2:13; 3:9-13**

And so we give thanks to God unceasingly, that having received the word of God, hearing it from us, you welcomed it not as a word of humans but as it truly is, the word of God, which is at work in you who believe…

How are we able to thank God in return for all the joy with which we rejoice because of you before our God, night and day praying exceedingly to see your face and to work with what is lacking in your faith? May God our Father and Jesus our Lord now direct our way to you.

And may the Lord make you to abound and to exceed in love for one another and all people, even as we also love you, to strengthen your hearts to be blameless and holy before God our Father in the presence of Jesus our Lord with all his saints.

RESPONSORY   Ps 141:2

When I call, Lord, hear my voice…

> *…which rises up to you.*

Like incense set before you…

> *…which rises up to you.*

Glory to the Father and to the Son and to the Holy Spirit:
> *…When I call, Lord, hear my voice, which rises up to you.*

Lord\, have mer-cy.

> *Christ\, have mer-cy.*

>> Lord\, have mer-cy.

MONDAY EVENING

+ *God, come to my assistance;*   Psalm 70:2
Lord, make haste to help me!

Glory…

For the/ beau-ty of the earth,
For the glo-ry of the skies,
For the/ love which from our birth
O-ver and a-round us lies.
Lord of all, to you we raise
This our song of grate-ful praise.

For the/ beau-ty of each hour,
Of the day and of the night,
Hill and/ val-ley, tree and flow'r,
Sun and moon and stars of light.
Lord of all, to you we raise
This our song of grate-ful praise.

For the/ joy of ear and eye,
For the heart and mind's de-light,
For the/ mys-tic har-mo-ny
Link-ing sense to sound and sight.
Lord of all, to you we raise
This our song of grate-ful praise.

For the/ joy of hu-man love,
Bro-ther, sis-ter, par-ent, child,
Friends on/ earth and friends a-bove,
Sa-cred res-pite from the wild.
Lord of all, to you we raise
This our song of grate-ful praise.

For your/ Church, that ev-er-more
Lifts its ho-ly hands a-bove,
Off-'ring/ up on ev-'ry shore
Faith and sac-rif-i-cial love.
Lord of all, to you we raise
This our song of grate-ful praise.

Per-fect/ gift of pres-ence thine
Won-drous gift so free-ly giv'n,
Gra-ces/ hu-man and div-ine,
Peace on earth and joy in heav'n.
Lord of all, to you we raise
This our song of grate-ful praise.

Text: Lyra Eucharistica, 1864; Folliot S. Pierpoint, 1864, altered
Music: 77 77 77, DIX, Conrad Kocher, 1838;
adapted by William H. Monk, 1823-99

PSALM 11

Antiphon *Blessed are you poor,*
for yours is the kingdom of God.   Lk 6:20b

In Adonai I take refuge.
How can you say to my self,
"Flee, bird, to your mountain
 for look, doers of bad now bend their bow,

 they set their arrow on the string
 to shoot from the shadow
 at the upright of heart.
 When foundations are destroyed,
 what can be done by the just?"

Adonai is in the holy temple,
on Adonai's throne in the heavens
with eyes observing, examining
the sons and daughters of humanity.

Adonai examines the righteous,
hating in the soul the love of violence,
will rain onto wicked ways
coal and brimstone sulphur on fire
and scorching wind, the lot of their cup,

for just is Adonai, loving justice;
we will see the faces of the Just One.

Glory...

                                                              Antiphon

PSALM 15

Antiphon *Blessed are the clean of heart,*
for they will see God.   Mt 5:8

Adonai, who may dwell in your tent?
Who may live on your holy hill?
One walking without blame,
one doing the right,
speaking truth in that one's heart,

whose tongue does not slander,
who does no wrong to a neighbor,
who casts no slur on a mutual human,
in whose eyes vile acts are despised

while those who fear Adonai are honored,
whose sworn oath is not changed even at cost,
who lends money without usury,
and accepts no bribe against the innocent.

One faithful in these
will be unshaken to forever.

Glory…

Antiphon

PSALM 45

Antiphon
*Rejoice on that day
and leap for joy,
for great is your reward in heaven.* Lk 6:23

My heart is stirred, a noble theme;
I recite my verses for the king;
my tongue is a pen of a skillful scribe.

You were anointed with grace on your lips,
more excellent among children of humanity.
For thus has God blessed you to forever.

Gird your sword upon your side, mighty one,
your splendor and your majesty.
Your majesty, be victorious!
Ride forth on behalf of truth and humility
and let justice display
awesome deeds of your right hand.

Your arrows are sharp;
let nations fall beneath you into the heart
of ones who choose enmity with the royal one
on God's throne forever and ever.
The scepter of the kingdom is a scepter of justice.

You love to see justice
and hate when people do bad things;
for this your God anointed you
above your companions with oil of joy,
with myrrh and aloes and cassias on your robes,
and from ivory palaces strings make you glad.

Children of royalty are honored among you
and the queen bride stands at your right hand,
honored in gold of Ophir.

Listen, daughter, and consider!
Give your ear and forget your people
and the house of your parents.

The king is enthralled for your beauty;
he is your lord, so honor him!
With the gift of your face, daughter of Tyre,
wealthy people will seek you.

The all-glorious daughter of the king is within
with interweavings of gold in her gown.
In embroidered garments she is led to the king;

her virgin companions following her
are being brought to you.
They are led in with joy and gladness;
they enter the palace of the king.

In the place of your parents will your children be,
as princes and princesses through all the land.
I will make perpetual the memory of your name
through all generations and generation.
For this the nations will praise you
ever and to forever.

Glory...

                                                Antiphon

PSALM 123

Antiphon
Talitha koun;
Little girl, I say to you, arise.   Mk 5:41

I lift up my eyes to you,
sitting in the heavens.
As eyes of slaves
are to the hand of their masters,

as the eyes of a maid
are to the hand of her mistress,
see, our eyes are to Adonai
till our God shows to us mercy.

Have mercy on us, Adonai, have mercy,
for we have endured much contempt.
Much ridicule of the proud
and contempt of arrogance
have we ourselves endured.

Glory...

Antiphon

PSALM 124

Antiphon *One finding one's own life will lose it,*
and one losing one's own life for my sake
will find it. Mt 10:39

If Adonai was not for us,
let Israel now say,
if Adonai was not for us
when human beings attacked against us,
then they would have swallowed us alive
when their fury flared against us.

Then the floods would have engulfed us,
the torrents would have swept over our selfs,
and the raging waters would have drowned us.

Blessed be Adonai,
who did not let us be torn by their teeth.
Our selfs, like a bird,
escaped from the snare of fowlers.

The snare being broken we escaped.
Our help is in the name of Adonai,
the Maker of heavens and earth.

Glory…

Antiphon

PSALM 136

Antiphon
*My food is that I may do
the will of the one who sent me.* John 4:34

Give thanks for Adonai who is good,
  mercy enduring to forever.
Give thanks to the One who is God of the "gods,"
  mercy enduring to forever.
Give thanks to the One who is Lord of the lords,
  mercy enduring to forever,

to the One who has done great wonders alone,
  mercy enduring to forever,
who made the heavens by understanding,
  mercy enduring to forever,
who spread out the earth upon the waters,
  mercy enduring to forever,

who made the great lights,
  mercy enduring to forever,
the sun as governor over the day,
  mercy enduring to forever,
the moon and stars as governors over the night,
  mercy enduring to forever,

who struck down Egypt in their firstborn,
  mercy enduring to forever,
who brought Israel out from their midst,
  mercy enduring to forever,
with mighty hand and outstretched arm,
  mercy enduring to forever,

who split the Reed Sea into halves,
  mercy enduring to forever,
and brought Israel through its midst,
  mercy enduring to forever,
but swept Pharoah and his army into the Reed Sea,
  mercy enduring to forever,

who then led the people through the desert,
  mercy enduring to forever,
who struck down great kings,
  mercy enduring to forever,
and slew mighty kings,
  mercy enduring to forever,

Sihon, king of the Amorites,
  mercy enduring to forever,
and Og, the king of Bashan,
  mercy enduring to forever,

who gave the land as an inheritance,
  mercy enduring to forever,
an inheritance to servant Israel,
  mercy enduring to forever,
who remembered us in our low estate,
  mercy enduring to forever,

and freed us from enmity,
  mercy enduring to forever,
who gives food to every creature,
  mercy enduring to forever.
Give thanks to El of the heavens,
  mercy indeed enduring to forever!

Glory...   Antiphon

EPHESIANS 1:3-10

Antiphon *Jesus called to himself the Twelve
and began to send them out two by two.* Mk 6:7a

Blessed be the God and Father
of our Lord Jesus Christ,
who has blessed us in Christ
with every spiritual blessing in the heavens.

God chose us in Christ
before the foundation of the world,
to be holy and free of blemish before him.

In love, God gave us a destiny:
as sons are adopted, through Jesus Christ himself,
in accord with the good pleasure of God's will
to the praise of the glory of grace
by which we are favored as God's beloved.

In Christ we have the redemption
through his blood, the forgiveness of sins,
in accord with the riches of his grace
which he made abound to us.

In all wisdom and intelligence
the mystery of God's will is made known to us
in accord with God's good pleasure and purpose:

A stewardship of the fullness of time,
heading up all things in Christ,
the things in the heavens and the things on earth.

Glory... Antiphon

READING **JAMES 4:1-12**

From where come wars and fights among you? Not from your pleasures soldiering in your members? You desire, and do not have; you murder and are jealous and are unable to obtain; you fight and you war. You have not because you ask not; you ask and receive not, because you ask badly, that you may spend in your pleasures.

Adulterers, do you not know that the friendship of the world is enmity of God? And so whoever resolves to be a friend of the world becomes an enemy of God. Or do you think that the scripture says in vain that, *the Spirit which dwelt in you yearns in envy*? But we are given greater grace, and so it says, *God resists the arrogant, but gives grace to the humble.*

And so be subject to God, but oppose the diabolo who will flee from you. Draw near to God, who will draw near to you. Cleanse your hands, sinners; and purify hearts, you two-souled. Be distressed and mourn and weep; let your laughter be turned to mourning and your joy to dejection. Be humbled before the Lord, who will exalt you.

Do not speak against each other, brothers and sisters. The one speaking against a brother or judging a sister speaks against the law and judges the law.

And if you judge the law, you are not a doer of law but a judge. One is the lawgiver and judge: the one able to save and to destroy. Who are you to be judging your neighbor?

RESPONSORY   Ps 41:5

You, Lord, are the one who can heal me…
             …*for it is you I have grieved.*
Lord, show to me your mercy…
             …*for it is you I have grieved.*
Glory to the Father and to the Son and to the Holy Spirit:
             …*You, Lord, are the one who can heal me,*
             for it is you I have grieved.

GOSPEL CANTICLE OF MARY   **LUKE 1:46-55**

Antiphon   *My soul is stretched full*
                    with praise of the Lord.

+ My soul is stretched full with praise of the Lord,
  and my spirit, beyond joy in God, my Savior,
  who chose to lay eyes on this humble servant.

  Behold, now and forward,
  each and every age will call me blessed,
  for the Mighty One did great things to me.
  Holy is the name and the mercy
  to generations and generations,
  the ones fearing the One,

  Who scattered the haughty of mind and heart,
  pulled the powerful off their high place,
  and lifted with dignity the humble in need.

The hungering are filled with good things,
the rich are sent away empty,
and servant Israel is given relief

with a memory of mercy to remember,
the promise spoken to our ancestors,
to Abraham and his descendants forever.

Glory…

Antiphon

INTERCESSIONS
- Lord, keep married couples in love…
- Grow our youth in wisdom and grace…
- For respect for the dignity of the human person…
- For all who have died…

- In gratitude for blessings…; Abba thank you.
- For the sins of this day…; Lord Jesus have mercy.
- With concerns over tomorrow…; Holy Spirit help.

OUR FATHER…

+ *May the Lord bless us, protect us from all evil,
and bring us to everlasting life.* ***Amen.***

MONDAY NIGHT

+ *God, come to my assistance;*　　　　　　　Psalm 70:2
Lord, make haste to help me!

Glory...

The Church's one foun-da-tion
Is Je-sus Christ, her Lord;
She is his new cre-a-tion   By wa-ter and the Word.
From heav'n he came and sought her
To be his ho-ly bride;
By blood re-deem-ing bought her,
And for her life he died.

E-lect from ev-'ry na-tion,   Yet one o'er all the earth,
Her char-ter of sal-va-tion One Lord, one faith, one birth.
One ho-ly name she bless-es,   Par-takes one ho-ly food,
And to one hope she press-es,
With ev-'ry grace en-dued.

Though with a scorn-ful won-der
Some see her sore op-pressed,
By schis-ms rent a-sun-der,   By her-e-sies dis-tressed,
Yet saints their watch are keep-ing;
Their cry goes up, "How long?"
And soon the night of weep-ing
Shall be the morn of song.

Mid toil and trib-u-la-tion   And tu-mult of her war
She waits the con-sum-ma-tion   Of peace for-ev-er-more,
Til with the vis-ion glo-ri-ous Her long-ing eyes are blest
And the great Church vic-tor-ious
Shall be the Church at rest.

Song text: see Ephesians 2:20; Samuel J. Stone, 1866, altered
Music: 76 76 D, AURELIA, Samuel S. Wesley, 1864

PSALM 86

Antiphon *Leave both the weed and the wheat*
to grow together
until the harvest. Mt 13:30

Hear in your ear, Adonai;
answer me for I am poor and in need.
Guard my life for I am devoted;
save your servant, my God,
the one trusting in you.

Be gracious to me, O Lord,
for to you I call all the day.
Bring joy to me, your servant,
for to you, Lord, I lift up my soul.

Indeed, Lord, you are good and forgiving
and abundant in mercy for all who call to you.
Hear my prayer, Adonai;
listen to the sound of my cries.

In the day of my trouble I will call to you
for you will answer me.
There is none like you among so-called "gods"
and there are no deeds like yours, O Lord.

PSALM 86, continued

All the nations you made will come
and they will worship before you, Lord,
and they will give honor to your name
for you are great and do marvelous deeds,
you, God, you alone.

Teach me, Adonai, your way
and I will walk in your truth.
Make my heart undivided
that I may revere your name.

I will praise you, Lord my God,
with all my heart
and I will glorify your name to forever
for great to me is your mercy
and you deliver my soul from the depth of Sheol.

Arrogant ones attack against me, God;
a band of ruthless people seek my life
and do not regard you before them.

But you, Lord El, Compassionate and Gracious,
slow of anger and abundant in mercy and fidelity:
Turn to me with your grace!

Grant your strength to your servant
and save the child of your handmaid!
Give to me a sign of goodness
that enmity may see and find shame,
for you, Adonai, help me and comfort me.

Glory…

MONDAY NIGHT

Antiphon *Leave both the weed and the wheat*
to grow together
until the harvest. Mt 13:30

READING **COLOSSIANS 1:9b-14**

May you be filled
with the full knowledge of God's will in all wisdom
and spiritual understanding, to walk worthily,
all-pleasing to the Lord in every good work
bearing fruit,
and growing in the full knowledge of God,
be empowered with all power
as the glory of God is mighty,
and endure all longsuffering with joy.
Give thanks to the Father who has made you fit
for your part of the lot of the saints in light,
who delivered us out of the authority of darkness
and transitioned us
into the kingdom of his beloved Son,
in whom we have redemption,
the forgiveness of our sins.

RESPONSORY Ps 31:6

Into your hands, Lord,… *…I commend my spirit.*

You have redeemed us, Lord God of truth.
…I commend my spirit.

Glory to the Father and to the Son and to the Holy Spirit:
…Into your hands, Lord, I commend my spirit.

Antiphon

> *Lord, save/ us!*
> *Save/ us while\ we are a-wake\,*
> *pro-tect us while we are a-sleep,*
> *that we may keep our watch/ with Christ/*
> *and when we sleep\, rest/ in his\ peace.*

GOSPEL CANTICLE of SIMEON **LUKE 2:29-32**

+ Now, Master, you set free your servant
according to your word in peace;

my eyes have seen your salvation,
which you have prepared
before the face of all the peoples,

a light for revelation to the nations
and glory for your people, Israel.

Glory

Antiphon

+ *May the all-powerful Lord*
grant us a restful night and a peaceful death. **Amen.**

Queen of heaven, rejoice, alleluia.
The Son whom you merited to bear, alleluia,
has risen as he said, alleluia.

Rejoice and be glad, O Virgin Mary, alleluia!
For the Lord has truly risen, alleluia.

TUESDAY READINGS

+ *Lord, open my lips*   Psalm 51:17
  and my mouth will declare your praise.

  Glory…

Praise the\ Lord, you/ heav'ns, a-dore\;
Praise you\ an-gels/ in the height;
Sun and\ Moon, re/-joice be-fore\;
Shine your\ praise, you/ stars of light.
Give praise\, for the Lord has\ spo-ken;
Might-y\ voice the worlds o\-beyed;
Laws which\ nev-er/ shall be bro-ken,
Guid-ance\ that the/ Lord has made.

Praise the\ Lord, the/ Lord is glo-rious,
Prom-is\-es that/ do not fail;
God has\ made the/ saints vic-tor-ious,
Sin and\ death shall/ not pre-vail.
Praise the\ God of our sal\-va-tion;
Hosts on\ high the pow'r pro\-claim;
Heav-en and earth and/ all cre-a-tion,
Praise and\ mag-ni/-fy the name.

Wor-ship\, hon-or/, glo-ry, bles-sing,
Lord, we\ off-er/ un-to thee;
Young and\ old, your/ praise ex-pres-sing,
In glad\ hom-age/ bend the knee.
All the\ saints in heav-en a-dore you,
We would\ bow be-fore your\ throne;
As your\ an-gels/ serve be-fore you,
So on\ earth your/ will be done.

Song text: Stan. 1,2, Foundling Hospital Collection,
1801; Stan. 3, Edward Osler, 1836, altered
Music: 87 87 D, PLEADING SAVIOR,
Joshua Leavitt, Christian Lyre, 1830
Popular melody for: *Sing of Mary, Pure and Lowly*

PSALM 10

Antiphon   *New wine is put into fresh wineskins.*   Mk 2:22

Why, Adonai, do you stand at far off
and hide in times of the trouble?
In arrogance doers of bad hunt the poor;
they are caught in schemes they devise.

Doers of badness boast of their greed,
blessing their hearts' cravings and reviling Adonai.
In pride they point their nose away
and seek God in none of their thoughts.

Their haughty ways prosper at all times,
your laws are ignored from a distance,
and they sneer at all enemies.

They say to themselves
"I will not be shaken, but happy,
 untroubled for generations to come."
Their mouths are full of oaths and lies and violence,
trouble and bad things kept under their tongue.

They lie in wait to ambush villages and murder,
their secret eyes on the innocent victim.
They lie in wait to ambush like a lion,
undercover lying in wait to catch the helpless
they catch and drag off in their nets.

The helpless are crushed and collapse,
falling under their strength.
They say to themselves "El has forgotten,
with faces covered, and sees nothing anymore."

Arise, Adonai! God, lift up your hand!
Do not forget the poor.
For why do those doing bad revile God and say,
to themselves, "God will not call an accounting"?

But you do see trouble and grief,
and consider taking the matter in hand;
to you the helpless commit themselves,
to you, the One helping the orphans.

Stop the arm of the doer of depravity;
call to account lest crimes be kept secret.
Adonai is King forever and ever;
the nations will perish from Adonai's land.

You hear, Adonai, the needs of the poor;
you encourage their heart and open your ear
to defend the orphans and oppressed.
May humanity repeat no terror on the earth.

Glory…

Antiphon

PSALM 12

Antiphon *A cloud came overshadowing them*
and a voice came out of the cloud:
This is my Son the Beloved; hear him. Mk 9:7

Help, Adonai,
for the godly are no more;
the faithful vanish from humanity's children.
They speak the lie to each of their neighbors,
lips of flattering with a double heart.

May Adonai close all flattering lips
and tongues speaking the boast that say:
"With our tongues we will triumph,
  our lips are with us; who is our master?"

But because of oppression of the weak,
because of groaning of the needy,
now Adonai says,
"I will arise and protect them."

Words of Adonai are flawless words,
like silver refined in the furnace of clay,
and being purified seven times over.

You, Adonai, you will keep them safe;
you are our protection to forever.
But doers of badness will still strut about
when vileness is honored among human beings.

Glory...

Antiphon

PSALM 37

Antiphon *There is nothing entering from outside
that can defile a human;
rather things that defile
come from within.* Mk 7:15

Fret not over those who do badness;
envy not those who do wrong.
For like grass their efforts wither,
and like the green plant they wilt away.

Trust in Adonai and do good!
Dwell in the land and enjoy safe pasture!
Find delight in Adonai
who will give the desires of your heart.

Commit your way and your trust
to Adonai who will do it:
making your righteousness shine like the dawn
and your justice like the noonday sun.

Be still before Adonai
and wait with patience.
Fret not over the ways of the prosperous,
over schemes carried out by human beings.

Refrain from anger and turn from wrath!
Fret not; it brings only harm,
for humans doing badness will be cut off,
but those who hope in Adonai
will inherit the land.

PSALM 37, continued

A little while and bad doings will be no more;
you will look and not find them in their places.
But the meek will inherit the land
and they will enjoy greatness of peace.

Plotters of bad things to do to the righteous
gnash their teeth at them.
But the Lord laughs at them,
knowing their day is coming.

They draw their sword
and they bend their bow
to bring down the poor and oppressed,
to slay those of the upright way.
Their sword will pierce into their own heart
and their bows will be broken.

Better the little bit of the righteous
than the wealth of many who do bad things,
for the powers of bad doers will be broken
while Adonai upholds the righteous.

Adonai knows the days of the blameless
and their inheritance will endure to forever.
They will not wither in times of disaster
and in days of famine they will enjoy plenty.

But wicked ways will perish
and those who choose enmity with Adonai
will vanish like the beauty of fields;
like smoke they will vanish.

A doer of badness borrows and does not repay,
but a righteous one is generous and giving.
The blessing on the righteous is to live in the land;
the curse of doing badness is to be cut off.

The steps of human beings are made firm
by Adonai who delights in their way.
Though we stumble, we will not fall
for Adonai upholds us by the hand.

I was young and now I am old,
yet never have I seen the righteous abandoned
or their children begging bread.
Generous and lending all the day,
their children are a blessing.

Turn from evil and do good!
Then live to always!
For Adonai loves justice
and will not abandon the faithful.
They will be protected to forever…
Righteous ones will inherit the land
and they will dwell in her to forever.

The mouth of the righteous he utters wisdom
and the tongue she speaks justice.
The law of their God is in their heart
and their feet do not slip.

PSALM 37, continued

Wicked ways lie in wait for the righteous
seeking to kill them;
Adonai will not leave them under this power
nor let them be condemned when on trial.

Wait for Adonai and keep to the way
of the one who will exalt you to possess the land,
and you will see wicked ways cut off.

I saw a ruthless human flourishing
like a native green tree,
but passing away is seen no more;
though I looked he was not to be found.

Consider the person of integrity
and observe the upright
for the future is for the person of peace.
But sinners sinning will be destroyed together;
the future of wicked ways will be cut off.

The salvation of the righteous is from Adonai,
their stronghold in times of trouble.
Their help and deliverance and salvation,
their deliverance from ways that are wicked,
is Adonai in whom they take refuge.

Glory...

Antiphon *There is nothing entering from outside*
that can defile a human;
rather things that defile
come from within.   Mk 7:15

PSALM 68

Antiphon *When you are invited, take the lowest place;*
one exalting the self will be humbled,
and one humbling the self will be exalted.

Lk 14:10,11

May God arise
and may foes in enmity flee and be scattered.
As smoke is blown, let it blow;
as wax melts before fire
may wicked ways perish from before God.

But may just ones be glad
and rejoice before God;
may they be happy with joy.
Sing to God! Sing praise to the name!
Extol the Rider of the Clouds,
and rejoice in the name Adonai,

Father of the fatherless
and defender of widows,
God dwelling in holiness,
God sets the lonely into a family
and leads prisoners forth with the songs,
but rebels live on sun-scorched land.

When you went out before your people, O God,
when you marched through the wasteland,
the earth shook and heavens poured rain
before the One God of Sinai,
before God, the God of Israel.

PSALM 68, continued

You gave a shower of abundances, O God,
on your inheritance;
even the weary you refreshed.
Your people settled in her, O God;
you provided for the poor from your bounty.

The Lord announced the word,
a great company of proclaimers.
Kings of armies flee, they flee,
and in camps of residence
plunder is divided.

While you sleep among campfires
wings of dove are sheathed with silver
and her feathers with the shine of gold.
When Shaddai scatters the kings,
the scattering is like snow on Zalmon.

A mountain of majesties,
the mountain of Bashan,
a rugged mountain is the mountain of Bashan.
Why gaze in envy, you rugged mountains,
at the mountain God chooses for the reign?
Indeed Adonai will dwell to forever.

Chariots of God are tens of thousands,
thousands of the multitude into the Sinai sanctuary.
You ascended to the height and led captive;
you received gifts from human beings,
and even from those rebelling,
to your dwelling, God Adonai.

Blessed be the Lord day to day,
bearing our burden is El our Savior.
Our El, the El of salvation,
the Lord Adonai is the escape from death.
Surely God will silence the plans of enmity,
in the crown of their hair where sins go on.

The Lord says, —
"From Bashan I will bring,
 fetch even from depths of the sea,
 that you may wash your foot in their defeat
 and the tongues of your dogs
 have their share from foes."

They view your processions, O God,
processions into the sanctuary
of my God and my King.
Singers are in front followed by harpists
among maidens with tambourines.

In great congregations, bless Adonai;
praise God in the assembly of Israel!
There little Benjamin leads the princes of Judah,
their throng the princes of Zebulun and Naphtali.

Your God summoned your power.
Show strength, God, as you did for us!
Because of your temple at Jerusalem,
to you the kings will bring gifts.

PSALM 68, continued

Rebuke the beast of the reeds,
the herd of bulls among calves of nations;
being humbled with bars of silver,
nations that delight in wars are scattered.
Envoys from Egypt will come;
Cush will submit their hands to God.

Kingdoms of the earth, sing to God!
Sing praise to the Lord!
To the Rider in the skies,
the ancient skies, see!
The voice thunders, the voice of might.

Proclaim the power of God over Israel,
the majesty and power in the skies.
Awesome are you, God, in your sanctuary;
the God of Israel gives power and strengths
to the people praising God.

Glory…

Antiphon   *When you are invited, take the lowest place;*
           one exalting the self will be humbled,
           and one humbling the self will be exalted.

Lk 14:10,11

PSALM 102

| Antiphon | *Whoever is not against you is for you.* | Lk 9:50 |

Adonai, hear my prayer
and let my cry for help come to you.
Hide not your faces from me
on the day of my distress.
Turn your ear to me on the day I call!
Quickly! Answer me!

My days vanish like smoke
and my bones burn like a glowing ember.
My heart is blighted like the grass
and so withered
that I forget to eat my food.
Because of my loud groaning
my bones cling to my skin.

I am like a desert owl;
like an owl of the ruins lying awake,
I became like a bird alone on the housetop.
Enmity taunts me all the day,
railing against me, cursing by me.

I eat ash as food
and mingle my drink with tears
because of your anger and your wrath,
for you took me up and threw me aside.
My days are like the long shadow,
and like the grass I wither away.

PSALM 102, continued

But you, Adonai, sit enthroned to forever,
and your renown is to generation and generation.
You will arise.
You will have compassion on Zion,
for the time to show favor to her,
the appointed time, has come,
for her stones are dear to your servants
and her dust moves them to pity.

The nations will fear the name of Adonai
and all the kings of the earth your glory,
for Adonai will rebuild Zion and appear in glory
and respond to the prayers of the destitute
and not despise their plea.

Let this be written for future generations
that people yet to be created may praise Yah.
Adonai looked down from the high sanctuary place
viewing from heavens to earth,
to hear the groans of prisoners
and release those to be put to death

to declare in Zion the name of Adonai
and give praise in Jerusalem
when peoples assemble together,
and kingdoms, to give worship.

Adonai broke my strength in mid-course
and cut short my days, and I said,
"My El,
  take me not away in the midst of my days.
  Your years are through generation of generations.

In the beginning you founded the earth
and the heavens, the work of your hands.
They will perish, but you remain
and they will all wear out like the garment;
like clothing you will change them
and they will be discarded.

But you: the same; your years will never end.
Children of your servants will live
and their descendants
will be established before you."

Glory...

| Antiphon | *Whoever is not against you is for you.* | Lk 9:50 |

READING **Year I**   **Year II**

week 1	Romans 1:18-32	Genesis 2:4-25
2	Romans 5:12-21	Genesis 12 &13
3	Romans 9:1-18	Genesis 21
4	Romans 13	Genesis 28 & 29
5	1 Corinthians 2	Genesis 42
6	1 Corinthians 7:25-40	1 Thessalonians 4
7	1 Corinthians 11:17-34	2 Corinthians 2:12-3:6
8	1 Corinthians 15:20-34	2 Corinthians 9
9	James 3:1-12	Galatians 2:11-3:14
10	Joshua 2	Philippians 1:27-2:11
11	Judges 4 & 5	Ezra 4 & 5
12	1 Samuel 1:1-19	Ezra 6
13	1 Samuel 9	Nehemiah 7 & 8
14	1 Samuel 19 & 20	Proverbs 8

15	2 Samuel 4 & 5	Job 3
16	2 Samuel 24	Job 13 & 14
17	1 Kings 11	Job 31
18	1 Kings 22	Joel 2
19	2 Kings 6	Zechariah 9
20	Ephesians 2:1-10	Ecclesiastes 3 & 4
21	Ephesians 5:8-20	Titus 3
22	Amos 2	1 Timothy 6:11-21
23	Amos 9	2 Peter 2:1-8
24	Hosea 10	Esther 4
25	Isaiah 5:8-30	Tobit 3
26	2 Kings 17:1-8	Judith 6 & 7
27	2 Kings 18	Sirach 3
28	Jeremiah 2	Sirach 14
29	2 Chronicles 35 & 36	Sirach 29 & 30 & 31
30	Jeremiah 36	Wisdom 3
31	Jeremiah 32	Wisdom 10 & 11
32	Ezekiel 8 & 9	2 Macabees 6
33	Ezekiel 18	1 Macabees 6
34	Ezekiel 37	Daniel 6

SHORT READING **ROMANS 13:11-14**

Know that this is the kairos-time, the hour for you to be raised out of sleep, for now our salvation is nearer than when we became believers. The night has advanced and the day draws near. Let us cast off therefore the deeds of the darkness, and let us put on the armor of the light. As in the new day, let us walk not in revellings to drunken bouts, not in sex to excesses, not in strife to jealousy, but put on the Lord Jesus Christ, and as for the flesh, give its lust no room to think.

Let us bless the Lord. *Thanks be to God.*

TUESDAY PROPHETS

Lord of all be-ing, throned a-far,
Your glo-ry flames from sun and star;
Cen-ter and soul of ev-'ry sphere\\,
And yet to lov-ing hearts how near.

Sun of our life, your liv-ing ray
Sheds on our path the glow of day;
Star of our hope, your gen-tle light\\
Shall ev-er cheer the long-est night.

Lord of all life, be-low, a-bove,
Whose light is truth, whose warmth is love;
Be-fore the bril-liance of your throne\\
We ask no lus-ter of our own.

Give us your grace to make us true,
And kind-ling hearts that burn for you,
Till all your liv-ing al-tars claim\\
One ho-ly light, one heav-'nly flame.

Text: Oliver Wendell Holmes, 1809-1894
Music: JESU DULCIS MEMORIA, LM; Model 1
Popular melody for: *O Radiant Light, O Sun Divine*

TOBIT 13:1b-8

Antiphon *Behold, I make all things new.* Rev 21:5b

Blessed be God who lives forever
and the kingdom of our God,
who scourges but then has mercy,
casts down to the deepest grave
and brings up from the great abyss.
No one can escape this hand.

Israelites, acknowledge before the nations
God who has scattered you among them
and even there shown you great mercy.

Let God be exalted by every living being
because our Lord is our God,
our Father and God forever.

Though scourged for your iniquities,
mercy will be on you all;
you will be gathered from all the nations
among whom you have been scattered.

With all your heart and soul
turn with honesty to the Lord
who will turn the face to you
and no longer hide.

See now what has been done for you,
and with full voice praise my Lord.
Bless the Lord of justice
and exalt the King of the ages.

In the land of my exile I acknowledge the Lord
and make known to a sinful nation
this power and majesty:
"Turn, you sinners, and do right before the Lord,
 who may look upon you with favor and mercy."

My God, I will exalt you
and rejoice in the King of Heaven.
Let all speak of this majesty
in Jerusalem with exaltation.

Glory...

Antiphon

ISAIAH 38:10-14,17b-20

Antiphon *The living alive praise Adonai.*

I asked, "Must I go in the prime of my days
 through the gates of Sheol;
 must I be robbed of the rest of my years?"

I said, "I will no longer see Adonai,
 Adonai in the land of the living.
 As a dweller of the place of cessation
 I will look on humanity no longer."

My house was pulled down
and taken from me like the tent of my shepherd;
I rolled up my life,
as a weaver cuts off from a loom.

ISAIAH 38, continued

From day to night you made an end of me.
I waited till dawn;
all my bones are broken as by a lion.
From day to night you made an end of me.

Like a swift or thrush I cried;
I moaned like the dove.
My eyes to the heavens grew weak.
Lord, troubles are at me;
come to my aid…

In your love you have kept my life
out of the pit of destruction;
indeed you put behind your back
all my sins.

Sheol cannot praise you
and death cannot sing to you praise,
nor can those going down the pit
hope for your kindness.

The living alive praise you,
as I do this day.
Fathers and mothers tell the children
all about your faithfulness.

Adonai saves us;
we will play our stringed instruments
and sing in the temple of Adonai
all the days of our lives.

Glory…

Antiphon   *The living alive praise Adonai.*

DANIEL 3:26-27,29,34-41b

Antiphon   *Lord, do not withhold your mercy.*

Blessed be you, Lord,
God of our ancestors,
your name worthy of praise
and glory forever.

For you are just in all you do;
all your deeds are true and your ways right,
and all your judgments are true…

We have sinned and broken your law
in turning from you;
in all ways possible we have sinned…

For the sake of your name,
do not give us up to forever
and do not void your covenant.

Do not take your mercy from us
for the sake of Abraham your beloved,
for the sake of your servant Isaac,
and Israel, your holy one,

to whom you promised to multiply
descendants like the stars of heaven
and like the sand on the shore of the sea.

For we, Lord, have become
least of the other nations
and are brought low in the world this day
because of our sins.

DANIEL 3:26-27,29,34-41b, continued

We have in our day
no ruler, prophet, or leader,
no burnt offering, sacrifice,
oblation or incense,
no place to make an offering before you
and so find your favor.

But with a contrite heart
and a humble spirit
may we be accepted
as if they were burnt offerings
of rams and bulls
or thousands of fat lambs.

As such may our sacrifice
be seen by you today
and may we follow you without reserve,
for no shame will come
to those who trust you.

And so we follow you
with all our heart;
we fear you
and seek your face.

Glory...

Antiphon   *Lord, do not withhold your mercy.*

ISAIAH 26:1b-4,7-9,12

Antiphon *My soul longs for you in the night;*
          within me my spirit yearns for you.

Our city is strong;
salvation makes walls and rampart.
Open gates, so the righteous nation may enter,
the one keeping faiths.

Your steadfast mind will keep peace,
peace because of trusting.
Trust in Adonai to forever,
for in God Adonai is the Rock of eternities…

The path of the righteous is level;
the Upright One smooths the way of the just.
Yes, in the way of your laws, Adonai,
we wait,
for your name and your renown
are the desire of our souls.

My soul yearns for you in the night;
within me my spirit longs for you.
Just as your judgments are on the earth,
so people of the world learn justice…

Adonai, you establish for us peace;
indeed all we have accomplished
you did for us.

Glory…

                                                Antiphon

READING **ISAIAH 55:1-11**

Yes! All you thirsty, come to the waters!
And you who have no money, come! Buy! And eat!
And come with no money
and buy wine and milk at no cost!
Why spend money on what is not bread,
and your labor on what does not satisfy?
Listen! Listen to me and eat the good,
and your soul will delight in the richness.
Give your ear, and come to me!
Hear, that your soul may live!
Indeed I will make with you an everlasting covenant,
the faithful loves of David.
See, a witness to the peoples I made him,
leader and commander of peoples.
Surely you will summon a nation you do not know,
and nations that do not know you will hasten to you,
because of your God Adonai,
and to the Holy One of Israel
who endowed you with splendor.
While Adonai can be found, seek!
And while near, call!
Let the doers of bad forsake their ways,
and the thinker of bad things turn to Adonai,
who will have mercy,
and to our God who makes great to pardon.
"For my thoughts are not your thoughts,
and nor are your ways my ways,"
declares Adonai;

"For as heavens are higher than the earth,
so are my ways higher than your ways
and my thoughts higher than your thoughts.
For just as the rain and the snow
come down from the heavens
and do not return there
without first watering the earth
and making her bud fruitful and fertile,
yielding seed for the sower and bread for the eater,
so is the word that goes out from my mouth.
My word will not return to me empty
but will accomplish what I desire
and will achieve the purpose for which I sent it."

RESPONSORY   Psalm 119:147

Lord, hear my voice,…
 …my hope is in your word and your promise.
Awake in the watch for dawn, I cry for help;…
 …my hope is in your word and your promise.
Glory to the Father and to Son and to the Holy Spirit:
 …Lord, hear my voice;
 my hope is in your word and your promise.

Let us bless the Lord.   *Thanks be to God.*

TUESDAY MORNING

+ *God, come to my assistance;*   Psalm 70:2
Lord, make haste to help me!

Glory...

We walk by faith, and not by sight;
No gra-cious words we hear
From him who spoke as none e'er spoke;
But we be-lieve him near.

We may not touch his hands and side,
Nor fol-low where he trod;
But in his prom-ise we re-joice,
And cry, "My Lord and God!"

Help then, O Lord, our un-be-lief;
And may our faith a-bound,
To call on you when you are near
And seek where you are found.

That, when our life of faith is done,
In realms of clear-er light
We may be-hold you as you are,
With full and end-less sight.

Text: CM, based on 2 Cor. 5:7 and John 20:24-29; Henry Alford, 1844,
altered. Music: ST. AGNES, CM; John B. Dykes, 1866
Popular melody for: *Shepherd of Souls*
or, SHANTI, by Marty Haugen, © GIA Publications, 1984,
is the current familiar tune.

PSALM 67

Antiphon *Woman (of Canaan),*
great is your faith;
let it be done as you desire.   Mt 15:28

May God be gracious to us and bless us,
may God's faces shine upon us.
How else can your ways be known on the earth
and your salvation among all the nations?

May the peoples praise you, O God,
may the peoples praise you, all of them.

May the nations be glad
and sing for joy
for you rule the peoples with justice
and guide nations of the earth.

May the peoples praise you, O God,
may the peoples praise you, all of them.

The land will yield her harvest,
our God will bless us,
and all the ends of the earth
will revere our God.

Glory...

Antiphon

PSALM 24

Antiphon   *She will bear a son,*
and you shall call his name Jesus;
he will save his people from their sins.   Mt 1:21

The earth and everything,
the world and all who are alive are to Adonai,
who founded the earth on the seas
and established the earth on the waters.

Who may ascend to the hill of Adonai?
And who may stand in the holy place?
The clean of hand and pure of heart
who do not lift the soul to an idol
and do not swear by falsehood
will receive the blessing from Adonai
and justice from the God who saves.

Such is the generation of ones who seek,
who seek your faces, God of Jacob.

Lift up your heads, you gates;
be lifted up you ancient doors,
that the King of glory may come in.

Who is this King of glory?
Adonai, strong and mighty,
Adonai, mighty of battle.

Lift up your heads, you gates;
lift up, you ancient doors,
that the King of glory may come in.

Who is this King of glory?
Adonai Sabaoth is the King of glory.

Glory...

                                                        Antiphon

PSALM 43

Antiphon   *Blessed are the ones mourning,*
                for they will be comforted.   Mt 5:4

O God, grant me justice;
plead my cause against a nation not godly;
rescue me from humans deceitful doing wicked.

God, my stronghold, why am I rejected?
Why must I go about mourning,
oppressed by enmity?

Send forth your light and fidelity;
let them guide me to your dwellings
and bring me to your holy mountain.

Then I will go to the altar of God,
to El, my joy and delight,
and I will praise you with harp, God, my God.

Why are you downcast, my soul?
Why do you groan within me?
Wait for God, whom I will yet praise,
the saving help of my face, my God.

Glory...

                                                        Antiphon

PSALM 33

Antiphon	*Where your treasure is,* *there also will your heart be.*	Lk 12:34

Sing joyfully to Adonai, righteous ones,
for praise is fitting for the upright.

Give thanks to Adonai with a harp,
make music on the lyre of ten.
Sing a new song with skill
and play with a shout of joy.

For right is the word of Adonai
and all the faithful deeds done.
Loving righteousness and justice,
the earth is full of Adonai's unfailing mercy.

The heavens were made by the word of Adonai
and all their hosts by the breath of этого mouth,
as one gathers in a heap the waters of the sea,
as one puts into the deep of the storehouses.

Let all the earth, let them fear,
let all alive in the world revere Adonai
who spoke and it came to be,
who commanded and it stood firm.

Adonai foils the plans of nations
and frustrates the designs of the peoples.
The plan of Adonai stands firm to forever,
heartfelt purpose to generation and generation.

Blessed is the nation for whom Adonai is God,
the people chosen for this inheritance.
From the heavens Adonai looks down and sees
all sons and daughters of Adam and Eve,

and from the place of dwelling watches
all those alive on the earth.
The one who formed our hearts
considers all our deeds.

No king is saved by the size of an army;
no warrior escapes by greatness of strength.
The horse is a vain hope for deliverance;
despite greatness of strength it cannot save.

See the eye of Adonai on those who place
their fear and hope in the unfailing mercy
that delivers them from death
and keeps them alive in the famine.

Our soul waits for Adonai,
who is our help and our shield,
in whom our heart rejoices,
the holy name in whom we trust.

Adonai, may you rest on us
your unfailing mercy
even as we hope in you.

Glory...

Antiphon

PSALM 65

Antiphon
*And that sown on the good soil
is the one hearing
and understanding the word,
who indeed bears fruit.*

Mt 13:23

For you, O God, silence
and praise in Zion;
to you will our vow be fulfilled.

To you hearing our prayer
all humanity will come.
Matters of sin overwhelmed over me;
you atoned for our transgressions.

Blessed are the ones you choose
and bring near to live in your courts.
We are filled with the goodness of your house
and the holiness of your temple.

Deeds awesome and just are your answer,
God of our salvation,
hope of all the ends of the earth
and of the far seas.

You form mountains by your power,
arming yourself with strength.
You still the roar of the seas,
the roar of their waves,
and the turmoil of nations.

Those who live in far away places
are in awe of your wonders;
in dawns of morning and in the evening
you call forth songs of joy.

You care for the land and water her;
with an abundance you enrich her.
God's stream is as you ordain the earth:
filled with waters, providing grain.

You drench its furrows
and level its ridges;
you soften her with showers
and bless the crops.

You crown the year with your bounty;
carts overflow with your abundance.
The desert grasslands are overflowing
and the hills are clothed with gladness.

The pastures are covered with the flock
and valleys are coated with grain.
They shout for joy;
for joy they sing.

Glory…

                                                  Antiphon

PSALM 85

Antiphon *Take courage; it is me. Come.* Mt 14:27,29

You showed favor, Adonai, to your land;
you restored the fortune of Jacob.
You forgave the guilt of your people;
you pardoned all of their sin.
You set aside all of your wrath;
you turned from your fierce anger.

Restore us, God of our salvation!
And put away your displeasure toward us.
Will you be angry with us to forever?
Will you prolong your anger
to generation and generation?

Will you not revive us again
that your people may rejoice in you?
Show us, Adonai, your unfailing mercy
and grant us your salvation.

I will listen for what El Adonai will say,
promising peace to the people, even to the saints,
but not letting them return to folly.
Surely near to ones fearing is salvation,
the glory to dwell in our land.

Love and Fidelity meet;
Peace and Justice kiss.
Fidelity springs forth from the earth
and Justice looks down from the heavens.

TUESDAY MORNING

Indeed Adonai will give the good
and our land will yield her harvest,
Justice going forward to prepare
the way for the steps of the Lord.

Glory…

Antiphon

PSALM 101

Antiphon

*A great prophet
is risen among us,
and God has visited
the people of God.*   Lk 7:16

I will sing of hesed-mercy and justice;
to you, Adonai, I will sing praise.
I will take care to be blameless in life.
When will you come to me?

I will walk with integrity of heart
in the midst of my house.
I hate and will not set before my eyes
vile things that faithless people do;
they will not cling to me.

The devious heart will be far from me;
I do not know evil.
I will silence the secret slandering of a neighbor;
haughty eyes and proud hearts I will not endure.

PSALM 101, continued

My eyes are on the faithful of the land,
to dwell with me;
one walking in a way of integrity
will minister to me.

Anyone practicing deceit
will not dwell in the midst of my house;
nor will one speaking falsehoods
stand before my eyes.

Each morning I will silence bad doers in the land
to cut off doings of badness
from the city of Adonai.

Glory…

Antiphon
*A great prophet
is risen among us,
and God has visited
the people of God.*   Lk 7:16

READING **1 JOHN 4:7-21**

Beloved, let us love one another, for love is of God, and everyone loving has been begotten of God and knows God. The one not loving did not know God, because God is love.

By this was God's love shown forth into us: God sent God's only begotten Son into the cosmos, that we might be alive through him. In this is love; not that we have loved God, but that God loved us and sent the Son as a sacrifice of reconciliation for our sins. Beloved, as God so loved us, we also ought to love one another.

No human has ever beheld God; if we love one another, God remains in us and God's love is perfected in us. By this we know that we remain in God and God in us, because of the Spirit of God given to us. And we have beheld and bear witness that the Father has sent the Son as Savior of the cosmos.

Whoever confesses that Jesus is the Son of God, God remains in that one, and that one in God. And we have known and have believed the love which God has in us.

God is love, and the one remaining in love remains in God and God remains in him or her. By this has love been perfected with us, that we may have confidence in the day of judgment, because as that one is, so also are we in this cosmos.

Fear is not in love, but perfect love casts out fear, because fear is about punishment, and the one fearing has not been perfected in love.

We love because God first loved us. If anyone says, "I love God," and hates a brother or sister, that one is a liar. For the one not loving a brother or sister who has been seen cannot love God who has not been seen.

And this commandment we have from God, that one who loves God loves also his or her brother and sister.

RESPONSORY   Ps 71:1,5

In you, Lord, I take refuge...   ...*you, Lord, are my hope.*
My trust, O Lord, from my youth...

                              ...*you, Lord, are my hope.*

Glory to the Father and to the Son and to the Holy Spirit:
   ...*In you, Lord, I take refuge; you, Lord, are my hope.*

GOSPEL READING OF THE DAY or GOSPEL CANTICLE
Antiphon   *God raised salvation in the house of David.*

CANTICLE OF ZECHARIAH   **LUKE 1:68-79**

+ Blessed be the Lord the God of Israel
  who chose a people,
  visited them to bring redemption,
  and raised salvation in the house of David,
  saving strength from God's own servant,

  speaking from the age of the prophets
  through the mouth of the holy prophet:
  Salvation out of enmity,
  even out of those who hate us,

  to show our ancestors how mercy works,
  and to remember the holy promise of the Lord,
  the covenant made for our father Abraham,
  calming our fear and making us free
  to serve God as holy and righteous and just
  in the Lord's presence all our days.

  And you also child
  will be called a prophet of the Most High
  for you will go before the Lord to prepare his way
  and give to his people a knowledge of salvation
  known in accepting forgiveness of their sins.

TUESDAY MORNING

From the deepness of God's mercy on us,
a sun rising from the height will visit to appear
to those who sit in the dark or shadow of death,
and to guide our feet into the way of peace.

Gospel Reading for Tuesday of

Week			
	1 Mark 1:21-28	**13** Matt 8:23-27	**25** Luke 8:19-21
	2 Mark 2:23-28	**14** Matt 9:32-38	**26** Luke 9:51-56
	3 Mark 3:31-35	**15** Matt 11:20-24	**27** Lk 10:38-42
	4 Mark 5:21-30	**16** Matt 12:46-50	**28** Lk 11:37-41
	5 Mark 7:1-13	**17** Matt 13:36-43	**29** Lk 12:35-38
	6 Mark 8:14-21	**18** Mt 15:1-2,10-14	**30** Lk 13:18-21
	7 Mark 9:30-37	**19** Mt 18:1-5,10,12-14	**31** Lk 14:15-24
	8 Mark 10:28-31	**20** Matt 19:23-30	**32** Luke 17:7-10
	9 Mark 12:13-17	**21** Matt 23:23-26	**33** Luke 19:1-10
	10 Matt 5:13-16	**22** Luke 4:31-37	**34** Luke 21:5-11
	11 Matt 5:43-48	**23** Luke 6:12-19	
	12 Matt 7:6,12-14	**24** Luke 7:11-17	

Glory... Antiphon

PETITIONS FOR THE CONSECRATION TO GOD
OF THE DAY AND ITS WORK
- For the Church and her ministry and apostolates...
- For secular authorities and all serving as stewards...
- For people who are poor or sick or in sorrow...
- For peace and the basic needs of each human being...

OUR FATHER...

+ *May the Lord bless us, protect us from all evil,
and bring us to everlasting life.* ***Amen***.

TUESDAY DAYTIME

+ *God, come to my assistance;* Psalm 70:2
  Lord, make haste to help me!

Glory…

In/ Christ there is no/ East or West,
In him no South\ or/ North;
But/ one com-mu-nion of God's love
Through/-out/ the whole\ wide earth.

In/ Christ shall true hearts/ ev'ry-where
Their high vo-ca\-tion/ find;
His/ ser-vice is the gold-en cord,
Close/ bind/-ing hu\-man-kind.

Join/ hands, then, mem-bers/ of the faith,
What-e'r your race\ may/ be!
Who/ serves my Fa-ther as his child
Is/ sure/-ly kin\ to me.

In/ Christ now meet both/ East and West,
In him meet South\ and/ North;
All/ souls of Christ are one in him
Through/-out/ the whole\ wide earth.

see Galatians 3:8
Text: William A. Dunkerley, 1908, under the pseudonym
of John Oxenham, altered
Music: MCKEE, CM; African American Spiritual,
arranged by Harry T. Burleigh, 1866-1949

PSALM 119:41-48
Waw

Antiphon *The Holy Spirit, the Paraclete, will teach you all things.* Jn 14:26

May your unfailing mercy come to me, Adonai,
your promised salvation.
Then will I answer my taunters
for I trust in your word.

Take not the word of truth from my mouth
for indeed I hope in your laws
and I will obey your law always
to forever and ever.

And I will walk in open freedom
for I sought out your precepts
and I will speak of your statutes
before kings without fear

for I delight in your commands
which I love,
reaching out my hands for your commands
which I love,
and I meditate on your decrees.

Glory…

Antiphon

PSALM 119:49-56
Zayin

Antiphon *Gather the fragments left over*
so that nothing is lost. Jn 6:12

Remember your word to your servant
for you give me hope.
This is my comfort in affliction:
your promise she makes me alive.

Arrogance mocks me to excess;
I do not turn from your law.
Remembering your ancient laws, Adonai,
I find comfort.

Indignation grabs me
for doers of bad forsake your law.
Your decrees are my songs
in the house of my lodging.

In the night I remember your name, Adonai,
and I will keep your law.
This is me:
obeying your precepts.

Glory...

Antiphon

PSALM 119:57-64
Heth

Antiphon *Be ready always*
for everyone asking you a word
concerning the hope in you.   1 Ptr 3:15b

Adonai, my portion,
I promise to obey your words.
I sought your faces with all my heart.
Have mercy on me as is your promise!

I pondered my ways
and I turned my steps to your statutes.
I will hasten and not delay
to obey your commands.

Though ropes of badness bind me
I will not forget your law.
I rise in the middle of the night
to give you thanks
for your righteous laws.

I am a friend to all who fear you
and those following your precepts.

The earth she is filled
with your mercy, Adonai;
teach me your decrees!

Glory…

Antiphon

PSALM 13

Antiphon   *Emmanuel!*
            God is with us!   Mt 1:23

Until when, Adonai?
Will you forget me forever?
Until when will you hide your faces from me?
Until when must I wrestle
with thoughts of my soul
and sorrow in my heart by day?
Until when will enmity triumph over me?

Look! Answer me, my God Adonai!
Give light to my eyes,
or I will sleep the death!
Or enmity will say,
"I overcame that one,"
and foes will rejoice when I fall.

But my trust is in your unfailing mercy;
my heart rejoices in your salvation.
I will sing to Adonai,
who is good to me.

Glory...

                                                Antiphon

PSALM 14

Antiphon
If we say we have no sin,
we deceive ourselves.
If we confess our sins,
God is faithful and forgiving.   1 Jn 1:8,9

The fool says in the heart, "There is no God."
They are corrupt, vile are their deeds;
no one is doing good.

Adonai looks down from the heavens
on sons and daughters of Adam and Eve
to see if one is wise,
if one is seeking God.

All turned aside together to corruption;
no one is doing good,
not even one.

Will the doers of bad things never learn?
Devouring my people as they eat bread,
they do not call on Adonai.

There they are, in dread of dread,
for God is in the company of the just.
They frustrate the plans of the poor,
but in Adonai the poor find their refuge.

Who from Zion could bring the salvation of Israel?
When Adonai restores the fortune to the people,
let Jacob rejoice, let Israel be glad.

Glory…   Antiphon

PSALM 53

Antiphon *Amen I tell you, whoever does
not receive the kingdom of God as a child
by no means may enter into it.*   Mk 10:15

In the heart of a fool is said, "There is no God."
The evil way is vile and corrupt;
there is no one doing good.

God looks from the heavens
on children of humanity
to see if there is one who understands,
one who is seeking God.

All of them turned away together;
they became corrupt;
there is no one doing good,
not even one.

Will the ones doing evil never learn?
Devouring my people, they eat bread;
they do not call on God.

There they dreaded and dread was not there,
for God scattered the bones of attackers
put to shame in God's rejection.

Who would be brought from Zion
for the salvation of Israel?
When God restores the fortunes of God's people,
let Jacob rejoice, let Israel be glad.

Glory... Antiphon

PSALM 54:1-6,8-9

Antiphon *The Son of humanity*
will be betrayed into human hands
and they will kill him,
and three days after being killed
he will rise up.   Mk 9:31

God, save me by your name
and by your might vindicate me.
God, hear my prayer!
Listen to the words of my mouth!

For strangers attack me
and ruthless people seek my life
without regard for God before them.
See, God is helping me!
The Lord is among those sustaining my life…

With a freewill offering
I will sacrifice to you;
I will give thanks, Adonai, to your good name,
for you delivered me from all trouble
and my eye has looked upon enmity.

Glory…

Antiphon

PSALM 74

Antiphon *He took our infirmities
and bore our diseases.*

Mt 8:17
Isaiah 53:4

Why, God, do you reject us to forever?
Your anger smolders against sheep of your pasture.
Remember your people you purchased of old
and redeemed, your tribe of inheritance,
Mount Zion where you dwelt.

Lift high your steps through everlasting ruin,
the enmity destruction to the sanctuary.
All who would be foes roared,
and in your meeting place
set up their standard signs.

They behaved like ones wielding at above
axes through a thicket of trees,
and now her carved panels
they smashed with axe and hatchet.
They sent your sanctuary to the ground with fire
and defiled the dwelling place of your Name.

They said in their heart,
"We will crush them."
Completely they burned in the land
all the places to worship God.
We see no miraculous signs;
there is no longer a prophet among us.
Until when? No one knows.

Until when, God, will foes in enmity
mock and revile your name?
To forever?
Why do you hold back your hand,
even your right hand
from the fold of your bosom?

But God, my King from of old,
bringing salvation onto the midst of the earth,
you split open the sea by your power,
you break the heads of monsters in the waters.

You crushed the heads of Leviathan,
giving him as food to people and desert creatures.
You opened up streams and springs
and dried up everflowing rivers.

To you is the day and to you is the night,
and you placed the moon and the sun.
You set all the boundaries of the earth;
summer and winter were made by you.

Remember those who in enmity mock Adonai
and the foolish people who revile your name.
Do not hand the life of your dove to the wild beast;
remember to forever the life of your afflicted ones.

Dark places of the land are filled with them
and haunts of violence.
Have regard for the covenant.
Let not the oppressed retreat, nor the disgraced;
may the poor and the needy praise your name.

PSALM 74, continued

Rise up, God! Defend your cause!
Remember the all-day mockery of fools.
Ignore not the clamor of foes,
nor those in enmity and continual uproar.

Glory…

Antiphon *He took our infirmities
and bore our diseases.* Mt 8:17; Is 53:4

READING **ROMANS 3:21-31**

Now without law
a righteousness of God has shown forth,
witnessed by the law and the prophets,
a righteousness of God
through faith in Jesus Christ for all who believe.
There is no difference, for all have sinned
and come short of the glory of God,
and are justified freely by God's grace
through the redemption in Christ Jesus,
in whom God set forth an expiation through faith
by his blood, for a showing forth of his righteousness
because of the passing by
of the sins previously committed,
in the forebearance of God,
for the showing forth
of righteousness in the present time,
that God should be just and justifying
those of faith in Jesus.

And so, where is the boasting? It was shut out.
Through what law? of works?
No, but through a law of faith.
For we reckon a person to be justified by faith
without works of the law.
Or is God of Jews only? Not also of nations?
Yes, also of nations, since there is one God
who will justify circumcision by faith
and uncircumcision through the faith.
And so, do we destroy law through faith?
May it not be. But we support the law.

RESPONSORY   Ps 16:11

You will make known to me the path of life,…
   …*fullness of joy in your presence.*

Eternal pleasure at your right hand,…
   …*fullness of joy in your presence.*

Glory to the Father and to the Son and to the Holy Spirit:
   …*You will make known to me the path of life,*
   fullness of joy in your presence.

Lord\, have mer-cy.
   Christ\, have mer-cy.
      Lord\, have mer-cy.

TUESDAY EVENING

+ *God, come to my assistance;*   Psalm 70:2
Lord, make haste to help me!

Glory...

Songs of thank-ful-ness and praise,
Jesus, Lord, to you we raise,
Man-i-fest-ed by the star
To the ma-gi from a-far;
Branch of roy/-al Da-vid's stem
In your birth at Beth-le-hem;
Prais-es be to you ad-dressed,
God in flesh made man-i-fest.

Man-i-fest at Jor-dan's stream,
Pro-phet, Priest and King su-preme;
And as Ca-na's wed-ding guest,
In your God-head man-i-fest;
Man-i-fest/ in pow'r div-ine,
Chang-ing wa-ter in-to wine;
Prais-es be to you ad-dressed,
God in flesh made man-i-fest.

Grant us grace to see you, Lord,
Mir-rored in your ho-ly Word;
May our im-i-ta-tion show,
In your like-ness may we go;
Pure and ho/-ly may we be
At your great E-pi-pha-ny;
May we praise you, ev-er blest,
God in flesh made man-i-fest.

PSALM 21:2-8,14

Antiphon *Jesus and his disciples*
ate at the house of Levi
and with them tax collectors and sinners;
many from there followed him.   Mk 2:15

In your strength, Adonai, the king rejoices,
and in your victory; how great is the joy!
You granted to him the desire of his heart
and did not withhold the request of his lips.

Indeed, you welcomed him with rich blessings
and placed on his head a crown of pure gold.
He asked from you life
and you gave length of days forever and ever.

Great is the glory through your victory;
on him you bestowed splendor and majesty.
Surely you granted him blessings for eternity
making him glad with joy in your presences,

for the king trusts in Adonai and will be unshaken
through the unfailing mercy of the Most High…
Be exalted, Adonai, in your strength!
We will sing and we will praise your might.

Glory…

Antiphon

Song text: Christopher Wordsworth, 1862, altered
Music: 77 77 D, SALZBURG; Jakob Hintze, 1678

PSALM 49

Antiphon *You cannot serve God and mammon;*
where your treasure is
there also will your heart be.   Mt 6:24b,21

Hear this all peoples!
Listen all alive in the world!
Men and women, all sons and daughters,
rich and poor alike:

My mouth will speak words of wisdom
and my heart utter the understanding of things.
I will turn an ear to a proverb;
I will expound my riddle with a harp.

Why should I fear in days of evil
the badness of deceivers who surround me,
the trusters of wealth,
and the boasters of the greatness of their riches?

No human can redeem redemption of another,
nor for oneself give a ransom to God.
Ransom of a soul is costly;
no ransom is ever enough
for one to live to forever
and not see the decay.

For we see that wise people die;
like the foolish and the senseless they perish,
and leave all their wealth to others.

Their thoughts are of their houses to forever
as their dwelling for generations and generation,
and so they call lands by their own names.

The human, despite riches,
does not endure,
but perishes just like the beasts.

This is their fate who trust in themselves
and their followers who give them approval.
Like the sheep they are destined for Sheol,
and death will feed on them too.

Upright ones will rule over them in the morning
and their form will decay in Sheol, their mansion.
But God will redeem my life
and take me from the hand of Sheol.

Be not overawed when human beings grow rich,
when they increase the splendor of their houses.
For in death they will take none of it;
with none of their splendor will they descend.

Though during their lives they blessed themselves,
and people do praise you when you prosper,
they will go to the generation of their ancestors
and never see light to forever.

Like the beast that must perish
so is a human with riches
but still poor in understanding.

Glory…

                                              Antiphon

PSALM 20

Antiphon   *The Spirit of the Lord is upon me;*
the Lord anointed me to evangelize the poor
and sent me to proclaim release to captives,
sight to the blind, and freedom to the crushed,
to proclaim a year of the Lord's acceptance.

Lk 4:18, and see Isaiah 61:1-2 & 58:6

May Adonai answer you on the day of distress.
May the name of the God of Jacob protect you,
send you help from the sanctuary,

support you from Zion,
remember all of your sacrifices,
accept your burnt offerings,
give to you as your heart desires,
and make all of your plans succeed.

We will shout for joy at your victory
and lift a banner in the name of our God;
may Adonai grant all your requests.

Now I know that Adonai saves the chosen anointed
and answers from the holy heavens
with a right hand of saving powers.

Some trust in the chariot
and others in the horses,
but we in the name of our God Adonai.
They kneel and they fall,
but we rise up and stand firm.

Adonai, save the king;
answer us on the day of our call.

Glory…

Antiphon

PSALM 125

Antiphon *If you know
to give good gifts to your children,
how much more will the heavenly Father
give the Holy Spirit to those who ask.* Lk 11:13

Ones trusting in Adonai
are like Mount Zion;
not to be shaken, they endure to forever.

As mountains surround around Jerusalem,
so Adonai surrounds around the people
from now and to forevermore.

Indeed the sceptor of badness will not remain
over the lot of the just
lest the hands of the just be used for bad.

Do good, Adonai, to the good,
even to those upright in their hearts!
But those who turn to crooked ways
Adonai will banish with those who do evil.

Peace be upon Israel!

Glory…

Antiphon

PSALM 131

Antiphon
*Scribes and Pharisees
preach and do not do it;
they put on human shoulders
heavy burdens bound,
but are unwilling to lift a finger
to move them.*   Mt 23:3b,4

Adonai, my heart is not proud
and my eyes are not haughty
and I am unconcerned
with the great matters,
with things so wonderful
as to be beyond me.

But indeed I have become still
and quiet in my soul
like a child with a mother, being weaned.
Like one being weaned
is my soul within me.

Israel, put your hope in Adonai
from now and to forevermore.

Glory…

Antiphon

PSALM 137:1-6

Antiphon *God so loved the cosmos,*
and so gave the only begotten Son
that everyone believing in him
may not perish
but have life eternal.   Jn 3:16

By rivers of Babylon,
there we sat and wept
as we remembered Zion;
On the poplars in their midst
we hung our harps,

for there our captors
asked us for words of song,
our tormentors for joy:
"Sing for us from the songs of Zion!"

How can we sing in a foreign land
a song of Adonai?
If I forget you, Jerusalem,
may my right hand forget its skill.

May my tongue cling
to the roof of my mouth
if I remember you not,
if I consider any but Jerusalem
as the height of my joy.

Glory…

                                        Antiphon

PSALM 138

Antiphon *Put out into the deep
and let down your nets for a catch.* Lk 5:4

I will thank you with all my heart.
Before those who would be "gods"
I will sing praise of you.
I will bow toward your holy temple
and I will praise your name
for your mercy and faithfulness.

You are exalted above all,
your name and your word.
On the day I called, then you answered me.
You made me bold and stout in my heart.

May all the kings of the earth praise you, Adonai,
when they hear the words of your mouth.
May they sing of the ways of Adonai,
for great is the glory of Adonai.

Though on high, Adonai looks upon the lowly
and knows the proud from afar.
Though I walk in the midst of trouble,
you keep me alive
against the anger of enmity.

You stretch out your hand,
your right hand, and you save me.
Adonai will fulfill me.
Your mercy, Adonai, is to forever.
Abandon not the works of your hands.

Glory...   Antiphon

REVELATION 4:11;5:9,10,12,13b

Antiphon *Holy, Holy, Holy,*
Lord God Almighty
who was and is and is to come.   Rev 4:8b

Worthy are you, our Lord and our God,
to receive the glory and honor and power,
because you have created all things,
and by your will all things were created and are.

Worthy are you to receive the scroll
and to open its seals,
because you were slain
and purchased for God by your blood
from every tribe and tongue and people and nation.

You made of them to our God
a kingdom and priests,
and they will reign over the earth.

Worthy is the Lamb, slain to receive
the power and riches and wisdom and strength
and honor and glory and blessing.

Glory…

Antiphon

READING   **1 JOHN 3:1-2**

See what manner of love the Father has given to us, that we may be called children of God, and we are. The world does not know us because it did not know him. Beloved, now we are children of God, and what we shall be has not yet been shown. We know that when it is shown, we will be like him because we will see him as he is.

Everyone who carries this hope is made pure as God is pure.

RESPONSORY   Ps 100:5

The love of the Lord endures to forever…

…for God is good.

Faithful love to all generations,…

…for God is good.

Glory to the Father and to the Son and to the Holy Spirit:
…The love of the Lord endures to forever, for God is good.

GOSPEL CANTICLE OF MARY   **LUKE 1:46-55**

Antiphon   *My spirit is beyond joy*
                         in God, my Savior.

+ My soul is stretched full with praise of the Lord,
   and my spirit, beyond joy in God, my Savior,
   who chose to lay eyes on this humble servant.

TUESDAY EVENING

Behold, now and forward,
each and every age will call me blessed,
for the Mighty One did great things to me.
Holy is the name and the mercy
to generations and generations,
the ones fearing the One,

Who scattered the haughty of mind and heart,
pulled the powerful off their high place,
and lifted with dignity the humble in need.

The hungering are filled with good things,
the rich are sent away empty,
and servant Israel is given relief

with a memory of mercy to remember,
the promise spoken to our ancestors,
to Abraham and his descendants forever.

Glory…

Antiphon

INTERCESSIONS
- For a culture of vocations all over the world…
- For all who have died…

- In gratitude for blessings…; Abba thank you.
- For the sins of this day…; Lord Jesus have mercy.
- With concerns over tomorrow…; Holy Spirit help.

OUR FATHER…

+ *May the Lord bless us, protect us from all evil,
and bring us to everlasting life.* ***Amen***.

TUESDAY NIGHT

+ *God, come to my assistance;*   Psalm 70:2
Lord, make haste to help me!

Glory…

What a Friend we have in Je-sus,
All our sins and griefs to bear!
What a priv-i-lege to car-ry
Ev-'ry-thing to God in prayer!
Oh, what peace we of-ten for-feit,
Oh, what need-less pain we bear,
All be-cause we do not car-ry
Ev-'ry-thing to God in prayer!

Glo-ry be to God the Fa-ther,
Son, and Spir-it ev-'ry-where.
Glo-ry be as the Be-got-ten
Son of Ab-ba hears our prayer
At the right hand of the Fa-ther,
Lamb of God, our mer-cy home.
Fa-ther, Son and Ho-ly Spir-it,
Glo-ry be to you a-lone.

Text: based on Matthew 21:22; Joseph Scriven, 1865;
verse 2 Stephen J. Wolf, 2011
Music: FRIEND; Charles C. Converse, 1868

TUESDAY NIGHT

PSALM 143:1-11

Antiphon   *Go into all the cosmos*
           and proclaim the gospel to all creation.   Mk 16:15

Adonai, hear my prayer!
Listen in your faithfulness to my cries!
Relieve me in your righteousness!
Bring not your servant into judgment
for not anyone alive is just before you.

Indeed enmity pursues my soul
and crushes my life to the ground
and makes me dwell in dark places
like dead ones of long ago.
My spirit grows faint within me;
within me my heart is dismayed.

I remember days of long ago
and meditate on all of your work
and ponder the deeds of your hands.
I stretch out my hands to you;
like land parched is my soul for you.

Be quick! Answer me, Adonai!
My spirit faints!
Hide not your faces from me
or I will be like and with ones going down the pit.

Bring in the morning your word of unfailing mercy,
for in you I put trust.
Show me the way I should go
for to you I lift up my life!

PSALM 143:1-11, continued

Rescue me, Adonai, from enmity; in you I hide.
Teach me to do your will, for you are my El.
May your good Spirit lead me on level ground.

For the sake of your Name, Adonai,
you keep me alive in your righteousness;
you bring my soul out from trouble.

Glory...

Antiphon   *Go into all the cosmos
and proclaim the gospel to all creation.*   Mk 16:15

READING **COLOSSIANS 3:5-17**

And so put to death what on the earth is in you:
fornication, uncleanness, lust, bad desire,
and greed that is idolatry.
The anger of God is coming because of these,
in which indeed you then walked
when you lived in these things.
But now put away all such things as anger, rage,
malice, blasphemy, abuse out of your mouth,
and do not lie to one another,
having put off the old human with its practices,
and having put on the new human
renewed in full knowledge
in the image of the one creating you,
where divisions have no place
whether Greek or Jew, circumcision or uncircumcision,
barbarian or Scythian, slave or free person,

but Christ is all and in all.
And so as God's chosen ones, holy and beloved,
put on yourselves bowels of compassion,
kindness, humility, meekness and patience.
Bear with one another
and if anyone has a complaint against anyone,
forgive.
As indeed the Lord forgave,
so also you.
Over all these things,
put on love,
which is the complete bonding.
And let rule in your hearts
the peace of Christ,
to which indeed you were called in one body,
and be thankful.
Let the word of Christ indwell in you richly,
teaching in all wisdom
and admonishing one another
in psalms, hymns and with spiritual songs
singing in your hearts to God.
And everything whatever you do
in word or in work,
do all things
in the name of the Lord Jesus,
giving thanks through him
to God the Father.

RESPONSORY   Ps 31:6

Into your hands, Lord,...   ...*I commend my spirit.*

You have redeemed us, Lord God of truth.
                                   ...*I commend my spirit.*

Glory to the Father and to the Son and to the Holy Spirit:
                                   ...*Into your hands, Lord,*
                                   I commend my spirit.

Antiphon

> *Lord, save/ us!*
> *Save/ us while\ we are a-wake\,*
> *pro-tect us while we are a-sleep,*
> *that we may keep our watch/ with Christ/*
> *and when we sleep\, rest/ in his\ peace.*

GOSPEL CANTICLE of SIMEON   **LUKE 2:29-32**

+ Now, Master, you set free your servant
  according to your word in peace;

  my eyes have seen your salvation,
  which you have prepared
  before the face of all the peoples,

  a light for revelation to the nations
  and glory for your people, Israel.

Glory   Antiphon

+ *May the all-powerful Lord*
  grant us a restful night and a peaceful death. **Amen**.

HAIL MARY...

WEDNESDAY READINGS

+ *Lord, open my lips* Psalm 51:17
  and my mouth will declare your praise.

  Glory…

All crea-tures of our God and King
Lift up your voice and with us sing,
  Al-le-lu-ia! Al-le-lu-ia!
You burn-ing sun with gold-en beam,
You sil-ver moon with soft-er gleam!
  Al-le-lu-ia! God, we praise you!
  Al-le-lu-ia! God, we praise you! Al-le-lu_-ia!

You flow-ing wa-ter, pure and clear,
Make mu-sic for your Lord to hear,
  Al-le-lu-ia! Al-le-lu-ia!
You fire so mas-ter-ful and bright,
Giv-ing the hu-man warmth and light.
  Al-le-lu-ia! God, we praise you!
  Al-le-lu-ia! God, we praise you! Al-le-lu_-ia!

Dear moth-er earth, who day by day
Un-fold your bless-ings on our way,
  Al-le-lu-ia! Al-le-lu-ia!
Flow-ers and fruits, all in you grown,
And God's own glo-ry let be shone.
  Al-le-lu-ia! God, we praise you!
  Al-le-lu-ia! God, we praise you! Al-le-lu_-ia!

You rush-ing winds that are so strong,
You clouds that sail in heav'n a-long,
   Al-le-lu-ia! Al-le-lu-ia!
You ri-sing moon, in praise re-joice,
You lights of eve-ning, find a voice!
   Al-le-lu-ia! God, we praise you!
   Al-le-lu-ia! God, we praise you! Al-le-lu_-ia!

And you most kind and gen-tle death,
Wait-ing to hush our la-test breath,
   Al-le-lu-ia! Al-le-lu-ia!
You lead to home the child of God,
As Christ our Lord the way has trod.
   Al-le-lu-ia! God, we praise you!
   Al-le-lu-ia! God, we praise you! Al-le-lu_-ia!

Let all things their Cre-a-tor bless,
And wor-ship God in hum-ble-ness,
   Al-le-lu-ia! Al-le-lu-ia!
Praise, praise the Fa-ther, praise the Son,
And praise the Spir-it, Three in One!
   Al-le-lu-ia! God, we praise you!
   Al-le-lu-ia! God, we praise you! Al-le-lu_-ia!

Text: Francis of Assisi, 1225; translated by William H. Draper,
Public School Hymn Book, 1919, altered.
Music: LASST UNS ERFREUEN, LM with alleluias;
Geistliche Kirchengesange, 1623

PSALM 18:2-30

Antiphon *You shall love the Lord, your God*
with all your heart and soul and mind,
and your neighbor as yourself.

Mt 22:37,39;
see Deuteronomy 6:5
and Leviticus 19:18

I love you, Adonai, my strength,
my rock Adonai, my fortress and deliverer;
in my God and Rock I take refuge,
my shield and horn,
my salvation and stronghold.

I call out praise to Adonai
and am saved from enmity.

They tangled me in cords of death
and overwhelmed me in torrents of destruction.
Cords of Sheol coiled around me
and snares of death confronted me.

In my distress I called "Adonai,"
I cried for help from my God,
who heard from the temple my voice;
my cry went into those ears.

The earth trembled and quaked
and foundations of mountains shook
and trembled because of wrath.
Smoke rose from the nostrils
and fire from the mouth consumed blazing coals.

PSALM 18:2-30, continued

The heavens parted
and dark clouds came down under the feet.
Mounted on the cherub,
flying and soaring on wings of wind,
a canopy of darkness covered all around,
dark waters in the clouds of the skies.

From the brightness of the presence
the clouds advanced
hailstone and lightning bolts.
Adonai thundered from the heavens,
the voice of the Most High resounding
as hailstone and lightning bolts.

Arrows shot, scattering them all;
with great lightning bolts they are dispersed.
Valleys of waters were exposed and laid bare,
foundations of earth at your rebuke.

At the blast of the breath of your nostril, Adonai,
you reached from on high and took hold of me
and drew me out from the deep waters;
you rescued me from enmity
and from powerful foes too strong for me.

They confronted me in the day of my disaster
but Adonai was my support,
brought me out to the spacious place
and rescued me because of delight in me.

Adonai dealt with me as my ways are righteous,
rewarded me as my hands are clean,
for I kept to the ways of Adonai.
Indeed all of God's laws are before me
and I did not turn from those decrees.

Honest before God,
I kept myself from sin
and seen by the eyes of Adonai
I am rewarded as my ways are right
and my hands are clean.

You show yourself faithful to the faithful,
to the honest you are honest,
and to the pure you show yourself pure,

but to the crooked you show yourself shrewd,
for you save humble people
but bring low the eyes of the haughty.
Indeed you make my lamp burn;
my God Adonai gives light in my darkness.

Indeed with you
I can advance against troops,
with my God
I can scale a wall.

Glory…

Antiphon *You shall love the Lord, your God*
with all your heart and soul and mind,
and your neighbor as yourself.

Mt 22:37,39

PSALM 18:31-51

Antiphon *Hear, Israel,*
the Lord our God is One. Mk 12:29

The ways of God are free of error,
the word of Adonai is flawless,
a shield for all who need refuge.
For who is God besides Adonai?
And who is the Rock except our God?

God arms me with strength,
keeps error out of my way,
makes my feet like the deer
and makes me to stand on my heights,
training my hands for the battle;
my arms can bend a bow of bronze.

You give to me your shield of victory,
your right hand sustains me,
and in stooping you make me great.
You broaden my path beneath me
so my ankles do not turn.

I pursued enemies and overtook them
and did not turn back until their defeat…
They fell beneath my feet.

You armed me with strength for conflict
and made the adversity bow at my feet.
You turned back enmity
and brought silence to foes.

They cried for help, but no one saved them.
Adonai did not answer them.
I beat them as dust on surfaces of wind;
like mud in the streets I poured them out.

You delivered me from strife of peoples,
you made me as a head of nations;
people I knew not are subject to me.

Hearing me in their ear they obey;
sons and daughters of foreigners
cringe before me and lose heart
and they tremble from their strongholds.

Adonai is alive!
Blessed be my Rock!
Exalted be God my Salvior!
God gives victory to me
and subdues nations under me,

saving me from enmity,
exalting me above foes,
and rescuing me from violence.
For this I will praise Adonai among the nations,
and to your name I will sing praise.

You make great victories of your king
and show unfailing mercy
to David your anointed
and his descendants to forever.

Glory…

Antiphon

PSALM 39

Antiphon　　　*You are the salt of the earth;*
　　　　　　　you are the light of the cosmos.　　Mt 5:13a,14a

I said, "I will watch my ways
　of sinning with my tongue;
　I will put on my mouth a muzzle
　as long as temptation is in my presence."

So in silent stillness I said nothing good,
and still my anguish increased.
My heart grew hot inside me;
in my meditation a fire burned.

I spoke with my tongue,
"Show me, Adonai, my end,
　the number of my days;
　let me know how fleeting I am.

See the handbreadths you made!
My days and my span
are as nothing before you.
Indeed, each of all humanity
stands as a breath.

Indeed, as a phantom the human goes out.
Indeed, vainly bustling about,
heaping up wealth
without knowing who will get it."

But what am I looking for now, Adonai?
My hope she is in you.
Save me from all my sins!
Make me not the scorn of fools.
I was silent and opened not my mouth,
for you, you have done it.

Remove your scourge from me;
from the blow of your hand I am overcome.
With a rebuke for sin
you discipline the human
and you consume our wealth like a moth;
indeed we are each but a breath.

Hear my prayer, Adonai,
and my cry for help;
listen, El, and be not deaf to my weeping.
For I am with you as an alien,
a stranger like all of my ancestors.
Look away from me that I may rejoice
before I depart and am no more.

Glory…

                                                         Antiphon

PSALM 103

Antiphon *Forgive each brother and sister
from your heart.* Mt 18:35

Bless Adonai, my soul!
All my inmost being, bless the holy Name!
Bless Adonai, my soul!
whose benefits are not to be forgotten:

forgiveness of all your sins,
healing of all your diseases,
redemption of your life from the pit,
crowning you with mercy and compassion,

satisfying your desire with good,
renewing your youths like the eagle,
working righteous deeds and justice
for all who are oppressed.

Adonai's ways are made known to Moses
and the deeds to peoples of Israel.

Compassionate and gracious is Adonai,
slow to anger and abundant in mercy,
neither accusing to always
nor harboring anger to forever,
neither treating us in accord with our sins
nor repaying us in accord with our wrongs.

As high as the heavens are above the earth
so great is the mercy for ones who fear Adonai.
As far as the east is from the west
so far from us are our transgressions removed.

As a father has compassion on his children,
so has Adonai compassion on ones fearing,
knowing our form
and remembering we are dust.

The days of a human are like the grass
flourishing like flowers of the field,
for wind blows over and it is no more
and the place remembers it no more.

But the mercy for those who fear Adonai
is from everlasting to everlasting.
Salvation is for children of the children
of those keeping the covenant
and those remembering to obey the precepts.

Adonai established a throne in the heavens
and rules over all the kingdoms.
Bless Adonai, all you angels,
you strong and mighty ones doing the bidding,
obeying the voice of the word.

Bless Adonai, all you hosts,
you serving and doing the will.
Bless Adonai, all you creatures,
in all places of the dominion.
Bless Adonai, my soul!

Glory...

                                                          Antiphon

PSALM 52

Antiphon *Laying his hands on each one brought to him,*
Jesus healed those ailing with diseases.

Lk 4:40b

Why, mighty one, do you boast of evil
to the disgrace of El all the day?
Your tongue plots destruction
like a sharpened razor, practicing deceit.

You love evil more than good,
falsehood rather than speaking truth.
Your tongue of deceit loves every confusing word.

Surely El will bring you down,
snatch you from your tent,
and uproot you from the land of the living.

Then the righteous will see and fear,
and they will laugh:
See the one who did not see God as refuge,
but grew strong by destruction
and trusted in the greatness of wealth.

But I am like an olive tree
flourishing in the house of God;
I trust in God's unfailing mercy forever and ever.

I will thank you to forever for what you have done,
and in the presence of your saints I will hope in you
for your name is good.

Glory...   Antiphon

WEDNESDAY READINGS

READING	Year I	Year II
week 1	Romans 2:1-16	Genesis 3
2	Romans 6:1-11	Genesis 14
3	Romans 9:19-33	Genesis 22
4	Romans 14	Genesis 31
5	1 Corinthians 3	Genesis 43
6	1 Corinthians 8	1 Thessalonians 5
7	1 Corinthians 12:1-11	2 Corinthians 3:7-4:4
8	1 Corinthians 15:35-58	2 Corinthians 10:1-11:6
9	James 3:13-18	Galatians 3:15-4:7
10	Joshua 3 & 4	Philippians 2:12-30
11	Judges 6	Haggai 1
12	1 Samuel 1:20-2:21	Ezra 7
13	1 Samuel 11	Nehemiah 9:1-21
14	1 Samuel 21 & 22	Proverbs 9
15	2 Samuel 6	Job 4
16	1 Chronicles 22	Job 18
17	1 Kings 12:1-19	Job 32 & 33
18	2 Kings 1	Joel 3
19	2 Kings 7 & 8	Zechariah 10
20	Ephesians 2:11-22	Ecclesiastes 5 & 6
21	Ephesians 5:21-33	1 Timothy 1
22	Amos 3	2 Timothy 1
23	Hosea 1 & 3	2 Peter 2:9-22
24	Hosea 11	Esther C
25	Isaiah 7	Tobit 4 & 5
26	2 Kings 17:24-41	Judith 8 & 9
27	2 Kings 19	Sirach 4
28	Jeremiah 3	Sirach 15
29	Habakuk 1 & 2	Sirach 35
30	Jeremiah 24	Wisdom 4
31	Jeremiah 30	Wisdom 12 & 13
32	Ezekiel 10 & 11	2 Macabees 7:1-19
33	Ezekiel 20	1 Macabees 9
34	Ezekiel 38	Daniel 8

or SHORT READING **ROMANS 8:35,37-39**

Who will separate us from the love of Christ? Affliction? Distress? Persecution? Famine? Nakedness? Peril? The Sword? But in all these things we over-conquer through the one who has loved us. For I am persuaded that not death, nor life, nor angels, nor rulers, nor present things, nor things coming, nor powers, nor height, nor depth, nor any other creature will be able to separate us from the love of God in Christ Jesus, our Lord.

Let us bless the Lord. *Thanks be to God.*

WEDNESDAY PROPHETS

Text: Matthias Claudius, 1782, hearing the words sung by farmers;
translated by Jane M. Campbell, 1861, altered
Music: 76 76 D, AURELIA, Samuel S. Wesley, 1864
Popular melody for: *The Church's One Foundation*

We plow the fields and scat-ter
the good seed on the land,
But it is fed and wa-tered
by God's al-migh-ty hand;
God sends the snow in win-ter,
the warmth to swell the grain,
The breezes and the sun-shine,
and soft refresh-ing rain.

God on-ly is the Ma-ker of all things near and far;
the Paint-er of the flow-er, the Ligh-ter of the star;
The winds and waves o-bey-ing,
while all the birds are fed;
Much more as God's own chil-dren
are giv-en dai-ly bread.

We thank you, then, O Fa-ther,
for all things bright and good,
The seed time and the har-vest,
our life, our health, our food;
No gifts have we to offer,
for all your love im-parts,
But that which you de-sire\,
our hum-ble, thank-ful hearts.

1 SAMUEL 2:1-10

Antiphon *My spirit rejoices
in God my Savior.* Lk 1:47

My heart rejoices in Adonai,
my horn is lifted high in Adonai.

My mouth boasts over enmity,
for I delight in being delivered.
There is no Holy One like Adonai,
indeed there is no one who compares;
there is no Rock like our God.

Arrogant pride is coming from their mouth.
Do not keep talking so proudly
or proudly let arrogance come from your mouth,
for Adonai is God who knows,
by whom all deeds are weighed.

Bows of warriors are broken
but those stumbling are armed with strength.
The full hire themselves out for more food,
but the hungry ones hunger no more.
She who was barren bore seven sons;
blessed with many sons,
she is pining away.

Adonai allows death
and is making alive,
brings down to Sheol
and is raising up.

Adonai allows poverty
and is sending wealth,
humbling and exalting,
raising the poor from the dust
and the needy from ash-heaps
to sit with princes
and inherit thrones of honor.

For the foundations of the earth are Adonai's,
setting the world upon them.
The feet of the saints will be guarded
but doers of badness will be silenced in darkness.

For not by strength does the human prevail;
Adonai shatters opposition,
thundering from the heavens.
Adonai will judge the ends of the earth,
give strength, and exalt the horn
of the one Chosen and Anointed.

Glory…

                                                      Antiphon

JUDITH 16:1,13-15

Antiphon *O Lord, you are great and glorious,*
wonderful in strength,
invincible.

Begin a song to my God with timbrels;
sing to the Lord with cymbals.
Sing to the Lord a new song;
exalt and acclaim the name.

I will sing to our God a new song;
O Lord, you are great and glorious,
wonderful in strength and unbeatable.

Let your every creature serve you,
for you spoke, and they were made.
You sent forth your spirit,
and they were created;
no one can resist your word.

Mountain foundations are shaken by waters
and rocks melt like wax at your glance.
But to those who fear you,
you show mercy.

Glory...

Antiphon

ISAIAH 33:13-16

Antiphon *Blessed is the one walking rightly*
and speaking right things.

Hear what I did,
you who are far away!
And acknowledge my power,
you who are near.

Sinners are terrified in Zion
and trembling grips the godless.
Who of us can dwell in fire that consumes?
Who of us can dwell in everlasting burning?

One walking rightly,
speaking right things,
rejecting the gain of extortions,
keeping hands from accepting the bribe,
stopping ears from hearing of blood,
shutting eyes against contemplation of evil:

That one will dwell on the heights
in a mountain fortress refuge,
supplied with bread
and waters unfailing.

Glory...

                                                          Antiphon

ISAIAH 61:10-62:5

Antiphon *My God has clothed me
in garments of salvation.*

To delight, I delight in Adonai,
my soul rejoices in my God,
who clothed me in garments of salvation
and arrayed me in a robe of justice,
as a bridegroom dresses his head like a priest
and a bride adorns herself with her jewels,

for as the soil makes the sprout come up
and as a garden makes seeds to grow
so will Sovereign Adonai
make justice spring up
and praise before all the nations.

For the sake of Zion, I will not keep silent;
for the sake of Jerusalem I will not remain quiet,
till righteousness comes out like the dawn
and salvation blazes like a torch.

The nations will see your righteousness
and all the kings your glory
and you will be called by a new name
that the mouth of Adonai will bestow.

You will be a crown of splendor
in the hand of our Lord
and a royal diadem
in the hand of your God.

No longer will you be called One Being Deserted,
nor will your name be called Desolation,
but you will be called My Delight Is In Her
and your land Espoused.
Adonai will delight in you
and your land will be married.

As a young man marries a maiden,
your Builder will marry you;
and as a bridegroom rejoices over a bride,
so will your God rejoice over you.

Glory...

Antiphon

READING **JOB 1:21**

Naked I came from the womb of my mother
and naked will I depart to there.
Adonai gave and Adonai takes away;
may the name of Adonai be praised.

RESPONSORY Ps 113:3,4

From the rising of the sun to its setting…
…praised be the name of the Lord.
The glory above the heavens,…
…praised be the name of the Lord.
Glory to the Father and to Son and to the Holy Spirit:
…From the rising of the sun to its setting;
praised be the name of the Lord.

Let us bless the Lord. *Thanks be to God.*

WEDNESDAY MORNING

+ *God, come to my assistance;*   Psalm 70:2
Lord, make haste to help me!

Glory...

Popular melody for: *Sing of Mary, Pure and Lowly*

Ho-ly\ **Jo-seph**/, **you sa-lut-ing**
Here we\ meet, with/ hearts sin-cere;
Bless-ed\ Jos-eph/, all u-nite and
Call on\ you to/ hear our prayer.

Refrain   Hap-py\ saint in hea-ven a-dor-ing
Je-sus\, Sa-vior of the\ race,
Hear your\ fos-ter/ sons and daugh-ters;
May we\ find with/ you our place.

You who\ faith-ful/-ly at-tend-ed
Him whom\ heav'n and/ earth a-dore;
Who with\ ten-der/ care de-fend-ed
Mar-y\, Vir-gin/ ev-er pure.
May our\ trust-ing voic-es\ lift-ing
Move you\ for our souls to\ pray;
May your\ smile of/ peace des-cend-ing,
Be-ne\-dic-tions/ on us lay.

Through this\ life, give/ watch a-round us!
Thank our\ Lord for/ ev-'ry breath,
And, when\ part-ing/ fear sur-rounds us,
Guide us\ e-ven/ through our death.

Refrain

PSALM 47

Antiphon *Behold, I am with you all the days*
until the completion of the eon. Mt 28:20

All you peoples, clap your hands!
Shout to God with cries of joy!
How awesome, Most High Adonai.

The great King over all the earth
subdued nations under us
and peoples under our feet,
and chose for us an inheritance,
the pride of Jacob the beloved.

God ascended with shouts of joy,
Adonai amid sound of trumpet.
Sing praises to God, sing praises.
Sing praises to our King, sing praises.

For God, King of all the earth, sing praises.
God reigns over the nations,
God sits on the holy throne.

Nobles of nations assemble,
the people of the God of Abraham.
God, shield of the earth, is greatly exalted.

Glory… Antiphon

Song text: anonymous, altered significantly
Music: 87 87 D, PLEADING SAVIOR,
Joshua Leavitt, *Christian Lyre*, 1830

PSALM 36

Antiphon *Blessed are your eyes for they see*
and your ears for they hear
what many prophets and just ones
longed to see and hear.   Mt 13:16,17a

An oracle of sin in the midst of my heart:
There is no fear of God in the eyes of a sinner,
whose own eyes are full of delusion,
who hates to detect sin.

Words of this mouth are empty and false:
Ceasing to be wise or do good,
this one plots evil while still in bed
and commits to a course not good
and rejects nothing that is wrong.

Adonai, to the heavens is your mercy
and your fidelity to the skies.
Your righteous might is like the mountains,
your justice deep and great.

Human and beast you preserve, Adonai.
How precious is your unfailing mercy.
High ones and humans find refuge
in the shadow of your wings.

They feast on the abundance of your house;
in the river of your delights you give them drink.
With you is the fountain of life,
and in your light we see light.

Continue your mercy to those who know you
and your just defense to the upright of heart.
Let the foot of pride not come to me
nor the hand of wicked ways drive me away.

See, doers of evil lie fallen;
they are thrown down
and unable to rise.

Glory...

                                                      Antiphon

PSALM 77

Antiphon *Blessed are those persecuted for what is right,*
for theirs is the kingdom of heaven.

Mt 5:10

My cry is for God,
indeed I cried for help.
My cry is for God to hear me.

In the day of my distress I sought the Lord,
my hand was stretched in the night without tiring;
my being refused to be comforted.
I remembered God and I groaned;
in meditation my spirit grew faint.

You kept open the lids of my eyes;
I was troubled and could not speak.
I thought of former days
and of years long ago.

I ponder my song in the night;
my heart in meditation
and inquired of my spirit,
"Will the Lord reject to forever,
never to show favor again?

Is the unfailing mercy vanished to forever?
Has the promise failed for all generations?
Has God forgotten to show mercy
or withheld compassion in anger?"

Then I thought, "My appeal is this,
  the years at the right hand of the Most High."
I will remember the deeds of Adonai;
yes, I will remember your long-ago miracles.
I will meditate on all your works
and consider your mighty deeds.

God in your holiness way,
what "god" is as great as God?
You are the God who does miracles;
you display among the peoples your power.
You redeemed your people with your arm,
the descendants of Jacob and Joseph.

The waters saw you, O God,
the waters saw you and writhed;
indeed the depths were convulsed.
Clouds poured down waters,
thunder resounded in the skies,
and your arrows flashed around.

Your thunder sounded in the whirlwind,
lightnings lit up the world;
the earth trembled and quaked.

Through the sea is your path,
and your way through mighty waters,
though your footprints were not seen.
You led your people like the flock
by the hand of Moses and Aaron.

Glory...

Antiphon

PSALM 97

Antiphon *Fill the water pots with water;*
now draw and carry some
to the master of the feast. Jn 2:7,8

Adonai reigns; let the earth be glad.
Let all the distant shores rejoice.
Clouds and thick darkness surround the throne
founded on righteousness and justice.

Fire goes before, consuming foes on every side.
Lightnings light up the world;
the earth sees and trembles.

Mountains melt like wax before Adonai,
before the Lord of all the earth.
The heavens proclaim God's justice
and all peoples see the glory.

Let those who serve idols be shamed,
those boasting in their images.
Worship God, all you "gods."

Zion hears and rejoices
and the villages of Judah are glad
because of your judgments, Adonai.
For you, Adonai, are Most High over all the earth,
far exalted above all the "gods."

Evil is despised by lovers of Adonai,
who guards the souls of the faithful
and delivers them from the hands of doers of bad.

Light dawns for the just
and joy on the honest of heart.
Rejoice in Adonai, you just,
and praise the holy name.

Glory…

Antiphon

PSALM 98

Antiphon *I will give you a mouth and wisdom
that will not be contradicted
or withstood.* Lk 21:15

Sing to Adonai a new song
who has done marvelous things,
working salvation at the right hand and holy arm.

Adonai made known salvation,
revealed for the eyes of the nations,
mercy remembered and faithfulness
to the house of Israel

and all the ends of the earth see
the salvation of our God.
Shout for joy to Adonai, all you earth!
Burst forth and sing and make music!

Make music to Adonai with harp,
with harp and the sound of singing,
with trumpets and blast of ram horn:
Shout for joy before the King Adonai!

PSALM 98, continued

Let the sea resound, the fullness of the world,
and those living in her.
Let the rivers clap hands,
let the mountains sing together for joy

before Adonai who comes to judge the earth,
who will judge the world with justice
and peoples with equity.

Glory...

Antiphon *I will give you a mouth and wisdom
that will not be contradicted
or withstood.* Lk 21:15

PSALM 108

Antiphon *The one doing the truth
comes to the light.* Jn 3:21

My heart is steadfast, God; I will sing
and even my soul will make music.
Awake the harp and lyre;
I will wake up the dawn!

I will praise you among the peoples, Adonai,
and I will sing of you among the peoples,
for greater than above the heavens is your mercy
and to the skies your faithfulness.

Be exalted above the heavens, O God,
your glory over all the earth
that your loved ones may be delivered.
Save your right hand, and help me!

God spoke from the sanctuary:
"I will triumph and parcel out Shechem,
 and measure the valley of Succoth;
 mine are Gilead and Manasseh,

Ephraim my head helmet,
Judah my scepter, and Moab my washbasin;
On Edom I toss my sandals
and over Philistia I shout in triumph."

Who will bring me to the Fortress City?
Who will lead me into Edom?
Have you, God, not rejected us,
and not gone out, God, with our armies?

Against enmity give to us aid,
for worthless is human help.
In God will we gain victory
and trample the enmity.

Glory…

Antiphon

PSALM 146

Antiphon   *Blessed are the meek,*
for they will inherit the earth.   Mt 5:5

Hallelujah! Praise Adonai, my soul!
I will praise Adonai during my life,
sing praise to my God while I still am.

PSALM 146, continued

Put your trust not in princes
nor in human beings in whom there is no salvation.
Their spirits depart,
and they return to the ground.
On that day their plans come to nothing.

Blessed are they whose help is the God of Jacob,
whose hope and God are Adonai,
the maker of heaven and earth
and the sea and all that is in them.

The one staying faithful to forever
defends justice for the oppressed
and gives food to the hungry.

Adonai sets prisoners free;
Adonai gives sight to the blind;
Adonai lifts those who are bowed down;
Adonai loves the righteous.

Adonai watches over alien strangers,
and sustains the orphan and the widow,
but frustrates the ways that are wicked.

Adonai reigns to forever,
your God, Zion, from generation to generation.
Hallelujah! Praise Adonai!

Glory…

Antiphon *Blessed are the meek,*
for they will inherit the earth. Mt 5:5

READING **1 THESSALONIANS 5:1-11**

Concerning the times and the seasons, brothers and sisters, you have no need to be written, for you know correctly that the day of the Lord comes as a thief in the night. Whenever they say, "peace and safety," then sudden destruction comes on them as the birth pang to a pregnant woman, and by no means may they escape. But you, brothers and sisters, are not in the darkness that the day should overtake you as a thief. For all of you are children of light and children of the day. We are not of the night nor of darkness. And so let us not sleep as the rest, but let us watch and be sober. For those sleeping by night sleep, and those being drunk by night are drunk. But being of the day, let us be sober, putting on a breastplate of faith and of love and a helmet of hope in salvation because God did not appoint us to wrath but to come to salvation through our Lord Jesus Christ, the one who died for us, in order that whether we watch or we sleep, together with him we may live. And so comfort one another and edify one another, as indeed you do.

RESPONSORY Tobit 1:13

The Most High has kept me in favor…
…with all my heart I will keep God in mind.
May the Most High rescue me from captivity…
…with all my heart I will keep God in mind.
Glory to the Father and to the Son and to the Holy Spirit:
…The Most High has kept me in favor;
with all my heart I will keep God in mind.

GOSPEL READING OF THE DAY or GOSPEL CANTICLE

Antiphon *Show us, Lord, how mercy works,
and remember your holy covenant.*

CANTICLE OF ZECHARIAH **LUKE 1:68-79**

+ Blessed be the Lord the God of Israel
who chose a people,
visited them to bring redemption,
and raised salvation in the house of David,
saving strength from God's own servant,

speaking from the age of the prophets
through the mouth of the holy prophet:
Salvation out of enmity,
even out of those who hate us,

to show our ancestors how mercy works,
and to remember the holy promise of the Lord,
the covenant made for our father Abraham,
calming our fear and making us free
to serve God as holy and righteous and just
in the Lord's presence all our days.

And you also child
will be called a prophet of the Most High
for you will go before the Lord to prepare his way
and give to his people a knowledge of salvation
known in accepting forgiveness of their sins.

WEDNESDAY MORNING

From the deepness of God's mercy on us,
a sun rising from the height will visit to appear
to those who sit in the dark or shadow of death,
and to guide our feet into the way of peace.

Gospel Reading for Wednesday of

Week			
1 Mark 1:29-39	**13** Matt 8:28-34	**25** Luke 9:1-6
2 Mark 3:1-6	**14** Matt 10:1-7	**26** Luke 9:57-62
3 Mark 4:1-20	**15** Matt 11:25-27	**27** Luke 11:1-4
4 Mark 6:1-6	**16** Matt 13:1-9	**28** Lk 11:42-46
5 Mark 7:14-23	**17** Matt 13:44-46	**29** Lk 12:39-48
6 Mark 8:22-26	**18** Matt 15:21-28	**30** Lk 13:22-30
7 Mark 9:38-40	**19** Matt 18:15-20	**31** Lk 14:25-33
8 Mark 10:32-45	**20** Matt 20:1-16	**32** Lk 17:11-19
9 Mark 12:18-27	**21** Matt 23:27-32	**33** Lk 19:11-28
10 Matt 5:17-19	**22** Luke 4:38-44	**34** Lk 21:12-19
11 Matt 6:1-6,16-18	**23** Luke 6:20-26	
12 Matt 7:15-20	**24** Luke 7:31-35	

Glory... Antiphon

PETITIONS FOR THE CONSECRATION TO GOD
OF THE DAY AND ITS WORK
- For the Church and her ministry and apostolates...
- For secular authorities and all serving as stewards...
- For people who are poor or sick or in sorrow...
- For peace and the basic needs of each human being...

OUR FATHER...

+ *May the Lord bless us, protect us from all evil,
and bring us to everlasting life.* ***Amen.***

WEDNESDAY DAYTIME

+ *God, come to my assistance;*   Psalm 70:2
Lord, make haste to help me!

Glory...

There's a wide/-ness in God's mer\-cy
Like the wide-ness of\ the sea;
There's a kind/-ness in God's jus\-tice
Which is more than lib\-er-ty.
There is plen\-ti-ful re-demp\-tion
In the blood/ that has\ been shed;
There\ is joy\ for all\ the mem//\-bers
In the sor\-rows of the Head.

For the love/ of God is broad\-er
Than the meas-ures of\ our mind,
And the heart/ of the E-ter\-nal
Be-yond won-der-ful\ and kind.
If our love\ were but more simp\-le
We might take/ him at\ his word,
And\ our lives\ would be\ thanks-giv//\-ing
For the good\-ness of the Lord.

Troub-led souls/, why will you scat\-ter
Like a crowd of fright\-ened sheep?
Fool-ish hearts/, why will you wan\-der
From a love so true\ and deep?
There is wel\-come for the sin\-ner
And more gra/-ces for\ the good;
There\ is mer\-cy with\ the Sa//\-vior,
There is heal\-ing in his food.

PSALM 119:65-72
Teth

Antiphon   *I have come to call not the righteous,*
          but sinners to conversion.   Lk 5:32

You do good to your servant, Adonai,
as is your word.
Teach me wisdom and knowledge
for I believe in your commands.

Before my affliction I went astray
but now I obey your word.
You are good and do the good;
teach me your decrees.

The arrogant smear on me lies;
with all my heart I keep your precepts.
Their hearts are fat and callous;
I delight in your law.

My affliction was good to me
so I might learn your decrees.
Law from your mouth is more precious to me
than thousands of gold and silver.

Glory...

                                           Antiphon

Song text: Frederick W. Fabor, 1814, 1863, altered
Music: 87 87 D, HYFRYDOL; Rowland Prichard, 1811-1887
Popular melody for: *Love Divine, All Love Excelling*

PSALM 119:73-80
Yodh

Antiphon *Give, and it will be given to you;
the measure you measure
will be measured to you.*   Lk 6:38

Your hands made me and formed me;
give me understanding to learn your commands.
Ones who fear you see me and rejoice
for in your word I hope.

I know, Adonai, your laws are righteous;
even in affliction you are faithful to me.
May your mercy now comfort me
as is your promise to your servant.

Let your compassions come to me for life,
as your law is my delight.
May arrogance be shamed
in wronging me without cause.
I will meditate on your precepts.

May those who fear you turn to me,
those understanding your statutes.
May my heart be all about your decrees
that I may be unashamed.

Glory...

Antiphon

PSALM 119:81-88
Kaph

Antiphon *Cast all your anxiety on God,
to whom everything about you matters.* 1 Ptr 5:7

My soul she longs for your salvation;
in your word I put my hope.
My eyes fail in the search for your promise
to say "When will you comfort me?"

Though like a wineskin dry in smoke,
I do not forget your decrees.
Where are the days of your servant?
When will you act on my persecutors?

The arrogant dig pitfalls for me
and not as are your laws.
All your commands are trustworthy.
They persecute me without cause; help me!

They almost wiped me from the earth
but I did not forsake your precepts.
As is your mercy-love, preserve me alive
and I will obey the statutes of your mouth.

Glory…

Antiphon

PSALM 17

Antiphon *The Lord is God of the living.* Lk 20:38

Hear, Adonai, a plea for justice;
listen to my cry.
Give ear to my prayer,
from lips without deceit.
May my vindication come from you;
may my eyes see right things.

You probe and examine
my heart in the night;
you test me and will find nothing.
By resolve my mouth will not sin.

By the word of your lips
my human deeds are kept from violent ways.
Holding my steps to your paths
my feet did not slip.

I call on you, El, for you will answer me.
Give your ear to me and hear my prayer.
Show the wonder of your great saving mercy,
at your right hand those taking refuge from foes.

Keep me as the apple daughter of your eye.
You hide me in the shade of your wings
from those who assail me in enmity,
surrounding around my life.
They close their callous hearts,
they speak their arrogant mouth.

Now they surround our tracks;
their eyes are alert, ready to throw to the ground.
They are like a lion hungry to tear prey,
like a great lion crouching undercover.

Rise up, Adonai!
Confront and bring down their ways.
Rescue my soul by your sword, Adonai,
by your hand from humans,
humans of the world whose reward is this life.

As for those who are cherished by you,
their bellies are full,
sons and daughters are plenty,
and they store up their wealth for their children.

In your justice,
I will see your faces and be satisfied
waking up to your likeness.

Glory…

    Antiphon

PSALM 70

Antiphon
*To one who strikes you
on the right cheek,
turn the other as well.*   Mt 5:39b

Save me, O God!
Adonai hasten to help me!
May plans to seek my life
be shamed and confused;

may the desire for my ruin
turn back in disgrace
and ones saying "aha!, aha!"
turn back in shame.

May all who seek you
rejoice in you and be glad
and may lovers of salvation say always,
"Let God be exalted."

Yet I am poor and needy;
God, come to me quickly
and do not delay, Adonai,
my help and my deliverer.

Glory…

Antiphon

PSALM 75

| Antiphon | *Let the one of you without sin be first to throw a stone.* | Jn 8:7 |

We give thanks to you, God;
we give thanks for your name is Near,
and tell of your wonderful deeds.

You choose and appoint the time
to be the upright judge.
The earth quakes, and all its people,
and you hold her pillars firm.

I say to the arrogant, "boast not,"
and to the bad doers, "lift not your horn;
 lift not your horns against the heavens
 nor speak with neck outstretched."

For there is no one from east or from west
and no one from the desert to exalt.
But God is the one judge,
bringing down this one and exalting another.

A cup is full in the hand of Adonai,
and wine foams and mixed spice pours out.
Indeed from this they drink to her dregs,
all the bad doers of the earth.

And I will declare to forever,
and sing praise to the God of Jacob.
All the horns of bad doings will be cut off,
and the horns of the righteous will be lifted up.

Glory... Antiphon

PSALM 94

Antiphon *Jesus touched her hand,*
the fever left her,
and rising she began serving them.   Mt 8:15

God of vindication,
Adonai, God of vindication, shine forth!
Rise up, One Judge of the earth!
Pay back desserts to the proud!

Until when, bad doers?
Until when, Adonai, will bad doers be jubilant?
They pour out and speak arrogance;
all the bad doers boast.

They crush your people, Adonai,
and they oppress your inheritance.
They slay the widow and alien;
they murder the orphan.

They say Adonai does not see
and the God of Jacob pays no heed.
Take heed, senseless ones among the people;
fools, when will you become wise?

Does the one who shapes the ear not hear?
Does the one who forms the eye not see?
Will the one who disciplines nations not punish?
Will the one who teaches have no knowledge?

Adonai knows the thoughts of humans,
that they are futile.

Blessed is the one whom you discipline, Adonai,
the one you teach from your law
to grant relief from days of trouble
till a pit is dug for bad doings,

for the people of Adonai will not be rejected,
the inheritance never abandoned.
Judgment will again be just,
after which will go all the upright of heart.

Who will rise up for me against bad doings?
Who will take a stand for me?
Unless Adonai helps me,
I would as soon dwell in the silence.

When I said, "My foot slips,"
your mercy, Adonai, supported me.
When my anxieties were great inside me
your consolations brought joy to my soul.

Can a throne of corruptions be allied with you,
one that brings misery by decree?
They band together against the just
and condemn the innocent to blood.

But Adonai became to me as a fortress,
and my God as a rock of refuge.
A rock of refuge is my God,
who will repay their sin to them
and destroy their wicked ways.
Our God, Adonai, will destroy them.

Glory... Antiphon

READING   **1 JOHN 2:1-6**

My little children, I write these things to you that you will not sin. If anyone does sin, we have an advocate with the Father: Jesus Christ the righteous, a propitiation for our sins, and not only for ours but also for those of all the world.

And by this we know that we have known him: if we keep his commandments. The one saying, "I have known him," not keeping his commandments, is a liar, and the truth is not in this one. But whoever keeps the word, truly in this one the love of God has been made complete.

By this we know that we are in him: The one claiming to remain in him ought walk as he himself walked.

RESPONSORY   Ps 17:8

Keep us, O Lord...   ...*as the apple of your eye.*

Hide us in the shade of your wings...
                             ...*as the apple of your eye.*

Glory to the Father and to the Son and to the Holy Spirit:
    ...*Keep us, O Lord, as the apple of your eye.*

Lord\, have mer-cy.
            Christ\, have mer-cy.
                        Lord\, have mer-cy.

WEDNESDAY EVENING

+ *God, come to my assistance;* Psalm 70:2
  Lord, make haste to help me!

  Glory...

Bles-sed be the God and Fa-ther
Of our Lord/ Je-sus Christ,
Who has blessed us in the Christ\,
bless-ings in their Spir-it breath.
As God chose us in the Mes-si-ah
be-fore/ found-ing sky or earth,
To be ho-ly, clean of blem-ish,
in God's eye: a-dop-tion worth.

In the Son we have re-demp-tion,
God's for-give-ness of our sin,
By the rich-es of his grace\
lav-ished on us gath-ered in.
Giv-ing wis-dom, know-ledge/, vis-ion,
mys-t'ry/ of the Fa-ther's will,
Sum-ming up all things in Je-sus,
fa-vored in the full-ness sent.

In our hear-ing of the gos-pel
word of our sal-va\-tion,
One by one we too were cho-sen,
joined as part-ners with the Son.
By the prom-is'd Ho-ly/ Spir-it,
signed and/ sealed as heirs of God,
God's pos-ses-sion, God's re-demp-tion,
God's be-lov-ed, Ab-ba's own.

Song text: Ephesians 1:3-14, Stephen J. Wolf, 2008,
with gratitude to the Institute for Priestly Formation
Music: 8787D, HYMN TO JOY, Ludwig van Beethoven, d. 1827;
adapted by Edward Hodges, 1824
Popular melody for: *Joyful, Joyful, We Adore Thee*

PSALM 27

Antiphon   *Come after me,*
            and I will make you fishers
            of human beings.   Mt 4:19

Adonai is my light and my salvation.
Whom shall I fear?
Adonai is the stronghold of my life.
Of whom shall I be afraid?

When people acting evil advance
against me to devour my flesh,
when enmity and foes go against me,
they will stumble and fall.

Though an army besiege against me,
my heart will not fear.
Though war break out against me,
in this I will be confident.

One thing I ask of Adonai:
to seek and to dwell in Adonai's house,
to gaze on Adonai's beauty
all the days of my life
as a seeker in the temple.

I will be kept safely dwelling,
hidden in the shelter of the tent,
on the day of trouble
set high upon rock.

Then will my head be exalted above enmity,
and I will sacrifice at the tent
the sacrifice of shouts of joy.
I will sing and make music to Adonai.

Hear, Adonai, my voice calling;
be merciful; answer me.
To you my heart says,
"My face seeks you."

Your faces, Adonai, I will seek.
Hide not your faces from me;
turn not away from your servant in anger.

You are my help;
neither reject nor forsake me,
God of my salvation.
Even if my father and my mother forsake me,
you, Adonai, will receive me.

Teach me your way, Adonai,
and lead me through oppression to a level path.
Do not give me over to the desire
of foes who rise with false witnesses
and breathers of violence.

PSALM 27, continued

Still I am confident: I will see
the goodness of Adonai
in the land of the living.
Wait for Adonai! And be strong!
Strengthen your heart and wait for Adonai!

Glory...

Antiphon *Come after me,
and I will make you fishers
of human beings.* Mt 4:19

PSALM 62

Antiphon *Do not worry about tomorrow
for tomorrow will worry about itself;
sufficient to the day is its own trouble.* Mt 6:34

My soul finds rest in God alone,
from whom is my salvation,
alone my salvation and my rock,
my fortress never to be shaken greatly.

Until when will you assault a human being,
will you throw down, all of you,
like a leaning wall or a tottering fence?

They fully intend
to topple from the lofty place;
they delight in lies
and bless with their mouth
and curse in their heart.

WEDNESDAY EVENING

My soul finds rest in God alone,
from whom is my hope,
alone my salvation and my rock,
my fortress not to be shaken.

From God is my salvation and my honor;
my mighty rock and refuge.
Trust in God at all times;
pour out your heart to God our refuge.

Sons and daughters of humanity are but a breath;
the so-called great ones are an illusion.
On balanced scales they both rise;
together they are only a breath.

Trust not in extortion
and take no pride in stolen things;
even when riches increase
do not set your heart on them.

One thing God has spoken,
two things I have heard:
that to God is strength
and to you, Lord, is mercy;
and surely you will reward to each
as are our deeds.

Glory…

                                                          Antiphon

PSALM 126

Antiphon *What do you wish me to do for you?*
...Go, your faith has healed you.   Mk 10:51,52

When Adonai returned Zion from captivity
we felt like people in a dream.
Then our mouth was filled with laughter,
and our tongue with a song of joy.

Then they said among the nations
"Their Adonai did greatness for them."
Adonai did greatness for us;
we were full of joy.

Restore our good fortune, Adonai,
like streams in the Negev desert.
Sowers are now in tears;
they will reap with a song of joy.

Going out, the sower goes out weeping,
carrying seeds for the sowing.
Returning, the sower will return
carrying sheaves with a song of joy.

Glory...

Antiphon

PSALM 127

Antiphon *Look at the birds of heaven and see:*
they do not sow or reap
or gather into barns
and your heavenly Father feeds them. Mt 6:26

If Adonai does not build the house,
the builders labor in vanity.
If Adonai does not watch over the city,
the watcher stands guard in vain.

It is vanity to rise early or stay up late,
or to eat the bread of hard toil;
the Lord provides as the beloved get their sleep.

See the heritage of Adonai:
Sons and daughters, a reward.
Like arrows in the hand of a warrior,
so are children of one's youth.

Blessed is the one
whose quiver is thus full;
they will not be shamed
when they contend at the gate with enmity.

Glory…

Antiphon

PSALM 139:1-18,23-24

Antiphon   *To you hearing I say,*
love your enemies
and do good to the ones hating you.   Lk 6:27

Adonai, you search me and you know me.
You know my sitting and my rising;
you perceive my thoughts from afar.
You discern my going and my lying down,
and you are familiar with all my ways.

When a word is not yet on my tongue
you see it, Adonai;
you know them all.

Behind and before you hem me in
and you lay your hand upon me.
Too wonderful for me is this knowledge,
more lofty than what I can attain.

Where can I go that is away from your Spirit?
Where could I flee from your presences?
If I go up to the heavens, you are there;
if I make a bed in Sheol, you I see!

If I rise on the wings of dawn,
if I settle on the far side of the sea,
even there your hand will guide me
and your right hand will hold me.

If I say, "Surely darkness will hide me
  and the night will light around me,"
even darkness will not be dark to you
and night will shine as the day;
as the darkness, so the light.

For you created my inmost beings;
you knit me together in my mother's womb.
I praise you because I am full of fear and wonder;
my self knows well how wonderful are your works.

My frame was not hidden from you
when I was made in the secret place,
woven together in the depths of earth.

Your eyes saw my body
and in your book were written and ordained
all the days before the first day was.

How precious to me, El, are your designs,
how vast are they, the sums of them;
if countable they number more than the sand.
Awake and still, I am with you…

Search me, El, and know my heart!
Test me, and know my anxious thoughts!
See if there is in me an offensive way,
then lead me on the ancient way!

Glory…

                                            Antiphon

COLOSSIANS 1:12-20

Antiphon   *Who follows me will have the light of life.*   Jn 8:12c

Give joyful thanks to the Father who made you fit
for your part of the lot of the saints in light,

who delivered us out of the authority of darkness
and transitioned us into
>   the kingdom of the beloved Son

in whom we have redemption,
the forgiveness of our sins.

The Son is the image of the invisible God,
the firstborn of all creation.
In him all things were created,
in the heavens and on the earth,
the visible and the invisible,
whether thrones, dominions, principalities or powers.

All things have been created through him and for him.
He is before all things,
and in him all things hold together.

He is the head of the body, the church,
and the beginning, the firstborn from the dead,
so that in all things he may hold the first place.

In him all the fullness was well pleased to dwell,
and through him reconciliation to himself of all things,
things on earth and things in the heavens,
making peace through the blood of his cross.

Glory...   Antiphon

WEDNESDAY EVENING

READING **EPHESIANS 3:16-21**

I pray that the Father may give to you according to the riches of his glory, by the power of his Spirit, to become strong in your inner humanity, that Christ may dwell in your hearts through faith, being rooted and founded in love, that you may have strength to comprehend with all the saints what is the breadth and length and height and depth, to know the love of Christ that excels knowledge, that you may be filled with the fullness of God. Now to the One who, by the power operating in us, is able to do superabundantly beyond all things we could ask or think, to him be the glory in the church and in Christ Jesus to all generations of the eon and of the eons.

RESPONSORY Ps 26:11,9

Redeem me, my Lord and my God,…
…and in your grace have mercy.

Sweep me not with those doing badness…
…and in your grace have mercy.

Glory to the Father and to the Son and to the Holy Spirit:
…Redeem me, my Lord and my God,
and in your grace have mercy.

GOSPEL CANTICLE OF MARY **LUKE 1:46-55**

Antiphon *Holy is the name and the mercy.*

+ My soul is stretched full with praise of the Lord,
  and my spirit, beyond joy in God, my Savior,
  who chose to lay eyes on this humble servant.

LUKE 1:46-55, continued

Behold, now and forward,
each and every age will call me blessed,
for the Mighty One did great things to me.
Holy is the name and the mercy
to generations and generations,
the ones fearing the One,

Who scattered the haughty of mind and heart,
pulled the powerful off their high place,
and lifted with dignity the humble in need.

The hungering are filled with good things,
the rich are sent away empty,
and servant Israel is given relief

with a memory of mercy to remember,
the promise spoken to our ancestors,
to Abraham and his descendants forever.

Glory…

Antiphon *Holy is the name and the mercy.*

INTERCESSIONS
- For all who have died…
- In gratitude for blessings…; Abba thank you.
- For the sins of this day…; Lord Jesus have mercy.
- With concerns over tomorrow…; Holy Spirit help.

OUR FATHER…

+ *May the Lord bless us, protect us from all evil,
and bring us to everlasting life.* **Amen**.

WEDNESDAY NIGHT

+ *God, come to my assistance;*   Psalm 70:2
  Lord, make haste to help me!

  Glory…

Cre-a-tor of the stars of night,
Your peo-ple's ev-er-last-ing light,
Re-deem-er Je-sus, save us all,
And hear your ser-vants when we call.

You griev-ing that the an-cient curse
Should doom to death a u-niv-erse,
Find now the med-i-cine of grace,
To save and heal the hu-man race.

See now the Bride-groom of the bride,
As drew the world to eve-ning tide;
Pro-ceed-ing from a vir-gin shrine,
As ful-ly hu-man and div-ine.

This Awe-some Name, ma-jes-tic now,
All knees to bend and hearts to bow;
All things ce-les-tial God does own,
And things ter-res-trial, God a-lone.

To God the Fa-ther, God the Son,
And God the Spir-it, Three in One,
Laud, ho-nor, might, and glo-ry be
From age to age e-ter-nal-ly.

Text: 7th Century unknown author; translated by John M. Neale, 1852, altered
Music: CONDITOR, LM; *Conditor Alme Siderum*, Sarum plainsong, Mode IV

PSALM 130

Antiphon *Whoever does the will of God
is my brother and sister and mother.* Mk 3:35

Out of the depths I cry to you, Adonai.
Lord, hear my voice.
Let your ears be attentive
to my cries for mercy.

If you kept a record of sins, Adonai,
Lord, who could stand?
But with you is the forgiveness,
and so you are revered in awe.

I wait, my soul waits for Adonai,
in whose word I put hope.
My soul waits for the Lord
more than watchers for the morning,
even watchers for the morning.

Put hope, Israel, in Adonai!
Unfailing mercy is from Adonai,
in whom is full redemption,
who will redeem Israel
from all the sins.

Glory...

Antiphon

WEDNESDAY NIGHT

READING · **JAMES 1:19-27**

Know, my beloved brothers and sisters; let every human be swift to hear, slow to speak, and slow to be angry, for human anger does not work toward God's righteous ways. So put away all filth and unnecessary waste and receive in meekness the word planted in you that is able to save your souls.

Become doers of the word and not hearers only misleading yourselves. The hearer of the word who is not a doer is like a human seeing in a mirror one's face of birth, and seeing oneself, goes away right away and forgets what sort he or she is.

But the one who looks into the perfect law of freedom and remains, becoming not a forgetful hearer but a doer of the work, blessed in the doing will this one be. Any who think themselves religious and do not bridle their tongue but deceive their heart, vain is their religion.

This is religion clean and undefiled before the God and Father: to care for orphans and widows in their affliction, and to keep oneself unspotted by the cosmos.

RESPONSORY · Ps 31:6

Into your hands, Lord,… …*I commend my spirit.*

You have redeemed us, Lord God of truth.
…*I commend my spirit.*

Glory to the Father and to the Son and to the Holy Spirit:
…*Into your hands, Lord, I commend my spirit.*

Antiphon

> *Lord, save/ us!*
> *Save/ us while\ we are a-wake\,*
> *pro-tect us while we are a-sleep,*
> *that we may keep our watch/ with Christ/*
> *and when we sleep\, rest/ in his\ peace.*

GOSPEL CANTICLE of SIMEON   **LUKE 2:29-32**

+ Now, Master, you set free your servant
  according to your word in peace;

  my eyes have seen your salvation,
  which you have prepared
  before the face of all the peoples,

  a light for revelation to the nations
  and glory for your people, Israel.

Glory   Antiphon

+ *May the all-powerful Lord*
  grant us a restful night and a peaceful death. **Amen.**

Hail Mary, full of grace, the Lord is with thee.
Blessed art thou among women,
and blessed is the fruit of thy womb, Jesus.
Holy Mary, mother of God, pray for us sinners
now and at the hour of our death.
Amen.

THURSDAY READINGS

+ *Lord, open my lips*   Psalm 51:17
  and my mouth will declare your praise.

  Glory…

Im-mort-al, in-vis-i-ble, God on-ly wise.
In light in-ac-ces-si-ble hid from our eyes,
Most bless-ed, most glo-rious, the An-cient of Days,
Your Son and your Spir-it, your great name we praise.

Un-rest-ing, un-hast-ing, and si-lent as light,
Nor want-ing, nor wast-ing, you rule day and night;
Your jus-tice like moun-tains high soar-ing a-bove
Your clouds which are foun-tains of bless-ing and love.

Great Fa-ther of glo-ry, Cre-a-tor of light,
Your an-gels a-dor-ing and saints in your sight;
Of all your rich gra-ces this grace, Lord, im-part:
Un-cov-er our fa-ces and make clean our heart.

All prais-es we ren-der; Lord help us to see
The splen-dor of light that is hid-den in thee,
And so let your glo-ry, Al-migh-ty, your art
Be told in the sto-ry of Christ to the heart.

Text: based on 1 Timothy 1:17
Walter C. Smith, *Hymns of Christ and the Christian Life*, 1876, altered
Music: 11 11 11 11, ST. DENIO, Welsh Melody, John Roberts,
Canaidau y Cyssagr, 1839

PSALM 44

Antiphon *The kingdom of heaven is like leaven*
a woman mixes into three measures of flour
until the whole is leavened. Mt 13:33

With our ears, God, we have heard,
our ancestors told us the deed
you did in their days, in days long ago.

You drove out nations by your hand
and you planted them;
you crushed peoples and made them flourish.
For they won victory not by their sword and arm,
but by your right hand and arm
and the light of your faces, for you loved them.

You are my King and my God;
decree the victories of Jacob.
Through you we push back enmity;
through your name we trample opposition.

Indeed I trust not in my bow
and my sword does not bring me victory,
but you give to us victory over enmity
and shame the adversity.
In God we boast all the day
and we will praise your name to forever.

But you let us be rejected and humbled
and you do not go out with our armies.
You turned us back before enmity
and adversaries plundered from us.

You gave us up like sheep devoured;
among the nations you scattered us.
You sold your people for no great price,
gaining nothing from their sale.

You made us a reproach to our neighbors,
scorn and mockery to those around us.
You made us a byword among the nations,
a shaking of heads among the peoples.

All the day my disgrace is before me
and my shame covers my face
at taunts of reproachers and revilers
because of avenging enmity.

All of this happened though we did not forget you
and were not false to your covenant.
Our hearts did not turn back
and our feet did not stray from your path,
but you pushed us into haunts of jackals
and you covered us over with deep darkness.

If we forgot the name of our God,
if we stretched out our hands to a foreign "god,"
would God not have discovered this,
the One knowing the secrets of the heart?
Yet for you we face death all the day;
we are considered as sheep for slaughter.

Wake up, Lord! Why do you sleep?
Rouse yourself! Do not reject us to forever.
Why do you hide your faces
and forget our oppression and misery?

PSALM 44, continued

Indeed our soul is brought down to the dust;
our body clings to the ground.
Rise up as our help and redeem us!
because of your unfailing mercy.

Glory...

Antiphon *The kingdom of heaven is like leaven*
a woman mixes into three measures of flour
until the whole is leavened. Mt 13:33

PSALM 89:2-38

Antiphon *One loving father or mother*
or son or daughter
more than me
is not worthy of me. Mt 10:37

Forever will I sing the mercy of Adonai;
with my mouth I will make known
your faithfulness to generation and generation.
Indeed I will declare forever
mercy standing firm,
your faithfulness established in the heavens.

"I made a covenant with my chosen ones,
 sworn to my servant David.
 I will establish your line to forever,
 and to generation and generation
 I will make firm your throne."

The heavens praise your wonder, Adonai,
and your loyalty in the holy assembly.
For who in the sky can compare to Adonai;
who is like Adonai among heavenly beings?

God is greatly feared in the council of holy ones
and is awesome over all who surround around.
Adonai Sabaoth, who is like you?
Mighty Adonai, your faithfulness is around you.

You rule over the surging of the sea;
when waves mount up you still them.
You crushed Rahab like the slain
and scattered enmity with the arm of your strength.

To you are the heavens
and to you is the earth;
the world and her fullness you founded.
North and South you created;
Tabor and Hermon sing for joy at your name.

To you is the arm strong with power;
your hand is exalted, your right hand.
Righteousness and Justice
are the foundation of your throne;
Mercy and Fidelity go before your faces.

Blessed are people who learn to acclaim Adonai;
they walk in the light of your presences.
In your name they rejoice all the day
and in your righteousness they exult,

PSALM 89:2-38, continued

for you are the glory of their strength
and by your favor you exalt our horn.
Indeed Adonai is our shield
and the Holy One of Israel is our king.

Once in a vision you spoke to your faithful:
"I bestowed strength on a warrior;
 I exalted from the people a young man.

I found David my servant,
I anointed him with my sacred oil,
and my hand will sustain him;
surely my arm will strengthen him.

No enemy will subject him to tribute
and no wicked people will defeat him.
Before him I will crush foes
and strike down adversity,

and my faithfulness and mercy are with him,
and through my hands will the horn be exalted.
And I will set his hand over the sea
and his right hand over the rivers.

He will call me out: 'You are my Father,
 my God and Rock of my salvation.'
I will also appoint him firstborn
and most exalted among kings of the earth.

I will maintain my mercy for him to forever
and my unfailing covenant with him.
I will establish his line to forever
and his throne as days of the heavens.

If his sons and daughters forsake my law
and do not follow my statutes,
if they violate my decrees
and keep not my commands,

then I will punish their sins with the rod
and their guilt with floggings.
But I will not take my mercy from them,
nor will I ever betray my faithfulness.

I will not violate my covenant
nor will I alter the promise of my lips.
Once I swore by my holiness;
I will not lie to David:

His line will continue to forever
and his throne like the sun before me.
Like the moon it is established forever,
a faithful witness in the sky."

Glory…

Antiphon	*One loving father or mother or son or daughter more than me is not worthy of me.*	Mt 10:37

PSALM 89:39-53

Antiphon *Who does not take his or her cross*
and follow after me
is not worthy of me. Mt 10:38

Lord, you have rejected and spurned,
you were angry with your anointed one.
You renounced the covenant of your servant,
the crown you defiled in the dust.

You broke through all of the walls
and reduced the strongholds to ruin.
Those passing on the way seized plunder
and the neighbors were full of scorn.

You exalted the right hand of foes
and made all the enemies rejoice.
You turned back the edge of our sword
and did not support us in battle.

You put an end to the splendor
and cast the throne to the ground.
You cut short the days of youth
and covered us over with shame.

Until when, Adonai?
Will you hide yourself to forever?
Will your wrath burn like fire?
Remember how fleeting am I!

For what futility you created
sons and daughters of Adam and Eve!
What human can live and not see death,
or save the soul from the power of Sheol?

Where, Lord, are your former great mercies
sworn to David in your faithfulness?
Remember, Lord, the mocking of your servants!
I bear this in my heart from many nations, Adonai:
the mockery of enmity,
the mockery of the steps of your anointed one.

Blessed be Adonai to forever.
Amen and amen.

Glory…

Antiphon

READING	Year I	Year II
week 1	Romans 2:17-29	Genesis 4
2	Romans 6:12-23	Genesis 15
3	Romans 10	Genesis 24:1-27
4	Romans 15:1-13	Genesis 32
5	1 Corinthians 4	Genesis 44
6	1 Corinthians 9:1-18	2 Thessalonians 1
7	1 Corinthians 12:12-31a	2 Corinthians 4:5-18
8	1 Corinthians 16	2 Corinthians 11:7-29
9	James 4:1-12	Galatians 4:8-31
10	Joshua 5 & 6	Philippians 3:1-16
11	Judges 7	Haggai 2
12	1 Samuel 2:22-36	Ezra 9 & 10
13	1 Samuel 12	Nehemiah 9:22-37

14	1 Samuel 25	Proverbs 10
15	2 Samuel 7	Job 5
16	1 Kings 1 & 2	Job 19
17	1 Kings 12:20-33	Job 38 & 39
18	2 Kings 2	Joel 4
19	2 Kings 9 & 10	Zechariah 11
20	Ephesians 3:1-13	Ecclesiastes 7 & 8
21	Ephesians 6:1-9	1 Timothy 2
22	Amos 4	2 Timothy 2:1-21
23	Hosea 2	2 Peter 3:1-10
24	Hosea 13	Esther 5 & 7
25	Isaiah 10	Tobit 6
26	2 Chronicles 29	Judith 10 & 11
27	Isaiah 37	Sirach 5
28	Jeremiah 4	Sirach 16
29	Habakuk 3	Sirach 38 & 39
30	Jeremiah 27	Wisdom 5
31	Jeremiah 31	Wisdom 14 & 15
32	Ezekiel 12	2 Macabees 7:20-42
33	Ezekiel 24	Daniel 1
34	Ezekiel 39	Daniel 9

or SHORT READING **ROMANS 8:14-27**

As many as are led by the Spirit of God, these are sons and daughters of God. For you did not receive a spirit of slavery, for fear again, but you received a spirit of adoption, by which we cry, "Abba, Father."

That very Spirit gives witness to our spirit that we are children of God. And if children, then also heirs, heirs on one hand of God, joint heirs on the other of Christ, since we suffer with him in order that we may also be glorified with him.

For I reckon that the sufferings of this time are not worthy of comparing with the coming glory to be revealed to us. For creation watches in anxiety and eager expectation for the revelation of the children of God. For creation was subjected to vanity, not of free will, but by that of the one subjecting, in hope, because even creation itself will be freed from the slavery of corruption to the freedom of the glory of the children of God.

We know that all creation groans together, in pain as in labor, until now. And not only this, but we ourselves, the firstfruit of the Spirit, groan within ourselves as we eagerly expect our adoption, the redemption of our bodies.

For by hope we were saved; but hope that is seen is not hope, for why would anyone hope for what is seen? But if we hope for what we do not see, through patience we eagerly wait.

And similarly also the Spirit shares in our weakness. For we do not know how to pray as is fitting, but the Spirit prays on our behalf with inexpressible groanings.

And the one searching our heart knows what is the mind of the Spirit, because the Spirit intercedes on behalf of saints according to the will of God.

Let us bless the Lord. *Thanks be to God.*

THURSDAY PROPHETS

O/ breathe on me, O/ breath of God,
Fill/ me with life a//-new,
That I may love what you have loved,
And do what you would do.

O/ breathe on me, O/ breath of God,
Un/-til my heart is// pure,
Un-til with you I will one will,
To do and to en-dure.

O/ breathe on me, O/ breath of God,
In/-spire my bu-sy// mind,
Un-til this earth-ly part of me
Glows with your fire div-ine.

O/ breathe on me, O/ breath of God,
My/ soul shall nev-er// die,
But live in your e-ter-nal life,
Your love the rea-son why.

Text: Edwin Hatch, 1878, altered
Music: ST. COLUMBA, CM; Gaelic Folk Melody
Popular melody for: *The King Of Love My Shepherd Is*

JEREMIAH 31:10-14

Antiphon *They will be my people and I will be their God*
for they will return to me with all their heart.

Jer 24:7b

Hear, nations, the word of Adonai;
proclaim it to distant coastlands and say:
"The One who scattered Israel
  will gather them and watch them
  as one who is shepherd to a flock."

For Adonai will ransom and redeem Jacob
from the hand of those with more strength.

They will come and they will shout
up on the height of Zion
and they will rejoice in the bounty of Adonai,
the grain and new wine and oil,
and younglings of the flock and herd;
and they themselves like a well-watered garden
will sorrow no more, not again.

Then young women will be glad in dance,
and young men together with the old.
I will turn their mourning into gladness;
I will comfort them and give joy instead of sorrow.
I will satisfy with abundance the self of the priests
and my people will be filled with my bounty,
declares Adonai.

Glory…

Antiphon

ISAIAH 12:1b-6

Antiphon *The crowds asked John the Baptist,*
What then shall we do? Lk 3:10

I give you thanks, Adonai.
Though you were angry with me,
your anger turned away
and you comforted me.

Surely God is my salvation!
I will trust and be not afraid
for God is my strength and my song.

Adonai became for me salvation
and you will draw with joy
waters from wells of salvation…

Give thanks to Adonai!
Call on the name!
Make the deeds known among the nations!
Proclaim that the name is exalted!

Sing to Adonai,
who has done glory!
Let this be known to all the world.

Shout! And sing for joy,
dwellers of Zion!
For great in your midst
is the Holy One of Israel.

Glory…

Antiphon

ISAIAH 40:10-17

Antiphon *A voice of one*
cried out in the desert:
Prepare the way of the Lord.   Mk 1:3

See! Sovereign Adonai comes with power,
and with a ruling arm.
See! And with reward
and accompanied with recompense.

Like a shepherd tending the flock
and gathering lambs in the arms,
carrying them in the heart
and leading gently those with young.

Who can measure the waters in a hand's hollow?
Or mark off the heavens with handbreadths?
Or hold the dust of the earth in a basket?
Or weigh mountains on a scale
or hills in a balance?

Who has understood the mind of Adonai?
What human has given counsel or instruction,
or whom was consulted for enlightenment
and teaching about what is right
and teaching knowledge?
Who can show the path of understanding?

Surely nations are like drops in a bucket
and are regarded as dust on a scale.
Surely islands are weighed like fine dust.

ISAIAH 40:10-17, continued

Even Lebanon is not sufficient to make fire,
nor their animals sufficient for burnt-offering.
Before God, all the nations are as nothing,
regarded as worthless and less than nothing.

Glory...

Antiphon
*A voice of one
cried out in the desert:
Prepare the way of the Lord.* Mk 1:3

ISAIAH 66:7-14a

Antiphon
*Know this:
The kingdom of God is at hand.* Lk 10:11b

"Before she goes into labor she gives birth;
 before pain comes upon her,
 she delivers a son.
 Who has heard of such as this?
 Who has seen such as these?

Can a country be born in one day
or a nation be brought forth in one moment?
Yet she is in labor,
then Zion gives birth to her children.

Do I bring to the moment of birth
and not give delivery?"
asks your God Adonai;
"Do I bring one to delivery
and then close up?

Rejoice with Jerusalem and be glad for her!
All who love her, rejoice with her!
Rejoice, all who mourn over her,

for you will nurse and you will be satisfied
at the breast of her comforts,
for you will drink deeply and you will delight
in the overflow of her abundance."

For this says Adonai:
"See, I extend peace to her like a river,
and wealth of nations like a flooding stream,
and you will nurse, being carried at her side,
and you will be playdanced on her knees.

As a child is comforted by a mother,
so will I comfort you
and over Jerusalem
you will be comforted.

When you see,
your heart will rejoice
and your bones will flourish like the grass."

Glory...

Antiphon

READING ISAIAH 66:1-2

This our Lord says,
"The heavens are my throne
and the earth is the footstool of my feet.
Where is this house that you will build for me?
Where is to be the place for my resting?
Even all these my hand made,
so all these came into being,"
declares our Lord.
"This I esteem:
the one humble and contrite spirit
who trembles at my word."

RESPONSORY Psalm 130:1

Out of the depths I cry to you…

…Lord, hear my voice!

My desire is to do your desire…

…Lord, hear my voice!

Glory to the Father and to Son and to the Holy Spirit:

*…Out of the depths I cry to you;
Lord, hear my voice!*

Let us bless the Lord. *Thanks be to God.*

THURSDAY MORNING

293

+ *God, come to my assistance;* Psalm 70:2
  Lord, make haste to help me!

  Glory…

The/ King of Love my/ Shep-herd is,
Whose/ good-ness fails me// nev-er;
I noth-ing lack if I am his
And he is mine for-ev-er.

Where/ streams of liv-ing/ wat-er flow,
Our/ ran-somed souls he// leads us,
And where the ver-dant pas-tures grow,
with food cel-es-tial feeds us.

Per/-verse and fool-ish/, do I stray,
But/ yet in love he// seeks me
To on his shoul-der gent-ly lay
And home, re-joic-ing, bring me.

You/ spread a ta-ble/ in our sight
Your/ unc-tion grace be//-stow-ing;
And, oh! the tran-sport of de-light
With our cup ov-er-flow-ing.

And/ so through all the/ length of days
Your/ good-ness fails us// nev-er.
Good Shep-herd, may we sing your praise
With-in your house for-ev-er!

Text: Psalm 23, Henry W. Baker, 1868, altered
Music: ST. COLUMBA, CM; Gaelic Folk Melody
Popular melody for: *O Breathe On Me, O Breath Of God*

PSALM 48

Antiphon *Take nothing on the way*
except only a staff,
sandals,
and a single tunic.   Mk 6:8

Great is Adonai, greatly being praised
in the city of our God,
on the holy mountain, beautiful loft,
the joy of all the earth,

Mount Zion, the upmost heights,
sacred mountain, the city of the Great King.
God in the citadels is shown as a fortress when,
see, the kings join forces and advance together.

They saw, were astounded, and fled in terror;
trembling seized them, pain like a woman in labor.
By the east wind you destroyed ships of Tarshish;

just as we heard, so we saw in the city
of Adonai Sabaoth, in the city of our God.
God makes her secure to forever.

In your temple we ponder your unfailing mercy.
Like your name, God, so your praise
goes to the ends of the earth;

your right hand is filled with justice.
Mount Zion rejoices because of your judgments;
the villages of Judah are glad.

Walk about Zion! Go around! Count her towers!
Consider at heart her ramparts!
And view her citadels!

So that you may tell to the next generation:
This God, our God, forever and ever
will guide us even to the end.

Glory…

Antiphon

PSALM 57

Antiphon
*This is my commandment,
that you love one another
as I have loved you.* Jn 15:12

Have mercy on me, God, have mercy on me,
for in you my life takes refuge
and in the shade of your wings I take refuge
until disasters pass.

I cry out to God Most High,
to El who fulfills me,
who sends from the heavens and saves me
and rebukes the one pursuing me.

God sends to my soul fidelity and mercy;
in the midst of ravenous lions I lie,
in the midst of human beings with teeth and spear
and arrows and tongues, their sharp swords.

PSALM 57, continued

Be exalted, God, above the heavens,
your glory over all the earth.

For my feet they spread a net
and my self was bowed down.
Before me they dug a pit
and fell inside it themselves.

My heart is steadfast, Elohim,
my heart is steadfast;
I will sing and make music.

Awake, my liver!
Wake up the harp and the lyre;
I will wake up the dawn.

Lord, I will praise you among the nations;
I will sing of you among the peoples,
for great to the heavens is your mercy
and to the skies is your fidelity.

God, be exalted above the heavens,
your glory over all the earth.

Glory…

Antiphon　　*This is my commandment,
that you love one another
as I have loved you.*　　Jn 15:12

PSALM 87

Antiphon *The Father and I are one.* Jn 10:30

On the holy mountain
is the foundation of Adonai,
who loves the gates of Zion
more than all of Jacob's dwellings.
Glorious things are being said of you, city of God.

"I will record Rahab and Babylon
 among those who know me;
 see Philistia and Tyre with Cush:
 this one was born there!"

Indeed of Zion it will be said,
"One and another were born in her,
 and the Most High will establish her."

Adonai will write when registering peoples,
"This one was born there."
And making music they will sing,
"All of my fountains are in you."

Glory...

Antiphon

PSALM 80

Antiphon *The Kingdom of God will be given
to a people who produce its fruit.* Mt 21:43

Hear us, One Shepherd of Israel,
you who lead Joseph like a flock.
From your throne on the cherubim, shine forth
before Ephraim, Benjamin and Manasseh!
Awaken your might! Come to our salvation!

O God, restore us!
Make your faces shine
that we may be saved!

Until when, Adonai, God of Hosts,
will you smolder against the prayer of your people?
You fed them with bread of tears
and you made them drink tears by the bowlful.
You made us a contention to our neighbors,
and enmity mocks us.

God of Hosts, restore us!
Make your faces shine
that we may be saved!

Out from Egypt, you brought a vine;
you drove out the nations and you planted it.
You cleared the ground before her;
her roots took root
and she filled the land.

Mountains were covered by her shade
and the mighty cedars by her branches.
She sent out her branches to the Sea,
and her shoots as far as the River.

Why have you broken down her walls?
All who pass by the way pick at her.
The boar from the forest ravages her,
and creatures of the field feed on her.

God of Hosts, return now!
Look down from heaven!
See and watch over this vine,
this root that your right hand planted,

and the son you raised up for yourself.
Some would burn it or cut it down;
at the rebuke of your faces
may those plans perish.

Let your hand be on the one at your right hand,
the descendant of Adam you raised up for yourself.
Then we will not turn away from you;
you revive us and we will call on your name.

Adonai, God of Hosts, restore us!
Make your faces shine
that we may be saved!

Glory…

Antiphon

PSALM 81

Antiphon *The sabbath was made*
for human beings,
not human beings
for the sabbath.   Mk 2:27

Sing for joy to God our strength!
Shout to the God of Jacob!

Begin the music! Strike the tambourine,
the melodious harp and the lyre!
Sound the ram horn at the new moon,
the full moon, the day of our feast!

For this is a decree for Israel,
an ordinance of the God of Jacob,
a statute established for Joseph
when time to go out from the land of Egypt
and the language we did not understand:

"I removed the burden from their shoulders,
 their hands were freed from the basket.
 In distress you called and I rescued you;

 I answered from the thundercloud
 and tested you at the waters of Meribah.
 Hear, my people, Israel, and I will warn you,
 if you will listen to me:

'No foreign "god" shall be among you;
you shall bow to no alien "god."
I am Adonai, your God,
who brought you out of the land of Egypt.
Open wide your mouth and I will fill it!'

But my people did not listen to my voice,
and Israel did not submit to me.
So I gave them to their stubborn heart
and they followed their devices.

If my people were listening to me,
if Israel would follow my ways,
as quickly would I subdue the enmity
and turn a firm hand to the foes.

Anyone hating Adonai would cringe
under punishment lasting to forever.
But I will feed my people with finest of wheat
and satisfy you with honey out of rock."

Glory…

                                                  Antiphon

PSALM 99

Antiphon
Were not ten lepers cleansed?
And this one foreigner alone
gives glory to God? Lk 17:17

Adonai reigns;
let the nations tremble.
The One sits enthroned on the cherubim;
let the earth shake.

Great in Zion is Adonai,
and exalted over all the nations.
Let them praise your great and awesome name,
"Holy are you, and mighty."

The King of justice loves you
and establishes equity and justice,
having done what is right in Jacob.

Exalt Adonai our God!
And worship at the feet on the footstool,
"Holy are you, and mighty."

Moses and Aaron are among the priests,
and Samuel among those calling the name,
calling on El Adonai, who answered them,
who spoke to them from the pillar of cloud.
They kept the statutes and decrees given to them.

Adonai, our God, you answered them.
You were the one Forgiving El to them,
though punishing their misdeeds.

Exalt Adonai our God!
And worship at the holy mountain,
for holy is our God Adonai!

Glory...

Antiphon

READING **1 PETER 4:7-11**

Now of all things the end has drawn near. And so be sober in mind and sober in prayer. Before yourselves in all things, have fervent love, because love covers a multitude of sins. Be hospitable to each other without murmuring.

As each one receives a gift to yourselves, minister it as good stewards of God's manifold grace. If anyone speaks, as words of God; if anyone ministers, as by strength supplied by God, so that in all things God may be glorified through Jesus Christ, to whom is the glory and the might to the eons of the eons. Amen.

RESPONSORY Ps 63:7,8

On my bed through the watch of night...
...O Lord, I think of you.

You who are my help,... *...O Lord, I think of you.*

Glory to the Father and to the Son and to the Holy Spirit:
...On my bed through the watch of night,
O Lord, I think of you.

GOSPEL READING OF THE DAY or GOSPEL CANTICLE

Antiphon *Lord, give us knowledge of salvation*
known in the forgiveness of our sins.

CANTICLE OF ZECHARIAH   **LUKE 1:68-79**

+ Blessed be the Lord the God of Israel
who chose a people,
visited them to bring redemption,
and raised salvation in the house of David,
saving strength from God's own servant,

speaking from the age of the prophets
through the mouth of the holy prophet:
Salvation out of enmity,
even out of those who hate us,

to show our ancestors how mercy works,
and to remember the holy promise of the Lord,
the covenant made for our father Abraham,
calming our fear and making us free
to serve God as holy and righteous and just
in the Lord's presence all our days.

And you also child
will be called a prophet of the Most High
for you will go before the Lord to prepare his way
and give to his people a knowledge of salvation
known in accepting forgiveness of their sins.

From the deepness of God's mercy on us,
a sun rising from the height will visit to appear
to those who sit in the dark or shadow of death,
and to guide our feet into the way of peace.

THURSDAY MORNING

Gospel Reading for Thursday of

Week			
	1 Mark 1:40-45	**13** Matt 9:1-8	**25** Luke 9:7-9
	2 Mark 3:7-12	**14** Matt 10:7-15	**26** Luke 10:1-12
	3 Mark 4:21-25	**15** Matt 11:28-30	**27** Luke 11:5-13
	4 Mark 6:7-13	**16** Matt 13:10-17	**28** Lk 11:47-54
	5 Mark 7:24-30	**17** Matt 13:47-53	**29** Lk 12:49-53
	6 Mark 8:27-33	**18** Matt 16:13-23	**30** Lk 13:31-35
	7 Mark 9:41-50	**19** Matt 18:21-19:1	**31** Luke 15:1-10
	8 Mark 10:46-52	**20** Matt 22:1-14	**32** Lk 17:20-25
	9 Mark 12:28-34	**21** Matt 24:42-51	**33** Lk 19:41-44
	10 Matt 5:20-26	**22** Luke 5:1-11	**34** Lk 21:20-28
	11 Matt 6:7-15	**23** Luke 6:27-38	
	12 Matt 7:21-29	**24** Luke 7:36-50	

Glory…

Antiphon

PETITIONS FOR THE CONSECRATION TO GOD OF THE DAY AND ITS WORK

- For the Church and her ministry and apostolates…
- For secular authorities and all serving as stewards…
- For people who are poor or sick or in sorrow…
- For peace and the basic needs of each human being…
- For a culture of vocations all over the world…

OUR FATHER…

+ *May the Lord bless us, protect us from all evil, and bring us to everlasting life.* ***Amen***.

THURSDAY DAYTIME

+ *God, come to my assistance;*   Psalm 70:2
  Lord, make haste to help me!

Glory...

Ho-ly God\, we praise/ your Name;
Lord of all\, we bow\ be-fore you!
All on earth\ your scep/-ter claim,
All in heav-en a-bove\ a-dore you;

    In-fin/-ite\ your vast do/-main,
    Ev-er-last\-ing is\ your reign.

Hark! the loud\ cel-es/-tial hymn
An-gel choirs\ a-bove\ are rais-ing,
Cher-u-bim\ and ser/-a-phim,
In un-ceas\-ing chor\-us prais-ing;

    Fill the/ heav-ens with sweet ac/-cord:
    Ho-ly, ho\-ly, ho\-ly Lord.

Ho-ly Fa\-ther, Ho/-ly Son,
Ho-ly Spir\-it, Three\ we name you;
While in ess\-ence on/-ly One,
Un-div-i\-ded God\ we claim you;

    And a/-dor\-ing bend the/ knee,
    While we en-ter the mys\-ter-y.

Text: Ignaz Franz, *Grosser Gott*, about 1774;
translated by Clarence Walworth, 1858, altered
Music: 78 78 77 GROSSER GOTT,
Katholisches Gesangbuch, Vienna, 1774

PSALM 119:89-96
Lamedh

Antiphon   *Why do you see*
the piece of dust in your neighbor's eye
but ignore the wood beam
in your own eye?   Lk 6:41

To eternity, Adonai,
your word stands firm in the heavens.
To generation and generation is your fidelity;
the earth you established endures.

Your laws endure the day
for all things are your servants.
If your law were not my delight
I would have perished in my affliction.

I will never forget your precepts
for by them you make me alive.
I am yours; save me
for I sought out your precepts.

Wicked ones wait to destroy me
but I will ponder your statutes.
I see a limit to all perfection
but your commands are without boundary.

Glory...

                                                        Antiphon

PSALM 119:97-104
Mem

Antiphon
Who do people say I am?
Who do you say I am? Mk 8:27,29

How I love your law,
my meditation all day long.
Your commands make me wiser than enmity
for they are with me to forever.

Greater than all my teachers is my insight
for I ponder your statutes.
I understand more than elders
for I obey your precepts.

I keep my feet off every evil path
to obey your word.
I turn not from your laws
for you have taught me.

How sweet to my taste are your promises,
sweeter than honey to my mouth.
I gain understanding from your precepts
for I hate every false path.

Glory...

Antiphon

PSALM 119:105-112
Nun

Antiphon *Every scribe*
discipled to the kingdom of heaven
is like a head of a household
who puts forth from the treasure
things both new and old. Mt 13:52

Your word is the lamp to my foot
and the light for my path.
I have made an oath and confirmation
to follow your righteous laws.

I have suffered much, Adonai;
make me alive as is your word.
Accept the willing praise of my mouth!
And now, Adonai, teach me your laws!

My life is constantly in my hand,
but I will not forget your law.
Doers of badness set a snare for me,
but I did not stray from your precepts.

I have your statutes as a heritage to forever,
they are indeed the joy of my heart.
I set my heart to keep your decrees
to forever, the very end.

Glory...

Antiphon

PSALM 25

Antiphon *The time is full*
and the kingdom of God has drawn near;
repent and believe in the gospel. Mk 1:15

To you, Adonai, I lift up my soul;
in you, my God, I trust;
let me not be shamed
and let enmity not triumph over me.

Indeed all who hope in you
will not be shamed;
shamed will be those doing
the defenseless treachery.

Show me your ways, Adonai;
teach me your paths.
Guide me in your fidelity and teach me,
for you are my saving God;
you are my hope all the day.

Remember your compassion, Adonai,
and your mercies, for they are from of old.
The sins of my youth and rebellious ways
you do not remember, as is your mercy.

You do remember me, Adonai, for you are good.
Good and upright is Adonai,
who instructs sinners in the way,
guides humble ones in rightness,
and teaches the way to the humble.

All the ways of Adonai are mercy and truth
for those who keep the covenant demands.
For the sake of your name, Adonai,
now you forgive my guilt, great as it is.

Who is the human who fears Adonai?
The one being instructed in the Lord's chosen way,
whose life will be days spent in prosperity,
whose descendants will inherit the land,
the confidence of Adonai is with those thus fearing;
the covenant is made known to them.

My eyes are ever on Adonai,
who will free my feet from the snare.
Turn to me! Be gracious to me!
For I am lonely and afflicted.

Troubles of my heart have multiplied;
free me from my anguish!
Look upon my affliction and distress!
Take away all my sins!

See the enmity, the increase of fierce hate!
Guard my life! Rescue me!
Let me not be shamed,
for I take refuge in you.

May integrity and uprightness protect me
because I hope in you.
Redeem Israel, God, from all our troubles.

Glory…

Antiphon

PSALM 56:2-7,9-14

Antiphon *The seed is the word of God.* Lk 8:11b

Be merciful to me, my God!
Human beings pursue me all the day,
attacking with oppression
and with slander all the day.

Indeed in their pride do the many attack me.
On the day I am afraid, in you I trust.
My praise is of God's word, in God I trust.
What can a mortal do to me? I will not be afraid.

All the day they twist my words against me;
all their plots are for harm.
They conspire, they lurk, they watch my steps;
they are eager for my life…

Record my lament,
put my tears in your wineskin;
are they not in your record?
Enmity will turn back on the day I call;

I will know that God is for me.
In God whose word I praise,
in Adonai whose word I praise, in God I trust.
What can a human do to me? I will not be afraid.

Upon me, God, are my vows to you;
I will present thank offerings to you
for you delivered my life from death
and my feet from stumbling,
to walk in God's presence in the light of the living.

Glory…   Antiphon

PSALM 79:1-5,9-11,13

Antiphon *If only you knew
what makes for peace.*   Lk 19:42a

God, the nations invaded
into your inheritance,
they defiled your holy temple,
they reduced Jerusalem to rubbles.

They gave the bodies of your servants
as food to birds of the air,
the flesh of your saints
to beasts of earth.

They poured out their blood
like the waters around Jerusalem
and no one is there burying.

We are a reproach to our neighbors,
scorn and derision to those around us.
Until when, Adonai, will you be angry?
Will the fire of your jealousy burn to forever?...

Hold not against us
the sins of our ancestors;
may your compassion be quick to meet us
for we are in desperate need.

PSALM 79:1-5,9-11,13, continued

Help us, God of our salvation,
for the glory of your name;
deliver us and pardon our sins
for the sake of your name.

Why should the nations say,
"Where is their God?"
Let vengeance be known among the nations
before our eyes for your servants,
for their blood being poured out.

May the groan of prisoners
come in before you;
by your strong arm
preserve the condemned...

We your people, the sheep of your pasture,
will give you thanks to forever.
Generation to generation
will recount your praise.

Glory...

Antiphon *If only you knew
what makes for peace.* Lk 19:42a

PSALM 128

Antiphon
*Everyone having
will be given more
and to abundance;
but the one not having,
even that will be taken.*   Mt 25:29

Blessed are all who fear Adonai
and walk in the way.
Indeed you will eat
from the labor of your hands.

To you will be blessings and prosperity,
and your spouse like a fruitful vine
inside and outside your house,
sons and daughters around your table
like shoots of the olives.

See: one who fears Adonai is blessed;
may Adonai bless you from Zion.
See and enjoy the prosperity of Jerusalem
all the days of your life,
and the joy of the children of your children.

Peace be upon Israel.

Glory...

Antiphon

PSALM 129

Antiphon *I am the bread of life;*
who comes to me does not hunger
and who believes in me
will never thirst.   Jn 6:35

"From my youths they oppressed me greatly,"
let Israel now say.
"From my youths they oppressed me greatly,
but over me gaining no victory.

On my back the plowers plowed;
their furrows they made long.
Righteous Adonai cut free
the cords of bad doers."

May all haters of Zion
be shamed and turned back;
May they be like grass on housetops,
which withers before it grows,

which cannot fill one hand of the reaper
nor an arm of the gatherer,
and passers-by will not say,
"Blessing of Adonai upon you!"

"We bless you in the name of Adonai!"

Glory…

Antiphon

1 PETER 2:21-24

Antiphon *May the God of peace,*
having led up out of the dead
by blood of the eternal covenant
the great shepherd of the sheep, our Lord Jesus,
form you in every good thing to do God's will,
doing in us through Jesus Christ
the thing well-pleasing before God,
to whom be the glory
unto the eons of the eons. Heb 13:20-21

To this you were called,
for indeed Christ suffered on behalf of you,
leaving to you an example to follow in his steps:

He did not sin, nor was guile found in his mouth;
he was reviled and did not revile in return;
suffering he did not threaten,
but delivered himself to the one judging justly.

Our sins he carried in his body up onto the tree,
that dying to sins, we might live for justice.
By his bruises, you are cured.

Glory…

Antiphon

READING — **1 PETER 1:22-25**

Your souls now purified by obedience to the truth
of unfeigned love for brothers and sisters,
love one another earnestly from the heart,
having been regenerated
not by corruptible seeds but incorruptible
through the living and abiding word of God.
All flesh is as grass,
and all its glory as a flower of grass;
the grass dried up and the flower fell out,
but the word of the Lord remains unto the eon.
This is the gospel word preached to you.

RESPONSORY — Ps 23:1

The Lord is my shepherd…   …*nothing shall I lack.*

My Lord lays me down in green pastures…
   …*nothing shall I lack.*

Glory to the Father and to the Son and to the Holy Spirit:
   …*The Lord is my shepherd; nothing shall I lack.*

Lord\, have mer-cy.
   Christ\, have mer-cy.
         Lord\, have mer-cy.

THURSDAY EVENING

+ *God, come to my assistance;* Psalm 70:2
  Lord, make haste to help me!

  Glory…

Beau-ti-ful Sa\\-**vior**, King of Cre-a\\-tion,
Son of\\ Ma-ry\\, Son of God!
Tru-ly I love\\ you, Tru-ly I'll serve\\ you,
Light of my soul, my Joy, my Crown.

Fair are the mea\\-dows, Fair are the wood\\-lands,
Robed in\\ flow-ers of bloom-ing spring;
Je-sus is fair\\-er, Je-sus is pur\\-er;
He makes our sad-dest spir-it sing.

Fair is the sun\\-shine, Fair is the moon\\-light,
Bright are the spark-ling\\ stars on high;
Je-sus shines bright\\-er, Je-sus shines pur\\-er,
Than all the an-gels in the sky.

Beau-ti-ful Sa\\-vior, Lord of the na\\-tions,
Full-y\\ hu-man\\, full-y God!
Praise, a-do-ra\\-tion, Glo-ry and ho\\-nor,
Now and for-ev-er-more, our Lord!

Text: based on Psalm 45:3; author unknown, 1677;
translated by Joseph A. Seiss, 1873, altered
Music: ST. ELIZABETH; Hoffman and Richter's
Schleisische Volkslieder, 1842

PSALM 30

Antiphon *Who touched my garments?* Mk 5:30

I will exalt you, Adonai,
for you lifted me up
and over me do not let enmity gloat.

Adonai, my God,
I cried to you for help and you healed me.
Adonai, you brought my self up from Sheol;
you spared me from going into the pit.

Sing to Adonai, you saints!
Sing praise to the holy name!
One moment in anger: lifetimes in the Lord's favor;
in the night weeping remains,
but joy comes in the morning

when I said in my security
I will be unshaken to forever.
In your favor, Adonai,
you made my mountain stand firm;
you hid your faces and I was dismayed.

To you, Adonai, I called
and to you, Lord, I cried for mercy.
What would be the gain in my destruction?
What is gained if I go into the pit?

Will the dust praise you?
Will the dust proclaim your fidelity?
Hear, Adonai! Be merciful to me!
Be my one helper, Adonai!

You turned my wailing
into dancing for me;
you removed my sackcloth
and clothed me in joy

so that my heart may sing to you,
and not be silent.
My God Adonai,
I will thank you to forever.

Glory…

    Antiphon

PSALM 32

Antiphon *Do you see this woman?*
Her many sins have been forgiven,
and so she has loved much. Lk 7:44,47

Blessed is the one forgiven of transgression,
who was covered with sin.
Blessed is the human against whom
Adonai does not count guilt,
and in whose spirit there is no deceit.

When I kept silent,
my bones wasted away
through my groaning all day.

For by day and night
your hand was heavy upon me;
my strength withered as in summer heat.

I acknowledged my sin to you,
and did not cover up my iniquity;
I said I will confess my transgressions to Adonai
and you forgave the guilt of my sin.

For this let every loyal one pray to you
at the time to find you.
Surely the rising of mighty waters
will not reach this one.

You are the hiding place for me;
you will protect me from trouble
and surround me with deliverance song.

I will instruct you and I will teach you
and counsel you in the way for you to go;
My eye is over you.

Do not be like a horse,
like your mule with no understanding;
by bit and bridle and harness they are controlled
or else they will not even come to you.

Many woes have the bad doers,
but the truster in Adonai
is surrounded in unfailing mercy.

Rejoice in Adonai!
Righteous ones, be glad!
And sing, all you upright of heart!

Glory…

                                          Antiphon

PSALM 72

Antiphon *Out of you, Bethlehem, will come forth a ruler*
who will shepherd my people Israel. Mt 2:6;
Micah 5:2

God, endow your justice to the king
and your righteousness to the royal heir,
to judge your people in righteousness
and your afflicted with justice.

Mountains will bring prosperity to the people,
the hills too in righteousness.
He will defend people oppressed,
save the children of the poor,
and crush the oppressor.

They will fear you as long as the sun,
as long as the moon,
from generation to generations.
He will be like rain falling on a mown field,
like showers watering the earth.

In his days the righteous will flourish
in prosperous abundance til the moon is no more.
He will rule from sea to sea
and from the River to the ends of the earth.

Before him will desert tribes bow
and enmity lick the dust.
The kings of Tarshish and the distant shores
will bring tribute and present gifts,
with kings of Sheba and Seba.
They will bow down to him;
all the kings of all the nations will thus serve.

For he will deliver the poor crying out
and the oppressed when no one is helping.
He will take pity on the poor and the needy
and will save the lives of the poor;

he will rescue their lives
from oppression and violence,
for their lifeblood is precious in his eyes.

May he live and be given gold of Sheba,
and may all ever pray
that he be blessed all the day.

May grain be abundant throughout the land,
on the tops of the hills,
swaying like the fruit of Lebanon,
and people flourish and thrive
like grass in a field.

May his name endure to forever
and continue as long as the sun;
and being thus blessed
may the nations bless him.

Blessed be God, Adonai, God of Israel,
alone doing marvelous deeds.
Blessed be the glory of the name to forever;
may the earth be filled with the glory of God.
Amen and amen.

Glory…

                                                  Antiphon

PSALM 132

Antiphon
*To the one who has,
more will be given;
from the one who has not,
even what that one has
will be taken away.*   Mk 4:25

Adonai, remember David
and all the hardships he endured,
the oath he swore to Adonai,
the vow he made to the Mighty One of Jacob.

I will not enter into the structure of my house;
I will not go to the mats of my bed;
I will not allow my eyes to sleep
nor let slumber come to my eyelids,
till I find a place for Adonai,
a dwelling for the Mighty One of Jacob.

See, we heard her in Ephrathah;
we came upon her in fields of Jaar.
"Let us go to the dwellings;
 let us worship at the feet on the footstool."

Arise, Adonai, to your rest,
you and the ark of your might.
May your priests be clothed in justice
and may your saints sing for joy.

For the sake of your servant David
reject not the face of your anointed.

Adonai swore an oath to David,
sure and not to be revoked.
"From the descendants of your body
 I will place on your throne.

 If your sons and daughters keep my covenant
 and my statutes that I teach them
 then their children to forever
 will sit on your throne."

For Adonai chose Zion
and desired her as a dwelling:
"This is my resting place to forever;
 here I will sit, for I desired her.

 To bless I will bless her provisions;
 her poor ones I will satisfy with bread,
 her priests I will clothe in salvation,
 and her saints will sing;
 they will sing for joy.

 Here I will make grow a horn for David;
 I will set up a lamp for my anointed.
 Enmity be clothed with shame.
 The crown on David will be resplendent."

Glory...

                                                Antiphon

PSALM 144

Antiphon *Zacchaeus, come down quickly,*
for this day it is fitting for me
to stay at your house. Lk 19:5

Blessed be Adonai, my Rock,
who trains my hands for war,
my fingers for battle,

my love and fortress,
my stronghold and deliverer,
my shield in whom I take refuge,
who subdues peoples under me.

What, Adonai, is a human that you care for us?
Children of humanity, that you think of them?
Like a breath is the human,
whose days like a shadow are fleeting.

Adonai, part your heavens and come down!
Touch the mountains so they smoke!
You send lightning, lightning, and scatter them!
Shoot your arrows and you rout them!

Reach your hands from on high!
Deliver me! Rescue me from the mighty waters
and from the hand of foreign peoples speaking lies,
whose right hands are the right hand of deceit.

I will sing a new song to you, O God,
and on the lyre of ten make music to you,
the One giving victory to the kings,
the One delivering from the deadly sword
your servant David.

Deliver me!
Rescue me from foreigners' hands,
whose mouths speak the lie,
whose right hands are the right hand of deceit.

Our sons in their youth
are like well nurtured plants,
our daughters like carved pillars
adorning a palace,

our barns filled with provisions from kind to kind,
our sheep becoming thousands
and tens of thousands in our fields,
and our oxen drawing loads,

no break in the walls and no exile
nor a cry of distress in the streets:
Blessed are the people of whom all this is true.
Blessed are the people whose God is Adonai.

Glory…

Antiphon

REVELATION 11:17-18, 12:10-12a

Antiphon
*I am the Alpha and the Omega,
says the Lord God,
the one who is and who was
and who is to come, the Almighty.*   Rev 1:8

We thank you, Lord God Almighty,
the One who is and who was;
you have taken your great power and reign.

The nations raged and your anger came,
and the time to judge the dead
and to reward your slaves and prophets,
the saints, and those fearing your name,
the small and the great…

Now have come the salvation and the power
and the kingdom of our God
and the authority of Christ the Anointed.
The accuser of our brothers and sisters was cast,
accusing them before our God day and night.

Their victory was because of the blood of the Lamb
and by the word of their witness.
They loved their life into their death,
and so be glad, you heavens,
and all you dwelling in them.

Glory…

Antiphon

READING **1 PETER 1:3-9**

Blessed be the God and Father of our Lord Jesus Christ, in whose great mercy we are given rebirth to a living hope through the resurrection of Jesus Christ from the dead, to the inheritance that is incorruptible, undefiled, and unfading, kept in heaven for you by the power of God, guarded through faith to a salvation ready to be revealed at the end time.

You exult in this, while yet you grieve if necessary for a little while by even many trials, for the proving of your faith, much more precious than gold that perishes even after being refined by fire, that you may be found giving praise and glory and honor at the revelation of Christ.

Without seeing him, you love him; still without seeing him you believe and exult with indescribable joy; and having been glorified, you are receiving the goal of your faith: the salvation of your souls.

RESPONSORY Ps 81:16b

The Lord our God feeds us…
...*...and with finest of wheat.*

Honey out of rock to satisfaction…
...*...and with finest of wheat.*

Glory to the Father and to the Son and to the Holy Spirit:
...*...The Lord our God feeds us,*
and with finest of wheat.

GOSPEL CANTICLE OF MARY **LUKE 1:46-55**

Antiphon *God has exalted with dignity
the humble in need.*

+ My soul is stretched full with praise of the Lord,
and my spirit, beyond joy in God, my Savior,
who chose to lay eyes on this humble servant.

Behold, now and forward,
each and every age will call me blessed,
for the Mighty One did great things to me.
Holy is the name and the mercy
to generations and generations,
the ones fearing the One,

Who scattered the haughty of mind and heart,
pulled the powerful off their high place,
and lifted with dignity the humble in need.

The hungering are filled with good things,
the rich are sent away empty,
and servant Israel is given relief

with a memory of mercy to remember,
the promise spoken to our ancestors,
to Abraham and his descendants forever.

Glory...   Antiphon

INTERCESSIONS

- In gratitude for blessings...; Abba thank you.
- For the sins of this day...; Lord Jesus have mercy.
- With concerns over tomorrow...; Holy Spirit help.

OUR FATHER...

+ *May the Lord bless us, protect us from all evil,
and bring us to everlasting life.* **Amen**.

THURSDAY NIGHT

+ *God, come to my assistance;*   Psalm 70:2
  Lord, make haste to help me!

  Glory...

Shep-herd of souls, re-fresh and bless
Your cho-sen pil-grim flock
With man-na in the wil-der-ness,
And wa-ter from the rock.

Hung-ry and thirs-ty, mor-tal, weak,
As you would come and go:
Our souls the joys of heav-en seek
Which from your pass-ion flow.

We would not live by bread a-lone,
But by your Word of grace,
In strength of which we trav-el on
To our a-bi-ding place.

Be known to us in break-ing bread,
But do not then de-part;
Sa-vior, a-bide with us and spread
Your ta-ble in our heart.

Text: James Mongtomery, 1825, altered
Music: ST. AGNES, CM, John B. Dykes, 1866

PSALM 16

Antiphon *Heaven and earth will pass away,*
but my words will not pass away. Mk 13:31

Keep me safe, El, for I take refuge in you.
I said to Adonai,
"You are my Lord;
 I have no good apart from you."

As for saints who are in the land,
even glorious ones,
all of my delight is in them.

Those who run after others
will multiply their sorrows;
I will not pour out their blood libations,
nor take up their names on my lips.

Adonai, you assign my portion and cup;
you make my lot secure.
Boundary lines fall for me in the pleasant places;
surely this inheritance is my delight.

I bless Adonai who counsels me;
even the nights instruct my heart.
With Adonai before me, always at my right hand,
I will not be shaken.

And so my heart is glad and my tongue rejoices.
My body will rest in security
because you will not abandon my soul to Sheol;
you will not let your holy one see decay.

> You will make known to me the path of living,
> fullness of joy in your presences,
> eternal pleasures at your right hand.

Glory…

Antiphon

READING   1 PETER 3:8-11

Now the end, all of you be of one mind, sympathetic, loving as siblings, compassionate, humble in mind, not giving back evil for evil to revile when reviled, but on the contrary a blessing, because to this you were called that you might inherit blessing.

Let the one wishing to love life and see good days restrain the tongue from evil and speak no guile by the lips, and turn aside from evil and do good. Let that one seek peace and pursue it.

RESPONSORY   Ps 31:6

Into your hands, Lord,…   *…I commend my spirit.*

You have redeemed us, Lord God of truth.
…I commend my spirit.

Glory to the Father and to the Son and to the Holy Spirit:
…Into your hands, Lord,
I commend my spirit.

Antiphon

> *Lord, save/ us!*
> *Save/ us while\ we are a-wake\,*
> *pro-tect us while we are a-sleep,*
> *that we may keep our watch/ with Christ/*
> *and when we sleep\, rest/ in his\ peace.*

GOSPEL CANTICLE of SIMEON   **LUKE 2:29-32**

+ Now, Master, you set free your servant
according to your word in peace;

   my eyes have seen your salvation,
which you have prepared
before the face of all the peoples,

   a light for revelation to the nations
and glory for your people, Israel.

Glory   Antiphon

+ *May the all-powerful Lord*
grant us a restful night and a peaceful death. **Amen.**

Loving Mother of the Redeemer,
gate of heaven, star of the sea,
assist your people who have fallen
yet strive to rise again.
To the wonderment of nature you bore your Creator,
yet remained a virgin after as before.
You who received Gabriel's joyful greeting,
have pity on us poor sinners. Amen.

FRIDAY READINGS

+ *Lord, open my lips*   Psalm 51:17
  and my mouth will declare your praise.

  Glory…

O sav-ing Vic-tim, o-pen wide
The gate of heav'n to us\ be-low;
Our foes press on/ from ev-'ry side;
Your aid sup-ply\; your strength be-stow.

To your great Name be end-less praise;
Im-mort-al God-head, One\ in Three;
Grant us for end/-less length of days,
In our true na\-tive land to be.

A-men.

Text: Thomas Aquinas, 1227-74;
Translated by Edward Caswall, 1849, altered
Music: O SALUTARIS HOSTIA, Abbe Duguet, about 1767

PSALM 35:1-2c,3c,9-19,22-23,27-28

Antiphon
> *The tax collector standing far off*
> *would not lift his eyes to heaven,*
> *but beat his breast saying,*
> *'God, be merciful to me, a sinner.'* Lk 18:13

Contend, Adonai, with my contenders!
Restrain those thinking to make war!
Take up shield and buckler and arise to my aid!...
Say to my soul, "I am your salvation."...

Then my soul will rejoice in Adonai
and take delight in salvation.
All of my bones will exclaim, "Adonai!
  Who like you rescues the poor from the powerful?
  Or the afflicted and the needy from the robbers?"

Ruthless witnesses come forward;
on things I do not know they question me.
They repay me evil for good;
forlorn is my soul.

Yet when they were ill
I clothed myself in sackcloth
and humbled myself with fasting
when my prayer had returned
to my breast unanswered.

As a friend and a sibling
I went about in grief,
bowing down like a mother in mourning.

But they took glee at my stumbling
and they gathered and gathered attackers
and did not cease to slander me unaware,
an ungodly circle of mockers
gnashing their teeth against me.

Until when, Lord? How long will you look on?
Rescue my life from their ravages,
my precious life from these lions.
I will give you thanks in the great assembly;
among people thronging I will praise you.

Let enmity neither gloat
without cause or reason
nor wink the eye at me…
You have seen, Adonai; be not silent.

Be not far from me, Lord.
Awake!, my God and Lord,
and rise to contend to my defense.
Vindicate me in your justice, Adonai…

May those who delight in my vindication
shout and be glad and always say,
"May Adonai be exalted,
 who delights in the peace of the servant."

And my tongue will speak your justice
and praise of you all the day.

Glory…

Antiphon

PSALM 38

Antiphon *If a house be divided against itself,
that house will be unable to stand.*   Mk 3:25

Adonai, rebuke me not in your anger
nor discipline me in your wrath,
for your arrows have pierced into me
and your hand has come down upon me.

There is no health in my body
because of your anger;
my bones are unsound because of my sin.
Indeed my guilts overwhelm my head
like a heavy burden,
too heavy for me.

I loathe them and they fester my wounds
because of my folly.
I am bowed down and brought very low;
all the day I go about mourning.

Indeed my loins are searing
and there is no health in my body.
Feeble and utterly crushed,
my heart groans in anguish.

Lord, before you is all of my longing;
my sighing is not hidden from you.
My heart pounds, my strength fails me,
and my eyes are without their light.

My friends and companions from the past
avoid being present to my woundedness,
and my neighbors stay far away.

People seeking my life set traps;
wanting to harm me, they talk of ruins
and plot deceptions all the day.

I am like a deaf man hearing nothing,
like a mute unable to open my mouth.
I became like one who does not hear,
like one whose mouth gives no answer.

Indeed, I wait for you, Adonai;
you will answer, Lord my God.
For I said, "let them not gloat over me;
  when my foot does slip, let them not exalt."

For my fall is ready for me
and my wounds are ever with me.
Indeed I confess my guilt;
I am troubled by my sin.

Vigorous ones seek enmity and for no reason,
many and numerous hating me.
Repaying the good with evil,
they slander me when I seek the good.

Forsake me not, Adonai;
my God, be not far from me.
Come quickly to my help,
my Lord and my salvation.

Glory…   Antiphon

PSALM 55:2-15,17-24

Antiphon
*Whoever receives me
receives the One who sent me.*   Mk 9:37b

Listen, Elohim, to my prayer!
Ignore not my plea, but hear me and answer me,
as I am troubled by my thoughts
and distraught at the voices of enmity,
at the stares of the faces of bad doers,
for they bring suffering down upon me
and revile me in anger.

My heart pounds within me
and the terrors of death assail me.
Fear and trembling harass me
and horror has overwhelmed me.

"Would that I had wings like the dove;
 I would fly away and find rest.
 See! I would flee far and stay in the desert.
 I would hurry to my place of shelter
 from the storm of the raging wind."

Confuse them, Lord; confound their speech,
for I see violence and strife in the city.
By day and by night they prowl about on her walls;
within her are mendacity and trouble.

Destructive forces are within her
and threats and lies never leave her streets.
It is not an enemy insulting me,
nor a foe rising against me
that I endure, from whom I hide;

but it is you, my other self,
my companion and my friend with whom
together we shared close companionship
walking with the throng at the house of Elohim…

To Elohim I call and am saved by Adonai
who hears my voice when I cry out in distress
in evening and in morning and at noon,
who redeems my soul in peace from the war
though many are opposing me.

El enthroned forever will hear and let be afflicted
those who never allow themselves to change,
who have no fear of God,
who send hands against friends,
and violate the covenant.

This one's mouth is smooth as butter,
yet war is in the heart,
speaking words more soothing than oil
that are yet drawn swords.

Cast your cares on Adonai,
who will sustain you
and to forever let not the righteous fall.

But you, God, will bring the bloody and deceitful
into the pit of corruption,
not living half their days.
And I will trust in you.

Glory…

Antiphon

PSALM 69:2-22,30-37

Antiphon   *Be not afraid of ones who can kill the body*
but are unable to kill the soul;
fear only the One able to destroy
both soul and body in gehenna.   Mt 10:28

Save me, Adonai,
for waters have come to my neck.
I sink into the deep mire; there is no foothold.
Into deep waters; the floods engulf me.

I am worn out from calling out;
my throat is parched and failing are my eyes
looking for my God.

Those hating me for no reason
are more numerous than the hairs of my head.
Many are the ones destroying me
in enmity for no reason.

What I did not steal must I then restore?
You, God, you know my folly
and my faults are not hidden from you.

May those who hope in you, God of Israel,
not be disgraced because of me.
For your sake I endure scorn
and disgrace covers my face.

I am a stranger to my brothers and sisters,
an alien to the children of my mother.
Zeal for your house consumes me
and insults of your insulters fall on me.

When I weep and fast
it leads only to scorn.
When I put on my clothing of sackcloth
then I am as sport to them.
Those sitting at the gate mock at me,
and drinkers of strong drink in their songs.

But I pray to you, Adonai,
in the time of favor;
in the greatness of your love, O God,
answer me with your sure salvation.

Rescue me from the mire and let me not sink;
let me be delivered from those who hate
and from the depths of the waters.

Let not the flood of waters engulf me,
nor the depth swallow me
nor the pit close its mouth over me.

Answer me, Adonai, for good is your love!
In the greatness of your mercies, turn to me!

Hide not your faces from your servant;
to my trouble, be quick! Answer me!
Come near because of the foes;
rescue my soul and redeem me!

You know my scorn and shame and disgrace;
all in enmity are before you.
Scorn broke my heart and I became helpless
and I looked for compassion but there was none,
and for comforters with none to be found.

PSALM 69:2-22,30-37, continued

Instead they put gall in my food
and for my thirst gave me vinegar to drink…
I am in pain and suffering;
may your salvation protect me, O God.

I will praise God's name in song and glory
with a thanksgiving more pleasing to Adonai
than ox or bull with horn and hoof.

The poor ones will see and be glad;
may your hearts now live, you seekers of God,
for Adonai hears the needy
and despises not the captives.

Let heaven and earth give praise
with the seas and all moving in them.
For God will rescue Zion
and rebuild the cities of Judah;

then they will settle there and possess her
and the children of God's servants will inherit her
and lovers of the Name
will dwell in her.

Glory…

Antiphon   *Be not afraid of ones who can kill the body
but are unable to kill the soul;
fear only the One able to destroy
both soul and body in gehenna.*   Mt 10:28

FRIDAY READINGS

READING	Year I	Year II
week 1	Romans 3:1-20	Genesis 6 & 7
2	Romans 7:1-13	Genesis 16
3	Romans 11:1-12	Genesis 24:33-67
4	Romans 15:14-33	Genesis 35
5	1 Corinthians 5	Genesis 45 & 46
6	1 Corinthians 9:19-27	2 Thessalonians 2
7	1 Corinthians 12:31b-13:13	2 Corinthians 5
8	James 1:1-18	2 Corinthians 11:30-12:13
9	James 4:13-5:11	Galatians 5
10	Joshua 7	Philippians 3:17-4:9
11	Judges 8 & 9	Zechariah 1
12	1 Samuel 3	Nehemiah 1
13	1 Samuel 15	Nehemiah 12
14	1 Samuel 26	Proverbs 15 & 16
15	2 Samuel 11	Job 6
16	1 Kings 3	Job 22
17	1 Kings 17	Job 40 & 41
18	2 Kings 3	Malachi 1 & 2
19	2 Kings 11 & 12	Zechariah 12 & 13
20	Ephesians 3:14-21	Ecclesiastes 9 & 10
21	Ephesians 6:10-24	1 Timothy 3
22	Amos 5	2 Timothy 2:22-3:17
23	Hosea 4 & 5	2 Peter 3:11-18
24	Hosea 14	Baruch 1 & 2
25	Isaiah 28	Tobit 7 & 8
26	Isaiah 20	Judith 12
27	2 Kings 21	Sirach 6
28	Jeremiah 7	Sirach 17
29	Jeremiah 22:10-30	Sirach 42 & 43
30	Jeremiah 28	Wisdom 6
31	Jeremiah 42 & 43	Wisdom 16 & 17
32	Ezekiel 13	1 Macabees 2
33	Ezekiel 28	Daniel 2
34	Ezekiel 40	Daniel 10

or SHORT READING **GALATIANS 2:15-21**

Jews by birth and not sinners of the ethnon-nations,
we know that a human is not justified by works of law
but through faith in Christ Jesus.
And we believed in Christ Jesus
that we might be justified by faith in Christ
and not by works of law,
because no flesh will be justified by works of law.
But if seeking to be justified in Christ
we were also found to be sinners,
then is Christ a minister of sin?
May it not be!
For if I build again the things I destroyed,
then I myself am a transgressor.
For through law I died to law,
that to God I might live.
I have been crucified with Christ,
and I live no longer I,
but Christ lives in me.
And what I live now in the flesh,
I live by faith in the Son of God,
loving me and giving up himself on my behalf.
I do not set aside the grace of God,
for if justification comes through law,
then Christ died for no reason.

Let us bless the Lord. *Thanks be to God.*

FRIDAY PROPHETS

My life flows on in end-less song
A-bove earth's lam-en-ta-tion.
I hear that near and far-off hymn,
It hails a new cre-a-tion:
Thru all the tu-mult and the strife
I hear that mu-sic ring-ing;
It finds an ech-o\ in my soul;
How can I keep from sing-ing?

What though my joys and com-forts fade
The Lord my Sa-vior liv-eth;
What though the shad-ows gath-er round
Songs in the night he giv-eth:
No storm can shake my in-most calm,
While to that ref-uge cling-ing;
Since Christ is Lord of\ heav'n and earth,
How can I keep from sing-ing?

I lift my eyes; the clouds grow thin;
I see the blue a-bove it;
And day by day clears way the path
Since first I learned to love it:
The peace of Christ makes fresh my heart,
A foun-tain ev-er spring-ing;
All things are mine since\ I am his;
How can I keep from sing-ing?

Text: Robert Lowry, 1860, altered
Music: 87 87, ENDLESS SONG, Quaker Hymn; Robert Lowry, 1860

ISAIAH 45:15-25

Antiphon *The kingdom of God
is justice and peace
and joy in the Holy Spirit.*   Rom 14:17

Truly, God, you hide yourself,
Saving God of Israel.
Makers of idols will know shame and disgrace,
all going off together in disgrace.

Israel will be saved by Adonai,
salvation everlasting.
You will not know shame
or disgrace to the ages.

For this says Adonai,
the one creating the heavens,
God who fashioned and made
and formed the earth,
creating it to be not an empty waste,
but formed to be inhabited,

"I am your Lord,
 and there is no other.
 Not in secret did I speak,
 from some place in a dark land,

 not saying to descendants of Jacob,
 'seek me in vain.'
 I, your Lord, speak justice
 and delare right things.

Gather together and come!
Assemble together, fugitives of the nations.
Those who carry idols of wood do not know:
they are praying to no-gods that cannot save.

Declare and present!
Let them counsel together!
Who foretold this from long ago?
Who declared this from the distant past?

Not I, your Lord?
There is no god apart from me,
God righteous and Saving;
there is none but me.

Turn to me and be saved,
all you ends of the earth,
for I am God and there is no other.

By myself I swore
integrity out of my mouth,
the word that will not be revoked.

Indeed, in front of me every knee will bow,
and every tongue will swear, and say,
'In our Lord alone are justice and strength,'

to whom will come and be shamed
all who have raged otherwise."
In Adonai they will be found righteous
and all the descendants of Israel will exult.

Glory…

                                              Antiphon

HABAKKUK 3:2-4,13a,15-19

Antiphon *Looking round on them with anger,*
Jesus grieved at their hardness of heart. Mk 3:5

Adonai, I heard your fame;
I stand in awe of your deeds, Adonai.
Now, in the midst of years, renew them!
In the midst of years, make them known!
Even in wrath you remember mercy.

Eloah came from Teman,
the Holy One from the Mount of Paran.
The heavens are covered with glory
and the earth is filled with praise

like the splendor of the rays of the sunrise
or the hand from a hiding place of power…
You came out to deliver your people,
to deliver your anointed one…

You trample on the sea,
your horses churning up the great waters.
I heard my heart and she trembled,
at the sound my lips quivered;

decay crept into my bones and my legs trembled.
Yet, I will wait patiently for the day,
calamity to come on the nation invading.

Though the fig tree does not bud
and there is no fruit on the vine,
the crops of the olive fail
and terraces produce no food,

the sheep cut themselves off from the fold
and there is no herd in the stalls,
yet will I rejoice in my Lord
and be joyful in the God of my salvation.

Sovereign Adonai, my strength,
makes my feet like that of the deer,
makes me go to the heights.

Glory...

                                                                             Antiphon

JEREMIAH 14:17b-22

Antiphon   *Before I formed you in the womb*
              I knew you.   Jer 1:5

Let my eyes overflow with tears
by night, by day, without cease,
for the grievous wounds suffered
by the virgin daughter of my people,
a very crushing blow.

If I go out in the country, see: ones slain by sword!
If I go into the city, see: the ravages of famine!
Indeed, both prophet and priest
have gone to a land they do not know.

To reject you rejected Judah?
Is Zion loathsome to you?
Why have you afflicted us
so we have no healing?

JEREMIAH 14:17b-22, continued

Our hope is for peace, but no good happens;
for a time of healing, but see: the terror!
We are aware, Adonai, of our no-good ways
and the guilt of our ancestors;
indeed we ourselves sin against you.

For the sake of your Name, neither reject us
nor dishonor the throne of your glory.
Remember, and break not your covenant with us!
Is there one among the worthless nations
that can bring rain or send showers from the skies?

Is that One not you, our God Adonai?
And so we hope in you,
for you do all these things.

Glory…

Antiphon *Before I formed you in the womb
I knew you.* Jer 1:5

TOBIT 13:8-11,13-15

Antiphon *One of the seven angels
showed me the holy city of Jerusalem
shining with the glory of God.* Rev 21:10,11

Acknowledge the Lord in Jerusalem.
You Jerusalem, Holy City, will be scourged
for the idol-works of your children.
The Lord will again have mercy
on the children of the righteous.

Acknowledge the Lord as is deserving
and bless the King of the ages,
that your tabernacle will be built in you again
with joy and cheer by all who were exiles,
and love for all generations
those who were distressed.

A bright light will shine to all the ends of the earth;
many nations will come from far away.
The inhabitants of the most remote parts of earth
will come to your holy Name
bearing in their hands gifts for the King of Heaven.

Generation to generation will give joyful praise
and the name of the Lord will be great forever…

Then, children of the righteous,
rejoice and exult and be gathered together
and bless the Lord of the ages.

Happy are those who love you
and happy will be those who rejoice in your peace.

Happy also are all who grieve over your afflictions
for they will rejoice with you
and give witness to your joy forever.

My soul, bless the Lord,
the great King.

Glory…

Antiphon

READING — **TOBIT 4:15a,16a,18a,19**

What you yourself dislike
do not do to anyone else.
Give some of your food to the hungry
and some of your clothing to the naked.
Seek advice from every wise person.
At all times bless and ask the Lord God
that your ways may be made straight
and that your plans may prosper.

RESPONSORY — Psalm 25:4

Push and pull my heart…   *…as is your will, my Lord.*

Keep my feet on your path…   *…as is your will, my Lord.*

Glory to the Father and to Son and to the Holy Spirit:
   …Push and pull my heart, as is your will, my Lord.

Let us bless the Lord.   *Thanks be to God.*

FRIDAY MORNING

+ *God, come to my assistance;*   Psalm 70:2
  Lord, make haste to help me!

Glory...

O Sa-cred Head, sur-round-ed
By crown of pierc\-ing thorn.
O Bleed-ing Head, so wound-ed,
Re-viled and put\ to scorn.
Our sins\ have marred the glo-ry
Of your most ho-ly Face,
Yet an/-gel hosts a-dor-ing
And trem-ble as they gaze.

I see your strength and vig-or
And death with cru-el rigor,
O ag\-o-ny and dy-ing!
Je-sus/, all grace sup-ply-ing,
All fa-ding in\ the strife,
Be-reav-ing you\ of life;
O love to sin-ner's free!
O turn your face on me.

In this, your bit-ter pass-ion,
Good Shep-herd, think\ of me
With your most sweet com-pass-ion,
un-wor-thy though\ I be:
Be-neath\ your cross a-bi-ding
For ev-er would I rest,
In your/ dear love con-fi-ding,
And in your pres-ence blest.

Text: Ascribed to Saint Bernard of Clairvaux, 1091-1153;
translated by Henry Baker, 1821-77
Music: 76 76 D, PASSION CHORALE; Hans Leo Hassler, 1601

PSALM 51

Antiphon   *If anyone serves me,*
            that one the Father will honor.   Jn 12:26b

Have mercy on me, O God,
in accord with your loving mercy;
in accord with the greatness of your compassion
blot out my transgressions.

Wash me of my guilt
and cleanse me from my sin,
for I know my transgressions
and my sin is before me always.

Against you yourself I sinned;
what I did is evil in your eyes.
You are proven right when you speak
and justified when you judge.
Surely we are sinners from birth,
from conception in a mother's womb.

Surely you desire truth in our inner parts;
in my inmost place you teach me wisdom.
You cleanse me with hyssop and I will be clean;
you wash me and I will be whiter than snow…

You let me hear joy and gladness;
let the bones you let be crushed now rejoice.
Hide your faces from my sins
and blot out all my iniquities.

A pure heart create in me, O God!
Renew inside me a spirit to be steadfast.
Do not cast me from your presences,
nor take from me your Holy Spirit.

Restore to me the joy of your salvation
and sustain in me a willing spirit.
I will teach transgressors your ways
and sinners will turn back to you.

Save me from bloodguilt, O God,
God of my salvation;
my tongue will sing of your justice.
Lord, open my lips
and my mouth will declare your praise.

Sacrifices give you no delight;
I could bring a burnt offering,
but it would give you no pleasure.
The sacrifices, God, you will not despise
are a contrite spirit and a humble heart.

Make Zion prosper in your pleasure,
and build up the walls of Jerusalem.
Then you will delight in the sacrifice of the just,
burnt offerings and whole offerings,
bulls offered on your altar.

Glory…

                                                Antiphon

PSALM 26

Antiphon *The tax collectors and prostitutes*
are going into the kingdom of God
before you.   Mt 21:31

Vindicate me, Adonai,
for I have walked in my life with integrity
and in Adonai I trusted without waver.

Search me, Adonai! And try me!
Examine my heart and my mind!
For your mercy is before my eyes
and I walk in your truth.

I do not sit with humans of deceit
nor consort with hypocrites.
I abhor the assembly of those who do evil
and do not sit with those who do wicked.

I wash my hands in innocence
and go about your altar, Adonai,
to proclaim a voice of praise
and to tell of all your wonderful deeds.

Adonai, I love the refuge of your house,
the dwelling place of your glory.

Take not my soul away with sinners
nor my life with people doing bloody things,
those who scheme in their hands
with their right hand full of bribes.

FRIDAY MORNING

But I walk in my life with integrity.
Redeem me! Be merciful to me!
My foot stands on level ground;
in great assemblies I will bless Adonai.

Glory…

Antiphon

PSALM 100

Antiphon — *Go to the lost sheep
of the house of Israel.*   Mt 10:6

Shout for joy to Adonai, all you earth!
Serve Adonai with gladness!
Come into the presence with joyful song.

Know that Adonai is God, who made us,
whose people we are,
in whose pasture we are the sheep.

Enter the gates with thanksgiving,
go into the courts with praise!
Give thanks and bless the Name!

Good is Adonai,
merciful to forever and faithful
through generations and generation.

Glory…

Antiphon

PSALM 28:1-3,6-9

Antiphon *Pray for all, even kings and those in authority,*
so our living may be
in quiet devotion and dignity. 1 Tim 2:2

To you I call, my Rock Adonai,
turn not to me a deaf ear.
For if you remain silent, away from me,
then I will be like one going into the pit.

Hear the sound of my cries for help
calling to you for help as I lift my hands
toward the Holy Place of your Holiness.

Do not drag me away with those who do bad,
who speak peace with their neighbors
but with malice in their heart.

Blessed be Adonai,
who heard the sound of my cries.

Adonai, my strength and my shield,
in whom my heart trusts,
I am helped and my heart leaps for joy
and in my song I will give thanks.

Adonai is the strength
and the saving refuge of the anointed.
Save your people! Bless your inheritance!
Be their shepherd and carry them to forever!

Glory...

Antiphon

PSALM 133

Antiphon　　*The multitude of believers*
　　　　　　was heart and soul one.　　Acts 4:32a

See how good
and how pleasant it is
to live as brothers and sisters,
united together.

Like the precious oil
running down on the head
and on the beard of Aaron,
running down on his collar and robes,

as if the dew of Hermon
was falling on Mount Zion,
there Adonai bestows
the blessing of life to forever.

Glory…

　　　　　　　　　　　　　　　　　　　　Antiphon

PSALM 147:1-11

Antiphon *Let me preach also in the villages near.* Mk 1:38

Hallelujah! Praise Adonai!
How good it is to sing praise to our God!
How pleasant and fitting to give praise!

Adonai builds up Jerusalem,
gathers Israel's exiles,
heals the ones with broken hearts
and binds up their wounds,
determines the number of the stars,
and calls to each of them by name.

Great and mighty in power is our Lord,
with unlimited understanding.
Adonai sustains the humble
and throws wickedness to the dust.
Sing to Adonai with thanksgiving!

Make music on the harp to our God,
who covers the skies with clouds
and supplies rain to the earth,
making grass to grow on the hills,
providing food for the cattle
and young ravens when they call.

Adonai finds pleasure
not in the strength of the horse
nor delight in the legs of the human,
but is delighting in those who fear Adonai
who hope in the unfailing mercy.

Glory...   Antiphon

PSALM 147:12-20

Antiphon *I am the living bread from heaven;*
anyone who eats of this bread
will live to the eon. Jn 6:51a

Extol Adonai, Jerusalem!
Zion, now give praise!

Your God strengthens the bars of your gates,
blesses your peoples within you,
grants peace to your border,
and satisfies you with finest of wheat.

Your God sends a command to the earth,
and in swiftness runs a word,
spreading snow like the wool
and scattering frost like the ash.

Hail is hurled like pebbles;
who can stand before the icy blast?
The word of the Lord is sent, and they melt;
wind stirs up and the waters flow.

The word of the Lord is revealed to Jacob,
decrees and laws of the Lord to Israel.
Not for any nation did the Lord do this;
they do not know these laws.
Hallelujah! Praise Adonai!

Glory...

Antiphon

READING — **EPHESIANS 4:25-32**

Put off the lie, and speak the truth to each neighbor,
for we are members of one another.
If you become angry, do not sin;
do not let the sun set on provocation,
and do not give a place for the diabolo.
Let the thief steal no more;
rather let the former stealer labor
working with his or her own hands, the good thing,
to share with the one who has need.
Keep every corrupt word
from coming out of your mouth,
but let the word be heard
that gives grace to the hearer who needs building up.
And do not grieve the Holy Spirit of God,
by whom you were sealed for the day of redemption.
Let all bitterness and rage and anger and fighting
and blasphemy be removed from you, with all evil.
Be kind to one another, tenderhearted,
and forgive yourselves
as also God in Christ has forgiven you.

RESPONSORY — Ps 143:8

Bring word at break of day…   …*in your unfailing love.*

Show the way for me to go…   …*in your unfailing love.*

Glory to the Father and to the Son and to the Holy Spirit:
   …*Bring word at break of day, in your unfailing love.*

FRIDAY MORNING

GOSPEL READING OF THE DAY or GOSPEL CANTICLE

Antiphon *God chose to visit God's people
and brought redemption.*

CANTICLE OF ZECHARIAH **LUKE 1:68-79**

+ Blessed be the Lord the God of Israel
who chose a people,
visited them to bring redemption,
and raised salvation in the house of David,
saving strength from God's own servant,

speaking from the age of the prophets
through the mouth of the holy prophet:
Salvation out of enmity,
even out of those who hate us,

to show our ancestors how mercy works,
and to remember the holy promise of the Lord,
the covenant made for our father Abraham,
calming our fear and making us free
to serve God as holy and righteous and just
in the Lord's presence all our days.

And you also child
will be called a prophet of the Most High
for you will go before the Lord to prepare his way
and give to his people a knowledge of salvation
known in accepting forgiveness of their sins.

From the deepness of God's mercy on us,
a sun rising from the height will visit to appear
to those who sit in the dark or shadow of death,
and to guide our feet into the way of peace.

Gospel Reading for Friday of

Week			
1	Mark 2:1-12	13 Matt 9:9-13	25 Luke 9:18-22
2	Mark 3:13-19	14 Matt 10:16-23	26 Lk 10:13-16
3	Mark 4:26-34	15 Matt 12:1-8	27 Lk 11:15-26
4	Mark 6:14-29	16 Matt 13:18-23	28 Luke 12:1-7
5	Mark 7:31-37	17 Matt 13:54-58	29 Lk 12:54-59
6	Mark 8:34 - 9:1	18 Matt 16:24-28	30 Luke 14:1-6
7	Mark 10:1-12	19 Matt 19:3-12	31 Luke 16:1-8
8	Mark 11:11-26	20 Matt 22:34-40	32 Lk 17:26-37
9	Mark 12:35-37	21 Matt 25:1-13	33 Lk 19:45-48
10	Matt 5:27-32	22 Luke 5:33-39	34 Lk 21:29-33
11	Matt 6:19-23	23 Luke 6:39-42	
12	Matt 8:1-4	24 Luke 8:1-3	

Glory...

Antiphon *God chose to visit God's people and brought redemption.*

PETITIONS FOR THE CONSECRATION TO GOD OF THE DAY AND ITS WORK

- For the Church and her ministry and apostolates...
- For secular authorities and all serving as stewards...
- For people who are poor or sick or in sorrow...
- For peace and the basic needs of each human being...
- For guardian angel intercession for those considering use of violence...
- For any elders or children who feel abandoned...
- In gratitude for blessings and grace...

OUR FATHER...

+ *May the Lord bless us, protect us from all evil, and bring us to everlasting life.* **Amen**.

FRIDAY DAYTIME

+ *God, come to my assistance;* Psalm 70:2
  Lord, make haste to help me!

  Glory...

Let all mor-tal flesh keep\ si-lence,
And with fear and trem-bling\ stand;
Pon-der noth-ing earth-ly\ mind-ed,
For with bless-ing in his\ hand,
Christ our God to earth de-scend//\-eth,
Our full hom-age to de/-mand.

King of kings, yet born of\ Ma-ry,
As of old on earth he\ stood,
Lord of lords, in hu-man\ ves-ture,
In the bo-dy and the\ blood;
He will give to all the faith//\-ful
His own self for heav-en-ly food.

Rank on rank the host of\ heav-en
Spreads its van-guard on the\ Way,
As the Light of light de\-scend-eth
From the realms of end-less\ day,
That the pow'rs of hell may van//\-ish
As the dark-ness clears a/-way.

Text: *Liturgy of St. James*, 5th Century; translated from Greek
by Gerard Moultrie, 1864
Music: 87 87 87 PICARDY, *Chansons Populaires
des Provinces de France*, 1860

PSALM 119:113-120
Samekh

Antiphon *Joy in heaven over one sinner repenting will exceed that over ninety-nine of the righteous with no need of repentance.*

Lk 15:7

I hate double-minded hypocrisy
but love your law.
My refuge and my shield,
in your word I put my hope.

Go away from me, doers of badness,
that I may keep my God's commands.
Sustain me as is your promise
and I will live.
Disappoint me not in my hope.

Hold me up and I will be delivered
and contemplate always your decrees.
You reject those who stray from your decrees
for vain is their deceit.

As dross you discard bad doers of earth
so I love your statutes.
My flesh trembles in fear of you;
I stand in awe of your laws.

Glory...

Antiphon

PSALM 119:121-128
Ayin

Antiphon *Unless the grain of wheat
falling to the ground dies,
it remains one grain;
but if it dies, it bears much fruit.* Jn 12:24

I have done righteousness and justice;
abandon me not to oppression.
Ensure the welfare of your servant;
let not the arrogance oppress me.

My eyes long to see your salvation
and the promise of your righteousness.
Deal with your servant as is your mercy
and teach me your decrees.

I am your servant, give me discernment
to understand your statutes.
They break your law;
it is time for Adonai to act.

For this I love your commands
more than gold, even pure gold;
for this I consider all your precepts right:
I hate every wrong path.

Glory...

Antiphon

PSALM 119:129-136
Pe

Antiphon   *When I am lifted up from the earth,*
              I will draw everyone to myself.   Jn 12:32

Your statutes are wonderful;
for this my self obeys them.
Your words enter giving light,
giving understanding to the simple.

I open my mouth in a sigh,
longing for your commands.
Turn to me with your grace,
your custom to lovers of your name.

Direct my footsteps by your word
and over me let no sin rule.
Redeem me from human oppression
that I may obey your precepts.

Shine your faces on your servant!
And teach me your decrees!
Streams of tears flow down my eyes
over disobedience to your law.

Glory...

                                                      Antiphon

PSALM 22

Antiphon *I am the true vine*
and my Father is the vinegrower.   Jn 15:1

My God, my God,
why have you abandoned me?
Far from my salvation
are the words of my groan.
My God, I cry out by day,
but you do not answer;
nor is silent my night.

Yet you Holy One are enthroned, praises Israel.
In you our ancestors trusted and were delivered.
To you they cried and they were saved.
In you they trusted and were not disappointed.

But I am a worm and not human,
the scorn of humanity and despised by people.
All those seeing me mock at me;
they shake their heads in insult:
"In the one you trust,
 let your Adonai rescue you;
 let the one who 'delights' in you deliver you!"

You brought me out from the womb,
to trust in you at the breasts of my mother.
From the womb I was cast upon you;
from the womb of my mother, you are my God.
Be not far from me,
for trouble is near with no one to help.

PSALM 22, continued

Many bulls surround me;
the strong of Bashan encircle me.
They open wide their mouths against me,
lions tearing up prey and roaring.

Like the waters I am poured out
and my bones are all out of joint.
My heart like wax
melts away within my insides.

Like a broken clay pot, my strength is dried up,
and my tongue is stuck in the roof of my mouth;
you lay me in the dust of death.

Dogs indeed surround around me,
a band of bad doers encircles me as a lion
ready to tear into my hands and my feet.

I can count all of my bones;
they stare and they gloat over me.
They divide my garments among them
and for my clothing they cast lots.

But you, Adonai, be not far off;
come quickly to help me, my Strength!
Deliver my soul from the sword
and from the power of the dog.
Rescue me from the mouth of the lion
and from the horns of wild oxen.

I will declare your name
to my brothers and sisters
and praise you in the assembly.

You fearing Adonai, give praise!
All you descendants of Jacob, give honor!
All you descendants of Israel, give reverence
before Adonai, who despised not, nor disdained,
nor hid the holy face from those suffering affliction,
but heard their cry for help.

From you is my praise within the great assembly;
my vows will I fulfill before those who fear you.
The poor anawim will eat to satisfaction,
and the seekers will praise Adonai;
may your heart live to forever.

All the ends of the earth will remember
and turn to Adonai,
and all the families of nations will bow down,
for to Adonai is the dominion, ruling over nations.

All those rich on the earth
will feast and worship and kneel,
all who go down to the dust,
all who cannot keep their own self alive.

Those to come will be served by being told,
and in the same way serve generations to come.
They will come and they will proclaim
the deeds of deliverance done by the Lord,
the story, to people yet to be born.

Glory...

Antiphon	*I am the true vine and my Father is the vinegrower.*	Jn 15:1

PSALM 59:2-5,10-11,17-18

Antiphon *The Kingdom of heaven is like a merchant*
who seeking fine pearls finds one precious pearl
and going away sells everything and buys it.
Mt 13:45,46

Deliver me from enmity;
protect me, God,
from those who rise up against me.
Deliver me from those who do evil
and save me from people of bloody ways.

See, they lie in wait for my life;
fierce people conspire against me
for no offense of me nor sin, Adonai.
For no wrong they make ready to attack;
arise to help me and look!...

For you, my Strength, I watch,
for you God, my fortress, you God are my love.

God will go before me
and gloat over ones who slander...

But I will sing of your strength
and I will sing in the morning of your mercy,
for you are my fortress
and my refuge in times of trouble.

To you, my Strength, I sing praise
for you God, my fortress, you God are my love.

Glory...

Antiphon

PSALM 60:3-14a

Antiphon *Do not judge,
lest you be judged.* Mt 7:1

God you rejected us and burst forth upon us;
you were angry, now revive us.

You shook the land and tore her open;
mend her fractures, for she quakes!
You showed your people a desperate time;
you made us drink wine to staggering.

For those who revere you, you raised a banner
to be unfurled against the bow,
that your beloved ones may be delivered.
Help us with your right hand and save us!

God spoke from the sanctuary:
"I will triumph and parcel out Shechem,
 and measure out the valley of Succoth;
 mine are Gilead and Manasseh,

 Ephraim my head helmet,
 Judah my scepter,
 and Moab my washbasin;
 On Edom I toss my sandal
 and over Philistia I shout in triumph."

Who will bring me to the Rock City?
Who will lead me into Edom?
Have you, God, not rejected us,
and not gone out, God, with our armies?

PSALM 60:3-14a, continued

Against enmity give to us aid,
For worthless is human help.
In the help of God
will we gain the victory…

Glory…

Antiphon *Do not judge,
lest you be judged.* Mt 7:1

PSALM 140:1-9,13-14

Antiphon *Blessed are you
when they disrespect and persecute
and tell all the lies against you for my sake;
rejoice and be glad,
for great is your reward in the heavens.* Mt 5:11

Rescue me, Adonai,
from humans doing badness;
protect me from humans of violence
who devise bad things in their hearts
and stir up wars every day.

They sharpen their tongues
like that of a serpent,
viper venom on their lips.

Keep me, Adonai,
from the hands of bad doers;
protect me from humans of violence
who plan to trip up my feet.

Proud ones have hidden a snare for me,
spread a net of ropes,
and set a trap for me
at the side of the path.

I say to Adonai, "You are my God!"
Hear, Adonai, the cry of my cries!
Lord Adonai, strength of my deliverance,
you shield over my head in the day of conflict.

Grant not, Adonai,
the desires of bad doers;
let not their plans succeed
or they will become proud…

I know that Adonai secures
justice for the poor
and the cause of the needy.
Surely the righteous will praise your Name;
the upright will live before your faces.

Glory…

Antiphon

READING **ROMANS 15:1-6**

We who are strong ought to bear the weaknesses
of those who are not strong,
and not to please ourselves.
Let each one of us please his or her neighbor
for good and for building up,
for even Christ pleased not himself.
As it has been written,
The reproaches of those reproaching you fell on me.
What was written for our teaching
was written that through patience
and through the comfort of the writings
we may have hope.
May the God of patience and comfort give to you
the same mind among yourselves
in accord with Christ Jesus.

RESPONSORY Rev 1:5,6

Loving us, Christ washed away our sins…
…in his own blood;

making us a kingdom and priests to our God…
…in his own blood;

Glory to the Father and to the Son and to the Holy Spirit:
*…Loving us, Christ washed away our sins,
in his own blood;*

Lord\, have mer-cy.
Christ\, have mer-cy.
Lord\, have mer-cy.

FRIDAY EVENING

+ *God, come to my assistance;*   Psalm 70:2
  Lord, make haste to help me!

Glory…

When/ I sur\-vey the/ **won**-drous cross
On which the Prince of glo-ry died,
My rich-est/ gain\ I count\ as loss,
And pour con-tempt on all my pride.

For/-bid it\, Lord, that/ I should boast,
Save in the death of Christ my God!
May all vain/ things\ that charm\ me most,
Be sac-ri-ficed as with his blood.

Were/ the whole\ realm of/ na-ture mine,
That trea-sure would be far too small;
Love so a/-ma\-zing, so\ div-ine,
De-mands my soul, my life, my all.

Text: Isaac Watts, *Hymns and Spiritual Songs*, 1707, altered
Music option: ERHALT UNS HERR, LM;
Klug's *Geistliche Lieder*, 1543;
Popular melody for: *The Glory Of These Forty Days*

PSALM 41

Antiphon *Is it easier to say to the paralytic,*
your sins are forgiven,
or to say, rise and walk?
That you may know that the Son of humanity
has authority to forgive sins on earth,
to you paralyzed I say,
'Rise; take your mat and go to your house.'

Mk 2:9-11

Blessed is the one concerned for the poor.
In the time of trouble Adonai will deliver.
Adonai will protect that one's life,
preserve it blessed in the land,
and give no surrender to the desire of foes.

Adonai will sustain on the sickbed,
and restore on that bed from all illness.
Adonai, take notice!
Heal my being for I have sinned against you!
Enmity asks in malice:

"When will that one die and the name perish?"
When they come to see me,
they speak with false hearts and gather slander,
and then go out to the outside to gossip.

Together against me they whisper,
imagining the worst for me:
"A vile disease has set in;
  that one will not recover."

Even my close friend
has lifted the heel against me,
the human being I trusted,
who ate my own bread.

But you, Adonai, take notice
and raise me up that I may repay them.
In this I know that with me you are pleased:
enmity does not triumph over my being.

In my integrity you hold me up
and set me in your presences to forever.

Blessed be Adonai, God of Israel,
from everlasting to the everlasting.
Amen and amen.

Glory… Antiphon

PSALM 46

Antiphon *Do you want to be whole?* Jn 5:6

God is our refuge and strength,
our help in troubles, ever present.
And so we will not fear,
even if earth were to give way,

even if mountains were to fall
into the heart of the sea,
even if sea waters foam
or mountains quake with their surging.

PSALM 46, continued

River streams make glad God's city,
the holy dwelling place of the Most High.
God is inside her and she will not fall.
God will help her at break of day.

Nations are in uproar, kingdoms fall;
the earth melts at the voice of God.
Adonai Sabaoth is with us;
the God of Jacob is our fortress.

Come and see the works of Adonai,
the desolations brought on the earth:
making wars to cease to the ends of the earth,
breaking the bow and shattering the spear
and burning with fire the chariot and shield.

"Be still! And know that I am God.
 I will be exalted among the nations;
 I will be exalted on the earth."

Adonai Sabaoth is with us;
the God of Jacob is our fortress.

Glory…

Antiphon *Do you want to be whole?* Jn 5:6

PSALM 121

Antiphon *But when the Son of humanity comes,*
will he find faith on earth?   Lk 18:8

I lift up my eyes to the hills.
From where does my help come?
My help is from and with Adonai,
Maker of heavens and earth,

who will not let your foot slip
nor slumber when watching over you.
Indeed the one watching over Israel
will not slumber and will not sleep.

Adonai watches over you,
your shade at your right hand.
By day the sun will not harm you,
nor the moon by the night.

Adonai will keep you from all harm
and watch over your soul.
Adonai will watch over your going and coming
from now and to forevermore.

Glory…

Antiphon

PSALM 135

Antiphon *What is the profit for a human
to gain the whole world
but lose his or her life?* Mt 16:26

Hallelujah! Praise Adonai!
Praise the name of Adonai!
Servants of Adonai, give praise!
You who minister in the house of Adonai,
in the courts of the house of our God,

praise Adonai, for good is Adonai!
Sing praise to the Name, for it is pleasant!
Adonai has chosen Jacob,
Israel the chosen treasure.

For I know that great is our Lord;
greater than all the "gods" is Adonai,
who does as Adonai pleases
in the heavens and on earth
and in the deep sea,

making storms to rise
from the ends of the earth,
sending lightning with the rain,
and bringing wind from the storehouses,

who struck down the firstborn of Egypt,
from human to beast,
sending signs and wonders to the midst of Egypt
against Pharaoh and against all of his servants,

FRIDAY EVENING

having struck down many nations and mighty kings:
Sihon, king of the Amorites,
and Og of Bashan,
and all the kingdoms of Canaan,
who gave their land as an inheritance,
an inheritance to Israel, the people of Adonai.

Your name, Adonai, is to forever,
your renown to generation and generation,
for you, Adonai, will defend your people
and will have compassion on your servants.

Idols of the nations are silver and gold,
the making of human hands.
A mouth to them but they cannot speak.
Eyes to them but they cannot see.

Ears to them but they cannot hear,
and there is no breath in their mouth.
Like them will be their makers
and all who trust in them.

House of Israel, bless Adonai!
House of Aaron, bless Adonai!
House of Levi, bless Adonai!
You who fear Adonai, bless Adonai!

Blessed be Adonai from Zion,
dwelling in Jerusalem.
Hallelujah! Praise Adonai!

Glory...

Antiphon

PSALM 145

Antiphon *The Son of humanity came
to seek and to save the lost.*   Lk 19:10

I will exalt you, my God the King,
and I will bless your Name to forever and ever.

In every day I will bless you
and I will extol your Name to forever and ever.
Great is Adonai, and greatly being praised,
an unfathomable greatness.

Generation to generation commend your works
and tell of your mighty acts
and the glorious splendor of your majesty,
and I will meditate on your wonderful deeds.

They will tell of the power of your awesome works
and I will proclaim your great deed.
They will celebrate and remember
the abundance of your goodness
and they will sing of your justice.

Gracious and compassionate is Adonai,
slow of angers and rich in mercy.
Good to all is Adonai,
whose compassions are on all who are made.

All whom you have made will thank you, Adonai,
and all your saints will bless you.
They will tell of the glory of your kingdom
and speak your might to make known

to sons and daughters of humanity your mighty acts
and the glorious splendor of your kingdom.
Your kingdom is the kingdom of all the everlastings
and your dominion is through all
generation and generation.

Adonai is faithful to all the promises
and loving to all who are made.
Adonai upholds all who are falling
and lifts up all who are being bowed.

The eyes of all look to you
and you give them their food in the season,
opening wide your hand and satisfying
the desire of every living thing.

Just is Adonai in all ways,
merciful to all who are made.
Near is Adonai to all who call,
to all who call in truth.

Fulfilled is the desire
of all who fear and love Adonai,
who hears their cry and saves them
and watches over them.
But wicked ways will be destroyed.

My mouth will speak praise of Adonai.
Let every creature bless the holy Name
to forever and ever.

Glory…

                                                        Antiphon

REVELATION 15:3b-4

Antiphon   *They sang the song*
            of Moses, the servant of God
            and the song of the Lamb.

Rev 15:3a

Great and wonderful are your works,
Lord God Almighty.
Just and true are your ways,
King of the nations.

Who will not fear, O Lord,
or glorify your name?
You alone are holy.

All the nations will come
and worship before you;
your ordinances are shown to all.

Glory...

Antiphon

READING   **1 CORINTHIANS 2:1-16**

Coming to you, brothers and sisters, I came without excellence of speech or of wisdom announcing to you the testimony of God. For I decided to know nothing among you except Jesus Christ, and this one having been crucified. And I was with you in weakness and fear and much trembling.

My speech and kerygma-proclamation was not persuasive words of wisdom, but a demonstration of spirit and power, that your faith may be not in human wisdom but in the power of God.

We speak wisdom among the mature, but wisdom not of this eon, nor of the leaders of this eon being brought to naught. But we speak of God, a wisdom in mystery, hidden, which God foreordained before the ages for our glory, which none of the leaders of this age has known. For if they knew, they would not have crucified the Lord of glory. But as it has been written,

things which eye has not seen and ear has not heard
and have not come upon the human heart,
how many are prepared for those loving God,

this is revealed to us by God through the Spirit. For the Spirit searches all things, even the deep things of God. Who of human beings knows the things of a human except the spirit in that human? So also no one has known the things of God except the Spirit of God. We have not received the spirit of the cosmos but the Spirit from God, that we may know the things freely given to us by God, which we also speak not in teach-

1 CORINTHIANS 2:1-16, continued

ing of human words of wisdom, but in teaching of the Spirit comparing spiritual things with spiritual things.

A natural human does not receive the things of the Spirit of God, for they are folly to one who cannot know what is discerned spiritually. But the spiritual human discerns on one hand all things; on the other the Spirit is discerned by no one: *For who has known the mind of the Lord and so who will instruct?* But we have the mind of Christ.

RESPONSORY 1 Cor 15:3; Rom 5:8; 1 Ptr 3:18

Christ died for our sins… …*while we were still sinners.*

Put to death, he rose to life in the Spirit…
  …*while we were still sinners.*

Glory to the Father and to the Son and to the Holy Spirit:
  …*Christ died for our sins, while we were still sinners.*

GOSPEL CANTICLE OF MARY **LUKE 1:46-55**

Antiphon *Remember your mercy, Lord.*

+ My soul is stretched full with praise of the Lord,
  and my spirit, beyond joy in God, my Savior,
  who chose to lay eyes on this humble servant.

FRIDAY EVENING

Behold, now and forward,
each and every age will call me blessed,
for the Mighty One did great things to me.
Holy is the name and the mercy
to generations and generations,
the ones fearing the One,

Who scattered the haughty of mind and heart,
pulled the powerful off their high place,
and lifted with dignity the humble in need.

The hungering are filled with good things,
the rich are sent away empty,
and servant Israel is given relief

with a memory of mercy to remember,
the promise spoken to our ancestors,
to Abraham and his descendants forever.

Glory…

Antiphon

INTERCESSIONS
- For all who have died…

- In gratitude for blessings…; Abba thank you.
- For the sins of this day…; Lord Jesus have mercy.
- With concerns over tomorrow…; Holy Spirit help.

OUR FATHER…

+ *May the Lord bless us, protect us from all evil,*
and bring us to everlasting life. **Amen**.

FRIDAY NIGHT

+ *God, come to my assistance;*   Psalm 70:2
Lord, make haste to help me!

Glory…

Text: Horatius Bonar, *Hymns Original and Selected*, 1846, altered
Music: KINGSFOLD, CMD, trad. English melody,
adapted by Ralph Vaughan Williams, 1906

I\ heard the voice of Je-sus say,
"Come/ un-to me\ and rest;
Lay\ down, you wea-ry one, lay down
Your/ head up-on\ my breast."
I/ came to Je\-sus as I was,
So/ wea-ry\, worn and sad;
I\ found in him a rest-ing place,
And/ he has made\ me glad.

I\ heard the voice of Je-sus say,
"Be/-hold, I free\-ly give
The\ liv-ing wa-ter; thirs-ty one,
Stoop/ down, and drink\ and live."
I/ came to Je\-sus, and I drank
Of/ that life\-giv-ing stream.
My\ thirst was quenched, my soul re-vived,
And/ now I live\ in him.

FRIDAY NIGHT

I\ heard the voice of Je-sus say,
"I/ am this dark\ world's light;
Look\ un-to me, your morn shall rise
And/ all your day\ be bright."
I/ looked to Je\-sus, and I found
In/ him my\ star, my sun;
And\ in that light of life I'll walk,
Till/ trav'l-ing days\ are done.

PSALM 88

Antiphon *Leave the dead to bury their own dead;*
you go proclaim the kingdom of God. Lk 9:60

Adonai, Elohay, my Savior,
I cry out day and night before you.
May my prayer come before you;
turn your ear to my cry.

My soul is full of troubles
and my life draws near to Sheol.
I am counted among those going down to the pit,
like a human with no strength,

set apart with the dead ones
like slain ones lying in the grave,
whom you no longer remember,
whom are cut off from your care.

PSALM 88, continued

You put me in the pit of the lowest,
in the darkest deep.
Your anger lies heavy upon me
and all your waves overwhelm.

You took away my friends
and made me repulsive to them;
in confinement I cannot escape.
My eye is dim from grief;
I call to you, Adonai,
and in every day stretch my hands to you.

Is it to the dead ones you show wonder?
Do the dead rise up and praise you?
Is your mercy declared in the grave
or your fidelity in the no-more?
Is your wonder known in the darkness
or your righteous deeds in the land of oblivion?

But to you, Adonai, I cry for help
and in the morning my prayer comes before you.
Why do you reject my soul, Adonai?
Why hide your faces from me?

Afflicted and coming close
to death and despairing,
from youth I have suffered your terrors.
Your anger has swept over me
and your terrors have destroyed me.

> They surround me all the day like the floods,
> engulfing over me completely.
> You took far away my loving companion;
> my one friend is darkness.

Glory…

| Antiphon | *Leave the dead to bury their own dead; you go proclaim the kingdom of God.* | Lk 9:60 |

READING **ROMANS 8:1-11**

Now there is no condemnation for the ones in Christ Jesus. For the law of the Spirit of life in Christ Jesus freed you from the law of sin and death. For the thing impossible by the law, weak through flesh, God did, sending God's own Son in the likeness of sinful flesh condemning sin in the flesh, that the ordering of the law might be fulfilled in us, walking not in accord with the flesh but in accord with the Spirit.

The ones in accord with the flesh, their minds are on the things of the flesh; but those of the ones in accord with the Spirit are on the things of the Spirit. For the mind of the flesh is death, but the mind of the Spirit is life and peace.

The mind of the flesh is enmity against God; it is not subject to the law of God, nor indeed can it be. And the ones in flesh cannot please God. But you are not in flesh but in Spirit, since the Spirit of God dwells in you.

ROMANS 8:1-11, continued

If anyone does not have the Spirit of Christ, this one is not of him. But if Christ is in you, the body is dead because of sin and the spirit is life because of righteousness.

If the Spirit of the one who raised Jesus from the dead dwells in you, the one who raised Christ Jesus from the dead will also give life to your mortal bodies through the indwelling of the Spirit in you.

RESPONSORY   Ps 31:6

Into your hands, Lord,...   ...*I commend my spirit.*

You have redeemed us, Lord God of truth.
                                  ...*I commend my spirit.*

Glory to the Father and to the Son and to the Holy Spirit:
                                  ...*Into your hands, Lord,*
                                  I commend my spirit.

Antiphon

> *Lord, save/ us!*
> *Save/ us while\ we are a-wake\,*
> *pro-tect us while we are a-sleep,*
> *that we may keep our watch/ with Christ/*
> *and when we sleep\, rest/ in his\ peace.*

GOSPEL CANTICLE of SIMEON — **LUKE 2:29-32**

+ Now, Master, you set free your servant
  according to your word in peace;

  my eyes have seen your salvation,
  which you have prepared
  before the face of all the peoples,

  a light for revelation to the nations
  and glory for your people, Israel.

Glory

Antiphon

+ *May the all-powerful Lord*
  grant us a restful night and a peaceful death. **Amen.**

Salve, **Regina**, mater misericordiae;
vita, dulcedo et spes nostra, salve.
Ad te clamamus, excules filii Evae.
Ad te suspiramus, gementes et flentes
in hac lacrimarum valle.

Eia ergo, advocata nostra,
illos tuos misericordes oculos
ad nos converte.
Et Iesum, benedictum fructum ventris tui,
nobis post hoc exsilium ostende.
O clemens, o pia, o dulcis Virgo Maria.

SATURDAY READINGS

+ *Lord, open my lips* Psalm 51:17
and my mouth will declare your praise.

Glory...

O sanc-tis-si-ma/,
O pi-is-si-ma/,
Dul-cis vir-go Ma-ri\-a!
Ma/-ter a-ma/-ta, In/ te-me-ra/-ta,
O\-ra\, O\-ra\ pro-no\-bis.

Ho-ly, ho-ly Ma-ry,
Strong and hum-ble Ma-ry,
Sweet-ness, vir-gin Ma-ri\-a!
Moth-er of our Sa/-vior,
In your fi-at "yes" and more,
O\-ra\, O\-ra\, pray\ for us.

Text: *Stimmen der Volker in Liedern*, 1807
Music: 55 7 55 7, O DU FROLICHE;
Tattersall's *Improved Psalmody*, 1704

PSALM 105

Antiphon *Simeon sang in the temple*
of seeing salvation,
a light for revelation to the nations.   Lk 2:29-32

Give thanks to Adonai;
call on the name.
Make known among the peoples the Lord's deeds!

Glory be to the holy name;
let the heart of the seeker of Adonai rejoice.
Look to Adonai, to the strength;
seek always the faces of the Lord.

Remember the deeds of wonder done,
the miracles and the judgments mouthed,
you descendants of God's servant Abraham,
you chosen ones of Jacob.

Adonai is our God, judge in all the earth,
remembering the covenant to forever
commanded for a thousand generations,
the word made with Abraham and the oath to Isaac

confirmed to Jacob as a decree,
to Israel as an everlasting covenant:
"I will give to you land of Canaan,
 a portion of your inheritance."

When they were few, few in numbers,
with strangers in their midst,
then they wandered from nation to nation,
from one kingdom to another people.

PSALM 105, continued

No one was allowed to oppress them
and for their sake kings were rebuked:
"Do not touch my anointed ones;
  do not harm my prophets."

Famine was allowed onto the land
and the king's grain supply was destroyed.
A man Joseph was sent before them,
sold as a slave;
they bruised his foot with the shackle

and his neck entered the irons
till the time foretold of him came to pass.
The word of Adonai proved him true.
The king sent for him and released him;

the ruler of the peoples set him free
and made him master of his household
and ruler over all his possessions
to discipline the princes as was his pleasure
and to teach the elders.

Then Israel entered Egypt;
Jacob lived as an alien in the land of Ham.
This people became very numerous,
more fruitful than their foes.
The hearts of the rulers were turned to hate
and conspired against this servant people.

Moses was sent as servant of the Lord
Aaron too as chosen of the Lord,
whose deeds they performed,
signs and wonders in the land of Ham.

The Lord sent darkness and it was dark;
for they rebelled against the word.
Their waters were turned into blood
which caused their fish to die.

Their land was teemed with frogs,
even the bedrooms of their rulers.
Swarms of flies were sent at a word,
gnats through all of their country.

Their rains were turned into hail
and lightning flamed through their land.
Their vine and fig tree were struck down
and the trees of their country were shattered.

Locusts came at the word
and grasshoppers without number.
Every green thing in their land was eaten up,
eaten up with the crops of their soil.

Then their firstborn were struck down, all of them,
the firstfruit of their humanity in all of their land.
The Lord brought them out with silver and gold
and no one faltered among the tribes.
Egypt was glad when they left, glad with dread.

A cloud as a cover was spread out
and fire to give them light at night.
They asked for quail and the Lord brought it
and satisfied them with bread from heaven.

PSALM 105, continued

The rock was opened and waters gushed out
flowing in the desert as a river,
for the holy promise was remembered,
the promise made to servant Abraham,
and the people were brought out rejoicing,
the chosen ones with shouts of joy.

They received the lands of nations
and inherited the wealth of peoples
so that they might keep the precepts
and observe the laws of the Lord.
Hallelujah! Praise Adonai!

Glory...

Antiphon   *Simeon sang in the temple
of seeing salvation,
a light for revelation to the nations.*   Lk 2:29-32

PSALM 106:1-16,19-48

Antiphon   *Whose sins you forgive,
they are forgiven;
whose sins you hold,
they are held.*   Jn 20:23

Hallelujah! Praise Adonai!
Give thanks to Adonai who is good,
whose mercy is to forever.

Who can proclaim the mighty acts of Adonai?
Who can declare the fullness of praise?
Blessed are they who maintain justice,
doing the right at all times.

Remember me, Adonai, as you favor your people!
In your salvation, come with your aid for me
to enjoy the prosperity of your chosen ones,
to have joy in the joy of your people,
and to give praise with your inheritance.

We have sinned as did our ancestors;
we have done wrong with bad actions.
Our ancestors when in Egypt
gave no thought to your miracle deeds,
did not remember your many kindnesses,
and rebelled by Yam Suf, the Sea of Reeds.

Still you saved them for the sake of your name,
to make known your power.
You rebuked the Sea of Reeds
drying it up.

You led them through the deep
as if it were a desert.
You saved them from the hands of foes
and redeemed them from the hand of enmity.

The waters covered the adversity;
not one of them survived.
Then they believed in the promises made;
they sang out praise.

PSALM 106:1-16,19-48

Soon did they forget those deeds
and would not wait for good counsel.
They craved cravings in the desert
and in the wasteland they tested their El,
who gave them their request
but sent a wasting disease on their life.

They envied Moses in the camp
and Aaron, the consecrated of Adonai...
They made a calf at Horeb
and gave worship to a cast idol.
They exchanged their Glory
for an image of a grass-eating bull.

They forgot El who had saved them,
doing great things in Egypt,
miracle deeds in the land of Ham
and awesome deeds by the Sea of Reeds.

By a word spoken they were to be destroyed,
except that Moses the chosen stood in the breach.
Then they despised the pleasant land
and did not believe the promise made.

They grumbled in their tents
and did not obey the voice of Adonai,
who lifted a hand to let them fall in the desert
and their descendants fall among the nations;
they were scattered through the lands.

They joined the rites of Baal of Peor
and they ate of sacrifices to ones lifeless.
They provoked anger by their deeds
and a plague broke out among them.

Phinehas stood up and intervened
and the plague was checked;
this was credited to him as righteousness
for generation and generations to forever.

They angered by the waters of Meribah,
the cause of trouble for Moses,
who spoke rashly with his lips
when they rebelled against the Spirit.

They did not defeat the peoples
as Adonai had commanded them,
but mingled with the nations
and adopted their customs.
They worshiped their idols
which became to them as a snare.

They sacrificed their sons and daughters.
They shed the innocent blood
of their own sons and daughters
whom they sacrificed to idols of Canaan,
desecrating the land by this bloodshed.

They defiled themselves by their deeds
and prostituted themselves by their deeds.
Against the people burned the anger of Adonai,
abhorring the promised inheritance.

PSALM 106:1-16,19-48

Into the hands of nations they were given,
ruled by their foes,
oppressed by enmity,
and made subject to their power.

Many times were they delivered,
but they rebelled in their decisions
and wasted away in their guilt.
But on hearing their cry

the Lord took note of their distress
and remembered for them the covenant,
and relented in greatness of love.
They gained empathy from all their captors.

Save us, Adonai our God!
Gather us from the nations
to give thanks to your holy name
and glory in your praise.

Blessed be Adonai, God of Israel
from everlasting to everlasting
and let all the people say, "Amen!"
Hallelujah! Praise Adonai!

Glory…

Antiphon *Whose sins you forgive,*
they are forgiven;
whose sins you hold,
they are held. Jn 20:23

SATURDAY READINGS

READING	Year I	Year II
week 1	Romans 3:21-31	Genesis 8
2	Romans 7:14-25	Genesis 17
3	Romans 11:13-24	Genesis 25
4	Romans 16	Genesis 37
5	1 Corinthians 6:1-11	Genesis 49
6	1 Corinthians 10:1-13	2 Thessalonians 3
7	1 Corinthians 14:1-19	2 Corinthians 6
8	James 1:19-27	2 Corinthians 12:14-21
9	James 5:12-20	Galatians 6
10	Joshua 10	Philippians 4:10-23
11	Judges 11	Zechariah 2
12	1 Samuel 4	Nehemiah 2
13	1 Samuel 16	Isaiah 59:1-14
14	1 Samuel 27 & 28	Proverbs 31
15	2 Samuel 12	Job 7
16	1 Kings 8	Job 23 & 24
17	1 Kings 18	Job 42
18	2 Kings 4:1-7	Malachi 3
19	2 Kings 13	Zechariah 14
20	Ephesians 4:1-16	Ecclesiastes 11 & 12
21	Philemon	1 Timothy 4
22	Amos 6	2 Timothy 4
23	Hosea 6 & 7	Jude
24	2 Kings 15 & 16	Baruch 3 & 4
25	Micah 1 & 2	Tobit 10 & 11
26	2 Kings 20	Judith 13
27	Zephaniah 1 & 2	Sirach 7
28	Jeremiah 9	Sirach 24
29	Jeremiah 19 & 20	Sirach 51
30	Jeremiah 29	Wisdom 7
31	Ezekiel 1	Wisdom 18 & 19
32	Ezekiel 14 & 15	1 Macabees 3
33	Ezekiel 34	Daniel 3
34	Ezekiel 47	Daniel 12

or SHORT READING **2 PETER 1:3-11**

The divine power has given us all things that go with life and piety through the full knowledge of the one who called us to this glory and virtue, through which the precious things and the very great promises have been given to us, so that through these you might come to share in the divine nature and escape from the corruption of worldly desire.

Also for this very thing bring all your diligence
> to supply your faith with virtue (*arete*),
> virtue with knowledge (*gnosis*),
> knowledge with self-control (*egkrateia*),
> self-control with endurance (*upomone*),
> endurance with piety (*eusebeia*),
> piety with friendship (*philadelphia*),
> and filial friendship with love (*agape*).

If these things abound in you, this will keep you from being barren and unfruitful in full knowledge of our Lord Jesus Christ. Blind and short sighted is the one who lacks these things, and forgetful of how his or her sins were cleansed.

And so, brothers and sisters, be diligent in your call and firm in your choice, and you will not fail in what you do. Richly supplied will be your entry into the eternal kingdom of our Lord and Savior Jesus Christ.

Let us bless the Lord. *Thanks be to God.*

SATURDAY PROPHETS

Text: based on Isaiah 40:1-8, for the Feast of John the Baptist,
Johann G. Olearius, d.1684, trans. by Catherine Winkworth, d.1878, altered
Music: 87 87 77 88, GENEVA 42, Claude Goudimel, Geneva Psalter, 1551

Com-fort, com-fort, O my peo-ple,
Speak of peace, thus says our God;
Com-fort those who sit in dark-ness,
Mourn-ing un-der sor-row's load;
Speak un-to Je-ru-sa-lem
Of the peace that waits for them;
Tell her all her sins I cov-er,
And that war-fare now is o-ver.

For the her-ald's voice is cry-ing
In the des-ert far and near,
Call-ing peo-ple to re-pen-tance
Since the king-dom now is here.
Now that warn-ing cry o-bey!
Now pre-pare for God a way!
Let the val-leys rise to meet him,
And the hills bow down to greet him.

Yes, all sins our God will par-don,
Blot-ting each con-fessed mis-deed;
All that well de-served the an-ger
God will no more see nor heed.
We have suf-fered ma-ny days,
Now our grief has passed a-way;
God will change our hea-vy sad-ness
In-to ev-er spring-ing glad-ness.

Make now straight what long was crook-ed,
Make the rough-er pla-ces plain;
Let our hearts be true and hum-ble,
As be-fits the ho-ly reign.
For the glo-ry of the Lord
Over earth is shed a-broad.
Hu-man be-ings, see the to-ken
That God's word is ne-ver bro-ken.

EXODUS 15:1b-4,8-13,17-18

Antiphon

*By faith they passed
through the Red Sea
as if it were dry land.*

Heb 11:29a

I will sing,
exalting exaltation to Adonai,
who hurled horse and rider into the sea.

My strength and my song,
Adonai has become to me salvation.
I will praise my God
and exalt the God of my ancestors.

Our Lord the warrior, named Adonai,
hurled Pharaoh's army of chariots into the sea...
By the blast of your nostrils the waters piled up;
like a wall they stood firm in the heart of the sea,
raging deep waters congealed.

The enemy boasted,
"I will pursue and overtake,
  divide the spoils and gorge on them myself;
  I will draw my sword;
  my hand will destroy them."

You blew with your breath
and they were covered by the sea;
they sank like lead
in the mighty waters.

Who is like you among "gods," Adonai?
Who like you is majestic and holy,
awesome in glory and working wonders?
You stretched your right hand
and let the earth swallow them.

You will lead in your hesed-love
the people you redeemed.
You will guide them in strength
to your holy dwelling…

You will bring them in and you will plant them
on the mountain of your inheritance,
the dwelling place you made, Adonai,
the sanctuary, Adonai, that your hands established.
Adonai will reign forever and ever.

Glory…

                                                            Antiphon

DEUTERONOMY 32:1-12

Antiphon   *Praise the greatness of our God.*

Listen, heavens, and I will speak:
Hear, earth, the words of my mouth.
Let my teaching soak in like the rain,
let my word descend like the dew,
like showers on grass,
like abundant rains on crops.

The name of Adonai I will proclaim,
and praise the greatness of our God.
The work of the Rock is perfect indeed;
all the ways of our faithful God are just
and without wrong, upright and just.

The children acted corruptly with no shame,
a generation warped and crooked.
Foolish and unwise people,
you repay Adonai in this way?
Did not your Father create you
and make you and form you?

Remember the days of old!
Consider the years of generation and generation!
Ask your parents and they will tell you!
Ask your elders and they will explain to you

how the Most High gave inheritance to nations,
dividing sons and daughters of humanity
and setting up boundaries of peoples
by numbers of sons and daughters of Israel.

For the portion of Adonai is the people,
Jacob the allotment of inheritance,
found in desert land, a barren and howling waste,
shielded with care, guarded as the apple of the eye,

like an eagle stirring up the nest
and hovering over the young ones,
spreading wings to catch them
and carrying them on its flight feathers.

Led by Adonai alone,
no foreign "god" was with them.

Glory…

Antiphon

WISDOM 9:1-6,9-11

Antiphon

*And Jesus advanced
in wisdom and age and favor
before God and humans.* Lk 2:52

God of my ancestors, Lord of mercy,
who made all things by your word
and through your wisdom framed humanity
to be master of the creatures you have created,
and to govern the world in holiness and justice
and judge justly and with an upright heart,

WISDOM 9:1-6,9-11, continued

Give me Wisdom,
your companion at your throne,
and do not reject me from among your children,
for I am your servant, born of your handmaid,
a feeble human with a short life
and a weak understanding of justice and laws.

Though a human be ever so perfect
in human eyes,
without your Wisdom that same one
will be of no account…

With you is Wisdom,
who knows your works
and was present when you created the world,
who knows what is pleasing in your eyes
and what is right in accord with your ordinances.

Send her forth from the holy heavens
and dispatch her from your glorious throne,
that she may labor beside me
and I may learn what pleases you.

For she knows and understands all things
and will guide me to prudence in my actions
and guard me in her glory.

Glory…

Antiphon *And Jesus advanced
in wisdom and age and favor
before God and humans.* Lk 2:52

EZEKIEL 36:24-28

Antiphon
*Let any who thirst
come to me and drink.* Jn 7:37

I will take you out of the nations
and I will gather you from all the countries,
and I will bring you back into your land.

I will sprinkle on you clean waters,
and you will be clean from all your impurities,
and from all your idols I will cleanse you.

I will give you a new heart
and I will put inside you a new spirit,
and I will remove the stone-heart from your flesh
and I will give you a flesh-heart,

and I will put inside you my Spirit
and I will move you to follow in my decrees
and my laws you will be careful to keep,

and you will live in the land I gave your ancestors,
and you will be my people
and I will be your God.

Glory...

Antiphon

READING **DEUTERONOMY 4:32-40**

Moses spoke,
"Ask now about the former days before you,
and from the day
when God created humanity on the earth,
and from the end of the heavens,
even to the end of the heavens:
Has a thing great as this ever happened?
Or has a thing like this been heard?
Has a people heard the voice of God
speaking out of fire as you heard
and lived?
Or has a "god" tried to take a nation out of a nation
by tests, by signs, by wonders, by war,
and by mighty hand and outstretched arm,
or by great awesome deeds
like all that your Lord God did for you
before your eyes in Egypt?
You were shown to know
that our Lord is God,
and none besides.
From the heavens you were made to hear
the voice of discipline,
and on the earth you were shown the great fire,
and you heard the words from out of the fire.
And because of love for your ancestors
and their chosen descendants after them,

> you were brought from Egypt
> by the Presence and Strength
> to drive out before you
> nations greater and stronger than you
> to bring you and give to you their land,
> an inheritance to this day.
> Acknowledge the day and take to your heart
> that our Lord is God
> in the heavens above and on earth below.
> There is no other.
> Keep the decrees and commands
> that I give you this day,
> that it may go well with you
> and with your children after you,
> and so that you may live long
> in the land that our Lord God gives you
> all the days."

RESPONSORY   Psalm 34:2

My soul will boast in the Lord…   *…and at all times.*

Praise always on my lips…   *…and at all times.*

Glory to the Father and to Son and to the Holy Spirit:
   …My soul will boast in the Lord, and at all times.

Let us bless the Lord.   *Thanks be to God.*

SATURDAY MORNING

+ *God, come to my assistance;*   Psalm 70:2
Lord, make haste to help me!

Glory…

Refrain

On\ this day, O beau-ti-ful Mo-ther,
On\ this day we give you our love.
Near you, Ma-don-na, fond-ly we hov-er,
Trust-ing your gen-tle care/ to prove.

Verse 1   **O**n this day we ask to share,
Dear-est Mo-ther, your sweet care;
Help us 'lest our feet\ a-stray\,
Wand-'ring from your guid-ing way.

Refrain

Verse 2   **Q**ueen of an-gels, deign to hear
Lisp-ing chil-dren's hum-ble pray'r;
Young hearts gain, O Vir\-gin pure\
Sweet-ly to your-self al-lure.

Refrain

Text: Louis Lambillotte, SJ, 1796-1855, altered
Music: 77 77, BEAUTIFUL MOTHER,
Rohr's *Favorite Catholic Melodies*, 1857

PSALM 8

Antiphon *I have much more to tell you,*
but you cannot bear it yet.   Jn 16:12

Adonai, our Lord!
How awesome is your name in all the earth!

Your glory is set above the heavens!
From lips of children and infants
you ordained strength to bring to silence
enmity, opposition and vengeance.

When I consider your heavens,
the works of your fingers,
the moon and stars which you set in place,
what is a human that you would be mindful,
a child of Adam and Eve that you would care?

And you made us little lower than a "god"
crowning us with glory and honor,
making us to rule over works of your hands,
putting everything under our feet,

flocks and herds, all of them,
and also beasts of the field,
birds of the air and fishes of the sea,
swimming through the paths of the seas.

Adonai, our Lord!
How awesome is your name in all the earth!

Glory...

Antiphon

PSALM 107

Antiphon *In awe, the disciples asked, Who then is this,*
whom both the wind and the sea obey? Mk 4:41

"Give thanks to Adonai, who is good,
  whose mercy is to forever."

Let this be said by the redeemed of Adonai,
who redeemed them from the hand of the foe
and gathered them from the lands,
from east and west, from north and the south sea.

Some wandered in the desert wasteland
finding no way to a city for settling,
hungry and thirsty, their life ebbing away.

Then they cried out to Adonai in their trouble,
who delivered them from their distresses,
who led them by a direct way
to go to a city for settling.

Let them give thanks to Adonai
for unfailing mercy, for deeds of wonder done
for sons and daughters of Adam and Eve,
for satisfying the throats of the thirsty
and filling the hungry with goodness.

Some sat in the dark and deep gloom,
prisoners of suffering and iron,
for they rebelled against the word of El
and despised the counsel of the Most High
who subjected their heart to the bitter labor,
and no one was there to help.

Then they cried in their trouble to Adonai,
who saved them from their distress,
brought them out from the dark and deep gloom,
and broke away their chains.

Let them give thanks to Adonai
for unfailing mercy, for deeds of wonder done
for sons and daughters of Adam and Eve,
for breaking down gates of bronze
and cutting through bars of iron.

Some were fools through their rebellious ways,
afflicted because of their sins.
Loathing all food,
they drew themselves near the gates of death.

Then they cried in their trouble to Adonai,
who saved them from their distress,
sending forth the word to heal them
and rescue them from their graves.

Let them give thanks to Adonai
for unfailing mercy, for deeds of wonder done
for sons and daughters of Adam and Eve,
and let them sacrifice offerings of thanksgiving
and tell of the works with songs of joy.

PSALM 107, continued

Some went to the sea in ships
to do trade on the mighty waters.
They saw the works in the deep,
the wonderful deeds of Adonai,
who spoke and stirred up a storm wind
and lifted up the waves.

They mounted up to the heavens
and went down to the deep;
in peril their courage melted away.
They reeled and staggered like drunkards,
all of them at their wits end.

Then they cried in their trouble to Adonai,
who brought them out from their distress,
hushing the storm to a whisper
and stilling the waves.
They were glad when it grew calm
and were guided to the haven they desired.

Let them give thanks to Adonai
for unfailing mercy, for deeds of wonder done
for sons and daughters of Adam and Eve,
and let them exalt in the assembly of the people,
and in the council of elders give praise.

Adonai turned rivers into desert,
springs of waters into thirsty ground,
and land of fruit into a salt waste
because of wicked ways of those living there.

Adonai then turned desert into pools of waters,
parched ground into springs of waters,
and brought hungry ones to live there.

They founded and settled a city,
sowed fields and planted vineyards,
and yielded the fruit of harvest.
They were blessed and they increased greatly,
and their herds were not allowed to diminish.

Then they decreased and were humbled
by oppression, calamity and sorrow
with contempt poured onto nobles,
made to wander in a trackless waste.

But the poor were lifted from affliction
and their families increased like a flock.
The upright saw this and rejoiced
but doers of badness shut their mouth.

Whoever is wise, heed these things
and ponder the great mercy of Adonai.

Glory…

Antiphon   *In awe, the disciples asked, Who then is this,*
   whom both the wind and the sea obey?   Mk 4:41

PSALM 92:1-9,11,13-16

Antiphon *The Kingdom of God is as when*
a human might throw seed on the earth
and sleep and rise night and day
and the seed sprouts and grows
without the human knowing how.   Mk 4:26,27

It is good to give thanks to Adonai,
to make music to your name, Most High,
to proclaim in the morning your love
and at night your faithfulness,

on the ten-string and on the lyre,
and the melody of the harp.
For you make me glad by your deeds, Adonai;
at the works of your hands I sing for joy.

How great are your works, Adonai;
very profound are your designs.
The senseless human does not know
and the fool does not understand.

Though wickedness springs up like grass
and doers of bad things seem to flourish,
their ways will be destroyed to forever.
But you, Adonai, are exalted to forever…

You gave me strength like a wild ox
and I was anointed with fine oil…
The just will flourish like the palm tree,
and grow like a cedar of Lebanon.

SATURDAY MORNING

Planted in the house of Adonai,
in the courts of our God they will flourish.
In old age they will still bear fruit,
fresh and green they will stay,
to proclaim –
"Adonai is just,
  in my Rock there is no wrong."

Glory…

Antiphon

PSALM 117

Antiphon
As the centurion responded:
I am unworthy
for you to enter under my roof
but only say the word
and let the servant be healed. Lk 7:6,7

Hallelujah! Praise Adonai, all you nations;
and extol, all you peoples.

Great is this steadfast mercy toward us,
the fidelity of Adonai to forever.
Hallelujah! Praise Adonai!

Glory…

Antiphon

READING **ROMANS 12:9-21**

Let love be unassumed. Shrinking from the bad, cleave to the good. Love one another warmly in filial love, giving preference in honor of one another, unslothful in zeal, burning in spirit, serving the Lord, rejoicing in hope, enduring in affliction, steadfast in prayer, imparting to the needs of the saints, and pursuing hospitality. Bless your persecutors; bless and do not curse them. Rejoice with those rejoicing; weep with those weeping. Be of the same mind toward one another, not attentive to the high things, but being present to the humble. Do not become wise in your own mind. Instead of returning evil for evil, don't. Provide for good things before all people. If possible, as far as it rests on you, seek peace with all human beings. Do not avenge yourselves, beloved, but leave room for the wrath, for it has been written: *Vengeance is mine; I will repay, says the Lord.* But if your enemy is hungry, feed him or her; or if they are thirsty, give them drink. In doing this you will heap on their heads coals of fire. Be not conquered by the kakon-bad, but conquer the evil by the agatho-good.

RESPONSORY Ps 92:4,2

Made glad, Lord, by your deeds...
   ...*I make music to your name.*
At the works of your hands I sing for joy;...
   ...*I make music to your name.*
Glory to the Father and to the Son and to the Holy Spirit:
   ...*Made glad, Lord, by your deeds, I make music to your name.*

SATURDAY MORNING

GOSPEL READING OF THE DAY or GOSPEL CANTICLE

Antiphon   *Lord, guide our feet into the way of peace.*

CANTICLE OF ZECHARIAH   **LUKE 1:68-79**

+ Blessed be the Lord the God of Israel
  who chose a people,
  visited them to bring redemption,
  and raised salvation in the house of David,
  saving strength from God's own servant,

  speaking from the age of the prophets
  through the mouth of the holy prophet:
  Salvation out of enmity,
  even out of those who hate us,

  to show our ancestors how mercy works,
  and to remember the holy promise of the Lord,
  the covenant made for our father Abraham,
  calming our fear and making us free
  to serve God as holy and righteous and just
  in the Lord's presence all our days.

  And you also child
  will be called a prophet of the Most High
  for you will go before the Lord to prepare his way
  and give to his people a knowledge of salvation
  known in accepting forgiveness of their sins.

  From the deepness of God's mercy on us,
  a sun rising from the height will visit to appear
  to those who sit in the dark or shadow of death,
  and to guide our feet into the way of peace.

Gospel Reading for Saturday of

Week			
1	Mark 2:13-17	13 Matt 9:14-17	25 Lk 9:43b-45
2	Mark 3:20-21	14 Matt 10:24-33	26 Lk 10:17-24
3	Mark 4:35-41	15 Matt 12:14-21	27 Lk 11:27-28
4	Mark 6:30-34	16 Matt 13:24-30	28 Luke 12:8-12
5	Mark 8:1-10	17 Matt 14:1-12	29 Luke 13:1-9
6	Mark 9:2-13	18 Matt 17:14-20	30 Lk 14:1,7-11
7	Mark 10:13-16	19 Matt 19:13-15	31 Luke 16:9-15
8	Mark 11:27-33	20 Matt 23:1-12	32 Luke 18:1-8
9	Mark 12:38-44	21 Matt 25:14-30	33 Lk 20:27-40
10	Matt 5:33-37	22 Luke 6:1-5	34 Lk 21:34-36
11	Matt 6:24-34	23 Luke 6:43-49	
12	Matt 8:5-17	24 Luke 8:4-15	

Glory...

Antiphon *Lord, guide our feet into the way of peace.*

PETITIONS FOR THE CONSECRATION TO GOD
OF THE DAY AND ITS WORK
- For the Church and her ministry and apostolates...
- For secular authorities and all serving as stewards...
- For people who are poor or sick or in sorrow...
- For the basic needs of each human being...
- For awareness of being created in the image of God...
- For discovery and discernment of our charisms...
- For consensus on both rights and responsibilities...
- For loving respect for folks who think differently...
- For God's healing of the core wounds of enemies...
- For the world peace that only God can give...

- For elders who feel abandoned…
- For justice for migrant workers and refugees…
- For the starving child awakening our conscience…
- For those suffering physical and mental torture…
- For people living in subhuman conditions…
- For human beings unjustly imprisoned or enslaved…
- For workers in degrading or unsafe conditions…
- For laborers where treated as mere tools for profit…
- For respect for those who think and act differently…
- For rejection of judging the inner guilt of others…
- For a culture of vocations all over the world…
- In gratitude for blessings and grace…
- For those who have asked for my prayer…
- For those for whom I have promised to pray…
- For those who weigh on my heart…

OUR FATHER…

+ *May the Lord bless us, protect us from all evil, and bring us to everlasting life.* **Amen**.

SATURDAY DAYTIME

+ *God, come to my assistance;*　　　　Psalm 70:2
Lord, make haste to help me!

Glory…

Je-ru-sa-lem/, **my hap-py home**\,
When shall I come/ to thee?
When shall my sor/-rows have an end\?
Your joys when shall\ I see?

The saints are crowned/ with glo-ry great\;
They see God face/ to face;
They tri-umph still/, they still re-joice\,
No grief or wor-ry their case.

King Da-vid stands/, his harp in hand\
As lea-der of/ the choir:
Ten thou-sand times/ that we be blessed\,
That we his mu\-sic hear.

Our La-dy sings/ Mag-ni-fi-cat\
With tune sur-pass/-ing sweet,
And all the vir/-gins bear their part\,
While sit-ting at\ her feet.

And Mag-da-len/ has left her grief\,
With cheer-ful joy/ does sing
And bless-ed saints/, their har-mo-ny\
To ev-'ry room\ they bring.

Je-ru-sa-lem/, Je-ru-sa-lem\,
God grant that I/ may see
Your end-less joy/, and of the same\
Par-ta-ker al\-ways be.

PSALM 119:137-144
Sadhe I

Antiphon   *There are last ones who will be first,*
               and there are first ones who will be last.

                                                     Lk 13:30

You are just, Adonai,
and just are your laws.
You laid down your statutes,
righteous and fully trustworthy.

My zeal wears me out
for enmity ignores your words.
Your promise is tested thoroughly
and your servant loves her.

Belittled and despised,
I forget not your precepts.
Your justice is right to everlasting
and your law is true.

Trouble and distress came upon me;
your commands are my delights.
Right are your statutes to forever;
give me understanding that I may live.

Glory…

                                                     Antiphon

Song text: F.B.P., London, around 1583, altered
Music: C.M., 86 86, LAND OF REST, traditional American melody

PSALM 119:145-152
Sadhe II

Antiphon   *Ask and it will be given you,*
seek and you will find,
knock and it will be opened to you.   Lk 11:9

I call with all my heart:
answer me, Adonai;
your decrees I will obey.
I call to you: save me,
that I may keep your statutes.

I rise before dawn and cry for help;
in your word I put my hope.
My eyes stay open in the night watch
to meditate on your promise.

Hear my voice,
as is your mercy, Adonai,
as your law makes me alive.
Scheming devisers are near,
but they are far from your law.

You are near, Adonai,
and all your commands are true.
I learned long ago from your statutes
that you established them to forever.

Glory…

Antiphon

PSALM 119:153-160
Resh

Antiphon *When coming, the Spirit of truth*
will guide you into all truth.   Jn 16:13

Look upon my affliction and deliver me
for your law I have not forgotten.
Defend my cause and redeem me
as your promise makes me alive!

Salvation is far from doers of badness
who do not seek out your decrees.
Your compassions are great, Adonai,
as your laws make me alive.

Many persecute me in enmity;
still I turn not from your statutes.
I look with perplexion on the faithless
who do not obey your word.

See how I love your precepts, Adonai,
as your mercy keeps me alive.
All your word is true
and to all eternity is your law of righteousness.

Glory…

Antiphon

PSALM 34

Antiphon
*The bread that I will give
is my flesh for the life of the cosmos.*   Jn 6:51b

I will bless Adonai at all times,
praise always on my lips.
My soul she will boast in Adonai,
let afflicted ones hear
and let them rejoice.

Glorify Adonai with me!
Let us exalt the name together.
I sought Adonai, who answered me
and delivered me from all my fears.

They look to the name and are radiant;
their faces are never covered with shame.
This poor human called and Adonai heard,
and saved this one from all troubles.

An angel encamps around to deliver
those who fear Adonai.
Taste and see that Adonai is good!
Blessed is the one who takes this refuge.

Fear Adonai, you saints;
for those who do so there is no lack.
Lions may grow poor and grow hungry,
but seekers of Adonai lack no good thing.

SATURDAY DAYTIME

Come, children! Listen to me!
I will teach you the fear of Adonai.
Who is the human who loves living?
Who desires days to see the good?

Keep your tongue from evil
and your lips from speaking the lie.
Turn from evil! And do good!
And pursue to seek peace!

The eyes of Adonai are on righteous ones
with ears open to their cry.
The faces of Adonai turn from those doing evil
to cut off from the earth their memory.

They cry and Adonai hears
and delivers them from all their troubles.
Close is Adonai to the brokenhearted,
saving those whose spirit is crushed.

Many are the troubles of the righteous
but Adonai delivers them from all of them,
protecting all of their bones;
not one of them will be broken.

Evil will slay the wicked and condemned will be
those who stay foes of the righteous.
The servants of Adonai are being redeemed
and there is no condemnation
of the souls who take this refuge.

Glory…

                                                    Antiphon

PSALM 61

Antiphon
*Come to me,
all who labor and are burdened,
and I will rest you.
My yoke is gentle
and my burden is light.*   Mt 11:28-30

Hear, God, my cry!
Listen to my prayer!
From the end of the earth I call to you
as my heart grows faint.

To the high rock you lead me
for you are my refuge
and tower of strength
against the foe.

I would dwell in your tent for forevers
and take refuge in the shelter of your wings.
For you, God, hearing my vows,
gave inheritance to those revering your name.

You add days upon days of the royal one,
and years for generation and generation,
enthroned in God's presences forever,
appointed and protected in God's love and fidelity.

I will sing praise of your name forever
to fulfill my vows day by day.

Glory...

Antiphon

PSALM 64

Antiphon *Father, forgive them,*
for they know not what they do.   Lk 23:34

Hear my voice, O God, in complaint;
you protect my life, threatened by enmity.
You hide me from conspiracies,
from the noisy crowd of people doing badness,

who sharpen their tongue like the sword,
aim their arrow of harmful words,
and shoot from ambush the innocent person;
they shoot suddenly and without fear.

They encourage those who plan harm,
and they talk of hidden snares,
saying, "who will see them?"
They plot injustices they call "the perfect plan!"
Surely the human mind and heart are cunning.

But God will shoot sudden arrows
striking down those plans.
Their ruin will be by their own tongues;
all who see them will shake heads.

All humanity will fear,
and come to proclaim the work of God,
and ponder the deeds of God.
Let the righteous rejoice and take refuge in Adonai;
let all the upright of heart give praise.

Glory...   Antiphon

READING **PHILIPPIANS 2:12-16**

My beloved, as always you obeyed, not only in my presence, but rather now even more in my absence, with fear and trembling you work out your salvation, for God is the one working in you both to will and to work on behalf of God's good will.

Do all things without murmurings and disputes, that you may be blameless and harmless, children of God faultless in the midst of a crooked generation.

Among those having been corrupted, you shine as luminaries in the world, holding up a word of life, a boast to me in the day of Christ, that not in vain did I run nor in vain labor.

RESPONSORY Ps 142:6,7a

I cry to you, my Lord,... *...you are my refuge.*

My portion in the land of the living,...
...you are my refuge.

Glory to the Father and to the Son and to the Holy Spirit:
...I cry to you, my Lord;
you are my refuge.

Lord\, have mer-cy.
Christ\, have mer-cy.
Lord\, have mer-cy.

SOLEMNITY GOSPELS in ORDINARY TIME

Holy Trinity Sunday (Sunday after Pentecost)
- A John 3:16-18
- B Matthew 28:16-20
- C John 16:12-15

Body and Blood (Sunday after Trinity Sunday)
- A John 6:51-58
- B Mark 14:12-16,22-26
- C Luke 9:11b-17

Sacred Heart (Friday after Body and Blood)
- A Matthew 11:25-30
- B John 19:31-37
- C Luke 15:3-7

Birth of John the Baptist (June 24)
Vigil: Luke 1:5-17
Day: Luke 1:57-66,80

Peter and Paul, Apostles (June 29)
Vigil: John 21:15-19
Day: Matthew 16:13-19

Assumption of Mary (August 15)
Vigil: Luke 11:27-28
Day: Luke 1:39-56

All Saints (November 1)
Matthew 5:1-12a

ACKNOWLEDGEMENTS

I have been asked by many people for an introduction to praying the psalms. *One Week in Ordinary Time* is one response to those requests.

The official translation approved by the Catholic Church for the *Liturgy of the Hours* is beautiful for chanting in monasteries and seminaries. As a parish priest, almost all of my time with the Psalter is with the church universal but alone with God, whether in my room, in the chapel, or in the woods. Praying in *Lectio Divina*, trying to listen to the Lord, I have found much prayerful fruit in several translations.

This meditation rendering follows consciously these four choices:

1. For the name YHVH, or *Yahweh*, the Hebrew word **Adonai** (ah-duh-nigh') meaning *My Lord*, is used; most real translations use THE LORD. In several places the words *El* or *Elyon* or *Elohim* are retrieved, as is *Sabaoth* instead of *Mighty* or *Hosts*.

2. Following the Christian understanding of one God in the three persons of the Trinity, masculine pronouns for God are avoided, except when God is referred to as Father, or specific references to Jesus.

3. In an admittedly imperfect effort to pray the gospel as well as the psalms, the word *enemy* is most often rendered as *enmity*.

4. Where people are referred to as *evil*, the emphasis is shifted to those who *do* evil, or *ways* that are evil or bad.

There are problems with all four of these choices, and these would be reasons to not consider this compilation for public liturgy. Still, in my judgment, the benefits overwhelm the problems.

The primary characater of this rendering is from the grace of twenty-four years of praying with the Psalter. May the Lord grant more of this grace.

Any errors in this rendering are entirely my own. Let us be grateful for all those who do the real work of translating sacred scripture.

Again, the primary source for this work is the grace of twenty-four years of praying the psalms, canticles and readings from several translations, including these:

The Liturgy of the Hours (Four Volumes)
Copyright © 1974 ICEL
International Committee on English in the Liturgy, Inc.

*New American Bible
with Revised New Testament and Revised Psalms*
Copyright © 1991, 1986, 1970 Confraternity of Christian Doctrine,
Inc. Washington, D.C. All rights reserved.
(*This is my favorite translation of the Psalms.*)

New American Bible Revised Edition (NABRE)
Copyright © 2010, 1986 Confraternity of Christian Doctrine,
Washington, D.C. All rights reserved.
(*480 words are from this newest Catholic translation.*)

New Revised Standard Version Bible: Catholic Edition
Copyright © 1993 and 1989 by the Division of Christian Education
of the National Council of the Churches of Christ in the U.S.A.

The New Jerusalem Bible
Copyright © 1985 by Darton, Longman & Todd, Ltd. & Doubleday,
a division of Bantam Doubleday Dell Publishing Group, Inc.

The Jewish Study Bible
Copyright © 1985, 1999 by the Jewish Publication Society

The Interlinear NIV Hebrew-English Old Testament
by John R. Kohlenberger III
Copyright © 1979, 1980, 1982, 1985, 1987
by the Zondervan Corporation

The NRSV-NIV Parallel New Testament in Greek and English
by Alfred Marshall
Copyright © 1990 by the Zondervan Corporation

I am especially grateful to all those who worked on the *New American Bible* and to Mr. Kohlenberger and Mr. Marshall.

444 ACKNOWLEDGEMENTS

These other works were consulted:

The New Jerome Biblical Commentary
edited by Raymond E. Brown, S.S., Joseph A. Fitzmyer, S.J.,
and Roland E. Murphy, O.Carm.
Copyright © 1990, 1968 by Prentice-Hall, Inc.

The following volumes from the Anchor Bible:
Psalms I (1-50); Psalms II (51-100); Psalms III (101-150)
The Anchor Bible, Volumes 16, 17, and 17A
by Mitchell Dahood, S.J.
Copyright © 1965,1966, © 1968, © 1970, Doubleday
The Wisdom of Ben Sira; The Anchor Bible, Vol. 39
by Patrick W. Skehan
Copyright © 1987, Doubleday & Company, Inc.
Tobit; The Anchor Bible, Vol. 40A
by Carey A. Moore
Copyright © 1996, Doubleday
The Wisdom of Solomon; The Anchor Bible, Vol. 43
by David Winston
Copyright © 1979, Doubleday & Company, Inc.
Daniel, Esther and Jeremiah, the Additions;
The Anchor Bible, Vol. 44
by Carey A. Moore
Copyright © 1977, Doubleday & Company, Inc.

And a stack of dictionaries.

Some of the morning **petitions** are drawn from *Guadium et Spes*,
"Pastoral Constitution on the Church in the Modern World,"
Vatican II, 1965, paragraph 27. Pages 430-31 includes them.

Some of the evening **intercessions** are from the *Liturgy of the Hours*.

The Trinitarian intercessions are from a simplified verson of the
consciousness examen of St. Ignatius of Loyola by Mark Link, SJ.

July 6, 2016   Stephen Joseph Wolf
Feast of Saint Maria Goretti   Clarksville, Tennessee

www.idjc.org

INDEX of SONGS

A Mighty Fortress: 87 87 66 66 7 EIN' FESTE BURG   Mon Morn., 96
All Creatures of Our God: LASST UNS ERFREUEN, LM w/alle's
                                                    Wed Readings, 213
Amazing Grace: 8686 CM, NEW BRITAIN   Mon Prophets, 90
Beautiful Savior: ST. ELIZABETH   Thu Evening, 319
Blessed Be: 8787D HYMN TO JOY   Wed Evening, 259
Come, Holy Spirit: LAMBILLOTTE, LM; with repeat
                                                        Sun Daytime, 54
Comfort, Comfort, O My People: 87 87 77 88, GENEVA 42
                                                       Sat Prophets, 411
Creator of the Stars of Night: CONDITOR, LM   Wed Night, 271
Faith Of Our Ancestors: ST. CATHERINE, LM with refrain
                                                      Mon Daytime, 112
For The Beauty Of The Earth: 77 77 77, DIX   Mon Evening, 126
From All That Dwells Below The Skies: DUKE STREET, LM
                                                      Mon Readings, 77
Holy God We Praise Your Name: 78 78 77 GROSSER GOTT
                                                        Thu Daytime, 306
Holy, Holy, Holy: 11 12 12 10 NICAEA   Sun Morning, 38
Holy Joseph: 87 87 D, PLEADING SAVIOR   Wed Morning, 234
How Can I Keep From Singing: 87 87, ENDLESS SONG
                                                      Fri Prophets, 349
I Heard the Voice of Jesus Say: KINGSFOLD, CMD   Fri Night, 394
Immortal, Invisible, God Only Wise: 11 11 11 11, ST. DENIO
                                                       Thu Readings, 275
In Christ There Is No East or West: 8686 CM, MCKEE
                                                        Tue Daytime, 184
Jerusalem My Happy Home: 86 86 CM, LAND OF REST
                                                        Sat Daytime, 432
Joyful, Joyful, We Adore You: 8787D HYMN TO JOY   Sun Night, 73
Let All Mortal Flesh Keep Silence: 87 87 87 PICARDY
                                                        Fri Daytime, 369
Lord of All Being Throned Afar: JESU DULCIS MEMORIA, LM
                                                       Tue Prophets, 161
Lord, Your Almighty Word: 664 6664, ITALIAN HYMN (MOSCOW)
                                                        Sun Evening, 63

445

INDEX of SONGS, continued

My Life Flows On In Endless Song: 87 87, ENDLESS SONG
                                                                Fri Prophets, 349
Now Thank We All Our God: 67 67 66 66, NUN DANKET
                                                                     Sun Vigil, 4
O Breathe On Me O Breath of God: ST. COLUMBA, CM
                                                              Thu Prophets, 286
O Lord of Life: 86 86 86 86 FOREST GREEN   Thu Daytime, 299
O Sacred Head Surrounded: 76 76 D, PASSION CHORALE
                                                                 Fri Morning, 357
O Sanctissima: 55 7 55 7, O DU FROLICHE   Sat Readings, 400
O Saving Victim: O SALUTARIS HOSTIA   Fri Readings, 337
On This Day the First of Days: 77 77, LUBECK   Sun Readings, 18
On This Day O Beautiful Mother: 77 77, BEAUTIFUL MOTHER
                                                                Sat Morning, 420
Praise God, from Whom All Blessings Flow: OLD HUNDREDTH, LM
                                                                 Sun Evening, 62
Praise the Lord, You Heavens Adore: 87 87 D, PLEADING SAVIOR
                                                                 Tue Readings, 145
Praise To The Lord: 14 14 4 7 8 LOBE DEN HERREN Sun Proph, 30
Shepherd of Souls: 8686 CM, ST. AGNES   Thu Night, 333
Songs of Thankfulness: 77 77 D, SALZBURG   Tue Daytime, 196
TE DEUM   Sun Prophets, 36
The Church's One Foundation: 76 76 D, AURELIA   Mon Night, 140
The King of Love My Shepherd Is: 8686 CM, ST. COLUMBA
                                                                 Thu Morning, 293
There's A Wideness In God's Mercy: 87 87 D, HYFRYDOL
                                                                 Wed Daytime, 248
We Plow the Fields and Scatter: 76 76 D, AURELIA Wed Proph, 227
We Walk By Faith: 8686 CM, ST. AGNES   Tue Morning, 170
What a Friend We Have In Jesus: FRIEND   Tue Night, 208
When I Survey The Wondrous Cross: ERHALT UNS HERR, LM
                                                                 Fri Evening, 381
Ye Sons and Daughters: 888, O FILII ET FILIAE   Sun Night, 14

These 46 songs were previously published in Hinge Hour Singer
and are thought by the publisher to be in the public domain.

447

INDEX of PSALMS

1 - Sun Readings, page 20
2 - Sun Readings, 21
3 - Sun Readings, 22
4 - Sat Night, 15
5 - Mon Morning, 97
6 - Mon Readings, 78
7 - Mon Daytime, 116
8 - Sat Morning, 421
9 - Mon Readings, 79
10 - Tue Readings, 146
11 - Mon Evening, 128
12 - Mon Readings, 148
13 - Tue Daytime, 188
14 - Tue Daytime, 189
15 - Mon Evening, 129
16 - Thu Night, 334
17 - Wed Daytime, 252
18 - Wed Rdgs, 215, 218
19 - Mon Morning, 99
20 - Tue Evening, 200
21 - Tue Evening, 197
22 - Fri Daytime, 373
23 - Sun Daytime, 57
24 - Tue Morning, 172
25 - Thu Daytime, 310
26 - Fri Morning, 360
27 - Wed Evening, 260
28 - Fri Morning, 362
29 - Mon Morning, 101
30 - Thu Evening, 320
31 - Mon Readings, 81
32 - Thu Evening, 322
33 - Tue Morning, 174
34 - Sat Daytime, 436
35 - Fri Readings, 338
36 - Wed Morning, 236
37 - Tue Readings, 149
38 - Fri Readings, 340
39 - Wed Readings, 220
40 - Mon Daytime, 118
41 - Fri Evening, 382
42 - Mon Morning, 102
43 - Tue Morning, 173
44 - Thu Readings, 276
45 - Mon Evening, 130
46 - Fri Evening, 383
47 - Wed Readings, 235
48 - Thu Morning, 294
49 - Tue Evening, 198

50 - Mon Readings, page 84
51 - Fri Morning, 358
52 - Wed Readings, 224
53 - Tue Daytime, 190
54 - Tue Daytime, 191
55 - Fri Readings, 342
56 - Thu Daytime, 312
57 - Thu Morning, 295
59 - Fri Daytime, 376
60 - Fri Daytime, 377
61 - Sun Daytime, 438
62 - Wed Evening, 262
63 - Sun Morning, 39
64 - Sat Daytime, 439
65 - Tue Morning, 176
66 - Sun Readings, 23
67 - Tue Morning, 171
68 - Tue Readings, 153
69 - Fri Readings, 344
70 - Wed Daytime, 254
71 - Mon Daytime, 120
72 - Thu Evening, 324
73 - Mon Readings, 86
74 - Tue Daytime, 192
75 - Wed Daytime, 255
76 - Sun Daytime, 58
77 - Wed Morning, 238
79 - Thu Daytime, 313
80 - Thu Morning, 298
81 - Thu Morning, 300
82 - Mon Daytime, 123
84 - Mon Morning, 104
85 - Tue Morning, 178
86 - Mon Night, 141
87 - Thu Morning, 297
88 - Fri Night, 395
89 - Thu Readings, 278
           282
90 - Mon Morning, 105
91 - Sun Night II, 74
92 - Sat Morning, 426
93 - Sun Morning, 42
94 - Sun Daytime, 256
95 - Sun Readings, 19
96 - Mon Morning, 107
97 - Wed Morning, 240
98 - Wed Morning, 241
99 - Thu Morning, 302
100 - Fri Morning, 361

101 - Tue Morning, page 179
102 - Tue Readings, 157
103 - Wed Readings, 222
104 - Sun Readings, 25
105 - Sat Readings, 401
106 - Sat Readings, 404
107 - Sat Readings, 422
108 - Wed Morning, 242
110 - Sun Evening, 64
111 - Sun Evening, 65
112 - Sun Evening, 66
113 - Sun Vigil, 5
114 - Sun Evening, 67
115 - Sun Evening, 68
116 - Sun Vigil, 6
117 - Sat Morning, 427
118 - Sun Morning, 43
119 - Sun-Sat Daytime
120 - Mon Daytime, 124
121 - Fri Evening, 385
122 - Sun Vigil, 7
123 - Mon Evening, 132
124 - Mon Evening, 133
125 - Tue Evening, 201
126 - Wed Evening, 264
127 - Wed Evening, 265
128 - Thu Daytime, 315
129 - Thu Daytime, 316
130 - Wed Night, 272
131 - Tue Evening, 202
132 - Thu Evening, 326
133 - Fri Morning, 363
134 - Sun Night I, 16
135 - Fri Evening, 386
136 - Mon Evening, 134
137 - Tue Evening, 203
138 - Tue Evening, 204
139 - Wed Evening, 266
140 - Fri Daytime, 378
141 - Sun Vigil, 8
142 - Sun Vigil, 9
143 - Thu Night, 209
144 - Thu Evening, 328
145 - Fri Evening, 388
146 - Wed Morning, 243
147 - Fri Morning, 364, 365
148 - Sun Morning, 46
149 - Sun Morning, 48
150 - Sun Morning, 49

"Sunday Vigil" is Saturday Evening.   Psalms 58, 83 & 109 are omitted; 78 is used in Lent.

INDEX of CANTICLES & READINGS

OLD TESTAMENT CANTICLES

Exodus 15:1b-4,8-13,17-18 - Sat Prophets, page 412
Deuteronomy 32:1-12 - Sat Prophets, 414
1 Samuel 2:1-10 - Wed Prophets, 228
1 Chronicles 29:10b-13 - Mon Prophets, 92
Tobit 13:1b-8 - Tue Prophets, 162
Tobit 13:8-11,13-15 - Fri Prophets, 354
Judith 16:1,13-15 - Wed Prophets, 230
Wisdom 9:1-6,9-11 - Sat Prophets, 415
Sirach 36:1-6,13-22 - Mon Prophets, 92
Isaiah 2:2-5 - Mon Prophets, 91
Isaiah 12:1b-6 - Thu Prophets, 288
Isaiah 26:1b-4,7-9,12 - Tue Prophets, 167
Isaiah 33:2-10 – Sun Prophets, 32
Isaiah 33:13-16 - Wed Prophets, 231
Isaiah 38:10-14,17b-20 - Tue Prophets, 163
Isaiah 40:10-17 - Thu Prophets, 289
Isaiah 42:10-16 - Mon Prophets, 94
Isaiah 45:15-25 - Fri Prophets, 350
Isaiah 61:10-62:5 - Wed Prophets, 232
Isaiah 66:7-14a - Thu Prophets, 290
Jeremiah 7:3b-7 – Sun Prophets, 34
Jeremiah 14:17b-22 - Fri Prophets, 353
Jeremiah 31:10-14 - Thu Prophets, 287
Ezekiel 36:24-28 - Sat Prophets, 417
Daniel 3:26-27,29,34-41 - Tue Prophets, 165
Daniel 3:52-57 - Sun Prophets, 31
Daniel 3:57-90 - Sun Morning, 40
Hosea 6:1-6 – Sun Prophets, 33
Habakkuk 3:2-4,13a,15-19 - Fri Prophets, 352

OLD TESTAMENT READINGS

Deuteronomy 4:32-40 - Sat Readings, page 418
Deuteronomy 6:4-7 - Sat Night, 16
Tobit 4:15-19 - Wed Prophets, 356
Job 1:21 - Wed Prophets, 233
Isaiah 55:1-11 - Tue Prophets, 168
Isaiah 66:1-2 - Thu Prophets, 292
Jeremiah 15:16 - Mon Prophets, 95
Ezekiel 37:1-14 - Sun Prophets, 35

MARIAN PRAYERS

Hail Mary, 274
Loving Mother of the Redeemer, 336
Queen of Heaven, 144
Salve Regina, 399

NEW TESTAMENT CANTICLES

Luke 1:46-55 - Evenings, page 12
Luke 1:68-79 - Mornings, 51
Luke 2:29-32 - Nights, 17
Ephesians 1 - Mon Evenings, 136
Philippians 2 - Sun Vigils, 10
Colossians 1 - Wed Evenings, 268
Revelation 4&5 - Tue Evenings, 205
Revelation 11&12 - Thur Evenings, 330
Revelation 15 - Fri Evenings, 390
Revelation 19 - Sun Evenings, 70
1 Peter 2:21-24 – Thu Daytime, 317

NEW TESTAMENT READINGS

Romans 3:21-31 - Tue Daytime, pg 194
Romans 8:1-11 - Fri Night, 397
Romans 8:14-27 - Thu Readings, 284
Romans 8:35,37-39 - Wed Readings, 226
Romans 11:30-36 - Sunday Vigil, 11
Romans 12:9-21 - Sat Morning, 428
Romans 13:11-14 - Tue Readings, 160
Romans 15:1-6 - Fri Daytime, 380
1 Corinthians 2:1-16 - Fri Evening, 391
2 Corinthians 1:3-7 - Sun Evening, 70
Galatians 2:15-21 - Fri Readings, 348
Ephesians 3:16-21 - Wed Evening, 269
Ephesians 4:25-32 - Fri Morning, 366
Philippians 2:12-16 - Sat Daytime, 440
Colossians 1:3-6 – Mon Readings, 89
Colossians 1:9b-14 - Mon Night, 143
Colossians 3:5-17 - Tue Night, 210
1 Thess 2:13; 3:9-13 - Mon Daytime, 125
1 Thessalonians 5:1-11 - Wed Morn, 245
2 Thessalonians 3:7-13 - Mon Morn, 109
1 Timothy 3:16 - Sun Night, 75
2 Timothy 2:1-13 - Sun Morning, 49
Hebrews 12:18-24 - Sun Daytime, 61
James 1:19-27 - Wed Night, 273
James 4:1-12 - Mon Evening, 137
1 Peter 1:3-9 - Thu Evening, 331
1 Peter 1:22-25 - Thu Daytime, 318
1 Peter 3:8-11 - Thu Night, 335
1 Peter 4:7-11 - Thu Morning, 303
2 Peter 1:3-11 - Sat Readings, 410
1 John 2:1-6 - Wed Daytime, 258
1 John 3:1-2 - Tue Evening, 206
1 John 4:7-21 - Tue Morning, 180
Revelation 7:9-12 - Sun Readings, 29

449

INDEX of ANTIPHON & RESPONSORY VERSES

Be not afraid., 16

Matthew 1:21, 172   Matthew 1:23, 188   Matthew 2:6, 324   Matthew 3:17, 101
Matthew 4:19, 260   Matthew 5:3, 20   Matthew 5:4, 173   Matthew 5:5, 243   Matthew 5:6, 66
Matthew 5:7, 8   Matthew 5:8, 129   Matthew 5:9, 91   Matthew 5:10, 238   Matthew 5:11, 378
Matthew 5:13,14, 220   Matthew 5:16, 9   Matthew 5:19, 22   Matthew 5:38,39, 55
Matthew 5:39b, 254   Matthew 5:40, 97   Matthew 6:6, 114   Matthew 6:24b,21, 198
Matthew 6:26, 265   Matthew 6:34, 262   Matthew 7:1, 377   Matthew 7:24, 81
Matthew 8:15, 256   Matthew 8:17, 192   Matthew 9:10, 33   Matthew 9:12,13b, 115
Matthew 9:13a, 12:7, 84   Matthew 10:6, 361   Matthew 10:28, 344   Matthew 10:37, 278
Matthew 10:38, 282   Matthew 10:39, 133   Matthew 11:28-30, 438   Matthew 13:16,17a, 236
Matthew 13:23, 176   Matthew 13:30, 141   Matthew 13:33, 276   Matthew 13:45,46, 376
Matthew 13:52, 309   Matthew 14:31, 64   Matthew 14:27,29, 178   Matthew 15:28, 171
Matthew 16:26, 386   Matthew 18:20, 19   Matthew 18:35, 222   Matthew 21:31, 360
Matthew 21:43, 298   Matthew 22:21, 107   Matthew 22:37,39, 215   Matthew 23:3b,4, 202
Matthew 25:13, 39   Matthew 25:29, 315   Matthew 25:35,36, 57   Matthew 28:20, 235

Mark 1:3, 289   Mark 1:15, 310   Mark 1:38, 364   Mark 2:9-11, 382   Mark 2:15, 197
Mark 2:22, 146   Mark 2:27, 300   Mark 2:28, 58   Mark 3:5, 352   Mark 3:25, 340
Mark 3:35, 272   Mark 4:25, 326   Mark 4:26,27, 426   Mark 4:41, 422   Mark 5:30, 320
Mark 5:41, 132   Mark 6:7a, 136   Mark 6:8, 294   Mark 6:31, 113   Mark 7:15, 149
Mark 8:27,29, 308   Mark 9:7, 148   Mark 9:31, 191   Mark 9:37b, 342   Mark 10:15, 190
Mark 10:45, 124   Mark 10:51,52, 264   Mark 12:29, 218   Mark 13:31, 334   Mark 16:15, 209

Luke 1:47, 228   Luke 2:29-32, 401   Luke 2:49, 104   Luke 2:52, 415   Luke 3:10, 288
Luke 4:4, 74   Luke 4:8, 56   Luke 4:18, 200   Luke 4:24, 120   Luke 4:40b, 224   Luke 5:4, 204
Luke 5:32, 249   Luke 6:20b, 128   Luke 6:23, 130   Luke 6:27, 266   Luke 6:36, 49
Luke 6:38, 250   Luke 6:41, 307   Luke 7:6,7, 427   Luke 7:14, 78   Luke 7:16, 179
Luke 7:44,47, 322   Luke 8:11b, 312   Luke 9:13, 59   Luke 9:14, 64   Luke 9:16, 40
Luke 9:50, 157   Luke 9:58, 79   Luke 9:60, 395   Luke 10:2, 23   Luke 10:11b, 290
Luke 10:37, 99   Luke 11:9, 434   Luke 11:13, 201   Luke 12:15, 105   Luke 12:34, 174
Luke 12:49, 118   Luke 13:30, 433   Luke 14:10,11, 153   Luke 14:33, 86   Luke 15:7, 370
Luke 16:13, 5   Luke 17:17, 302   Luke 18:8, 385   Luke 18:13, 338   Luke 18:13; 22:69, 36
Luke 18:22, 67   Luke 19:5, 328   Luke 19:10, 388   Luke 19:42a. 313   Luke 20:38, 252
Luke 21:15, 241   Luke 23:34, 439   Luke 23:43, 7   Luke 24:46, 15

John 2:7,8, 240   John 3:8, 20   John 3:16, 203   John 3:17, 31   John 3:21, 242   John 3:30, 48
John 4:34, 134   John 5:6, 383   John 6:12, 186   John 6:35, 316   John 6:51a, 365   John 6:51b, 436
John 7:37, 116, 417   John 8:7, 255   John 8:12c, 268   John 10:4, 102   John 10:14, 43
John 10:30, 297   John 12:24, 371   John 12:26b, 358   John 12:32, 372   John 13:14, 6
John 14:23, 68   John 14:26, 185   John 15:1, 373   John 15:12, 295   John 15:17, 46
John 16:12, 421   John 16:13, 435   John 18:34, 42   John 20:21, 25   John 20:23, 404
John 20:29, 60

Acts 4:32a, 363   Romans 14:17, 350   1 Cor 15:3; Rom 5:8; 1 Ptr 3:18, 392   1 Timothy 2:2, 362
Phil 2:3, 10   Heb 11:29a, 412   Heb 13:20-21, 317   James 4:12, 123   1 Ptr 3:15b, 187
1 Ptr 5:7, 251   1 John 1:8,9, 189   Revelation 1:8, 330   Revelation 1:5,6, 380   Rev. 4:8b, 205
Revelation 15:3a, 390   Revelation 21:5b, 162   Revelation 21:10,11, 354   St. Augustine, 70

1 Chronicles 29:14b, 92   Psalm 16:11, 195   Psalm 17:8, 258   Psalm 23:1, 318   Psalm 25:4, 356
Psalm 26:11,9, 269   Psalm 31:6, 17   Psalm 34, 92   Psalm 34:2, 419   Psalm 41:5, 138
Psalm 51:17, 18   Psalm 63:7,8, 303   Psalm 70:2, 4   Psalm 71:1,5, 182   Psalm 72:18,19, 109
Psalm 81:16b, 331   Psalm 92:4,2, 428   Psalm 100:5, 206   Psalm 111:2,4, 11   Psalm 113:3,4, 233
Psalm 119:147, 169   Psalm 130:1, 292   Psalm 138:4,5, 71   Psalm 141:2, 125
Psalm 142:6,7a, 440   Psalm 143:8, 366   Psalm 147:2, 95   Psalm 147:5, 61
Isaiah 12:4,5, 50   Isaiah 42:6a, 94
Jeremiah 1:5, 353   Jeremiah 7:5b,6, 34   Jeremiah 24:7b, 287   Tobit 1:13, 245

PSALTER COMPARISON

Psalms of One Week in Ordinary Time

	Office of Readings	*Morning Prayer*
SUN	95 1 2 3 66 104	63 93 118 148 149 150
MON	6 9 31 50 73	5 19 29 42 84 90 96
TUE	10 12 37 68 102	67 24 33 43 65 85 101
WED	18 39 52 103	36 47 77 97 98 108 146
THU	44 89	48 57 80 81 87 99
FRI	35 38 55 69	51 26 28 100 133 147
SAT	105 106	8 107 92 117

Psalms of the Four-Week Psalter

	Office of Readings				*Morning Prayer*			
	I	II	III	IV	I	II	III	IV
SUN	1 2 3	104	145	24 66	63 149	118 150	93 148	118 150
MON	6 9A	31	50	73	5 29	42 19A	84 96	90 135
TUE	10 12	37	68	102	24 33	43 65	85 67	101 144
WED	18A	39 52	89A	103	36 47	77 97	86 98	108 146
THU	18B	44	89B 90	44	57 48	80 81	87 99	143 147A
FRI	35	38	69	55	51 100	51 147B	51 100	51 147B
SAT	132	136	107	50	119-19 117	92 8	119-14 117	92 8

ORDINARY TIME

PSALTER COMPARISON

Psalms of One Week in Ordinary Time

	Daytime Prayer	Evening Prayer	Night
SUN	119 23 76 119	110 111 112 114 115	91
MON	119 7 40 71 82 120	11 15 45 123 124 136	86
TUE	119 13 14 53 54 74	20 21 49 125 131 137 138	143
WED	119 17 70 75 94	27 62 126 127 139	130
THU	119 25 56 79 128 129	30 32 72 132 144	16
FRI	119 22 59 60 140	41 46 121 135 145	88
SAT	119 34 61 64	113 116 122 141 142	4 134

Psalms of the Four-Week Psalter

	Daytime Prayer				Evening Prayer				Night
	I	II	III	IV	I	II	III	IV	
SUN	118	23 76	118	23 76	110 114	110 115	110 111	110 112	91
MON	19B 7	119-6 40	119-12 71	119-17 82 120	11 15	45	123 124	136	86
TUE	119-1 13 14	119-7 53 54	119-13 74	119-18 88	20 21	49	125 131	137 138	143
WED	119-2 17	119-8 55	119-14 70 75	119-19 94	27	62 67	126 127	139	31 130
THU	119-3 25	119-9 56 57 79 80	119-15 128 129	119-20	30 32	72	132	144	16
FRI	119-4 26 28	119-10 59 60	22	119-21 133 140	41 46	116A 121	135	145	88
SAT	119-5 34	119-11 61 64	119-10 34	119-22 45	119-14 16	113 116B	122 130	141 142	4 134

www.ingramcontent.com/pod-product-compliance
Lightning Source LLC
Chambersburg PA
CBHW071553080526
44588CB00010B/893